Michael Moncur

SAMS
Teach Yourself

JavaScript
in 24 Hours

SAMS

201 West 103rd St., Indianapolis, Indiana, 46290 USA

Sams Teach Yourself JavaScript in 24 Hours

Copyright © 2002 by Sams Publishing

International Standard Book Number: 0-672-32406-7

Library of Congress Catalog Card Number: 20002104732

Printed in the United States of America

First Printing: June 2002

05   04   03   02   4   3   2   1

Trademarks

Warning and Disclaimer

ACQUISITIONS EDITOR
Scott Meyers

MANAGING EDITOR
Charlotte Clapp

PROJECT EDITOR
George E. Nedeff

INDEXER
Mandie Frank

PROOFREADER
Abby VanHuss

TECHNICAL EDITOR
Philip Karras

TEAM COORDINATOR
Amy Patton

MULTIMEDIA DEVELOPER
Dan Scherf

INTERIOR DESIGNER
Gary Adair

COVER DESIGNER
Aren Howell

Contents at a Glance

Contents

About the Author

MICHAEL MONCUR is a freelance Webmaster and author, and has worked with the Internet since Gopher was still a cool thing. He wrote *Sams Teach Yourself DHTML in 24 Hours*, and has also written several bestselling books about networking and the CNE and MCSE programs. In his spare time (about an hour per year) he composes music and builds model rockets.

Dedication

To my family, and especially Laura. Thanks for all your love and support.

Acknowledgments

I'd like to thank everyone at Sams for their help with this book, and for the opportunity to write it. In particular, Scott Meyers and Mark Taber helped me get started. Jeff Schultz and Amy Patton managed the project and kept things moving along. George Nedeff, the project editor, managed the editing process. The technical reviewer, Phil Karras, helped keep the writing grounded in reality.

I am grateful to everyone involved with previous editions of this book, including David Mayhew, Sean Medlock, Susan Hobbs, and Michelle Wyner. I'd also like to thank David and Sherry Rogelberg and the rest of the team at Studio B for their help throughout this project.

Finally, personal thanks go to my wife, Laura, my parents, Gary and Susan Moncur, the rest of the family (not to forget Matt, Melanie, Ian, and Kristen) and my friends, particularly Chuck Perkins, Matt Strebe, Cory Storm, Robert Parsons, Dylan Winslow, Scott Durbin, Ray Jones, James Chellis, Curt Siffert, Richard Easlick, and Henry J. Tillman. I couldn't have done it without your support.

We Want to Hear from You!

As the reader of this book, *you* are our most important critic and commentator. We value your opinion and want to know what we're doing right, what we could do better, what areas you'd like to see us publish in, and any other words of wisdom you're willing to pass our way.

You can email or write me directly to let me know what you did or didn't like about this book—as well as what we can do to make our books better.

Please note that I cannot help you with technical problems related to the topic of this book, and that due to the high volume of mail I receive, I might not be able to reply to every message.

When you write, please be sure to include this book's title and author as well as your name, email address, and phone number. I will carefully review your comments and share them with the author and editors who worked on the book.

Email: webdev@samspublishing.com

Mail: Mark Taber
           Associate Publisher
           Sams Publishing
           201 West 103rd Street
           Indianapolis, IN 46290 USA

Reader Services

For more information about this book or another Sams Publishing title, visit our Web site at www.samspublishing.com. Type the ISBN (excluding hyphens) or the title of a book in the Search field to find the page you're looking for.

Introduction

The World Wide Web began as a simple repository for information, but it has grown into much more—it entertains, teaches, advertises, and communicates. As the Web has evolved, the tools have also evolved. Simple markup tools such as HTML have been joined by true programming languages—including JavaScript.

Now don't let the word "programming" scare you. For many, the term conjures up images of long nights staring at the screen, trying to remember which sequence of punctuation marks will produce the effect you need. (Don't get me wrong. Some of us enjoy that sort of thing.)

Although JavaScript is programming, it's a very simple language. As a matter of fact, if you haven't programmed before, it makes a great introduction to programming. It requires very little knowledge to start programming with JavaScript—you'll write your first program in Hour 2, "Creating a Simple Script."

If you can create a Web page with HTML, you can easily use JavaScript to improve a page. JavaScript programs can range from a single line to a full-scale application. In this book, you'll start with simple scripts, and proceed to complex applications, such as a card game.

If you've spent much time developing pages for the Web, you know that the Web is constantly changing, and it can be hard to keep up with the latest languages and tools. This book will help you add JavaScript to your Web development toolbox, and I think you'll enjoy learning it.

I really had fun writing this book—and believe it or not, writing isn't always fun. I hope you'll have as much fun as you experiment with JavaScript and its capabilities.

How to Use This Book

This book is divided into 24 lessons. Each covers a single JavaScript topic, and should take about an hour to complete. The lessons start with the basics of JavaScript, and continue with more advanced topics. You can study an hour a day, or whatever pace suits you. (If you choose to forego sleep and do your studying in a single 24-hour period, you may have what it takes to be a computer book author.)

Q&A, Quiz, and Exercises

At the end of each hour's lesson, you'll find three final sections. Q&A answers a few of the most common questions about the hour's topic. The Quiz includes three questions to test your knowledge, and the Exercises offer ways for you to gain more experience with the techniques the hour covers.

This Book's Web Site

Since JavaScript and the Web are constantly changing, you'll need to stay up-to-date after reading this book. This book's Web site, maintained by author Michael Moncur, includes the latest updates. The site also includes downloadable versions of the listings and graphics for the examples in this book. Here's the address:

`http://www.jsworkshop.com/`

If you have questions or comments about this book, have noticed an error, or have trouble getting one of the scripts to work, you can also reach the author by email at `js3@starlingtech.com`. (Please check the Web site first to see if your question has been answered.)

PART I

Getting Started

Hour

HOUR 1

Understanding JavaScript

The World Wide Web (WWW) began as a text-only medium—the first version of the HTML (Hypertext Markup Language) specification didn't even have the capability to include graphics on a page. Although it's still not quite ready to give television a run for its money, the Web has come a long way.

Today's Web sites can include a wealth of features: graphics, sounds, animation, video, and sometimes even useful content. Web scripting languages, such as JavaScript, are one of the easiest ways to spice up a Web page and to interact with users in new ways.

The first hour of this book introduces the concept of Web scripting and the JavaScript language. It also describes how JavaScript, Java, and other Web languages fit into the scheme of things. The following topics will be covered in this hour:

- What Web scripting is, and what it's good for

- How scripting and programming are different (and similar)

- What JavaScript is
- How to include JavaScript commands in a Web page
- How different Web browsers handle JavaScript
- Choosing between JavaScript and alternative languages

Learning Web Scripting Basics

In the world of science fiction movies (and many other movies that have no excuse), computers are often seen obeying commands in English. While this may indeed happen in the near future, computers currently find it easier to understand languages like BASIC, C, and Java.

If you know how to use HTML to create a Web document, you've already worked with one computer language. You use HTML tags to describe how you want your document formatted, and the browser obeys your commands and shows the formatted document to the user.

Since HTML is a simple text markup language, it can't respond to the user, make decisions, or automate repetitive tasks. Interactive tasks like these require a more complex language: a programming language, or a *scripting* language.

While many programming languages are complex, scripting languages are generally simple. They have a simple syntax, can perform tasks with a minimum of commands, and are easy to learn. Web scripting languages allow you to combine scripting with HTML to create interactive Web pages.

Scripts and Programs

A movie or play follows a script—a list of actions (or lines) for the actors to perform. A Web script provides the same type of instructions for the browser. A script in JavaScript can range from a single line to a full-scale application. (In either case, JavaScript scripts almost always run within a browser.)

So what's the difference between scripting and programming? It depends on who you ask. We'll refer to scripting throughout this book, but feel free to include JavaScript Programming on your resume after you've finished this book.

Some programming languages must be *compiled*, or translated into machine code, before they can be executed. JavaScript, on the other hand, is an *interpreted* language: The browser executes each line of script as it comes to it.

There is one main advantage to interpreted languages: writing or changing a script is very simple. Changing a JavaScript script is as easy as changing a typical HTML document, and the change is enacted as soon as you reload the document in the browser.

> Interpreted languages have their disadvantages—they can't execute very quickly, so they're not ideally suited for complicated work like graphics. Also, they require the interpreter (in JavaScript's case, usually a browser) in order to work.

Introducing JavaScript

JavaScript was developed by Netscape Communications Corporation, the makers of the popular Netscape Web browser. JavaScript was the first Web scripting language to be introduced, and it is still by far the most popular.

> JavaScript was originally called LiveScript and was first introduced in Netscape Navigator 2.0 in 1995. It was soon renamed JavaScript to indicate a marketing relationship with Java.

JavaScript is almost as easy to learn as HTML, and it can be included directly in HTML documents. Here are a few of the things you can do with JavaScript:

- Add scrolling or changing messages to the browser's status line.
- Validate the contents of a form and make calculations. (For example, an order form can automatically display a running total as you enter item quantities.)
- Display messages to the user, either as part of a Web page or in alert boxes.
- Animate images or create images that change when you move the mouse over them.
- Create ad banners that interact with the user, rather than simply displaying a graphic.
- Detect the browser in use and display different content for different browsers.
- Detect installed plug-ins and notify the user if a plug-in is required.

You can do all this and more with JavaScript, including creating entire applications. We'll explore the uses of JavaScript throughout this book.

How JavaScript Fits into a Web Page

As you hopefully already know, HTML is the language you use to create Web documents. To refresh your memory, Listing 1.1 shows a short but sadly typical Web document.

LISTING 1.1 A simple HTML document

```
<html>
<head>
<title>Our Home Page</title>
</head>
<body>
<h1>The American Eggplant Society</h1>
<p>Welcome to our Web page. Unfortunately,
it's still under construction.</p>
</body>
</html>
```

This document consists of a header within the <head> tags and the body of the page within the <body> tags. To add JavaScript to a page, you'll use a similar tag: <script>.

The <script> tag tells the browser to start treating the text as a script, and the closing </script> tag tells the browser to return to HTML mode. In most cases, you can't use JavaScript statements except within <script> tags. The exception is event handlers, described later in this chapter.

Using the <script> tag, you can add a short script (in this case, just one line) to a Web document, as shown in Listing 1.2.

If you want to try this example in a browser but don't want to type it, the HTML document is available on this book's Web site, http://www.jsworkshop.com/ (as are all of the other listings).

LISTING 1.2 A simple HTML document with a simple script

```
<html>
<head>
<title>Our Home Page</title>
```

LISTING 1.2 Continued

```
</head>
<body>
<h1>The American Eggplant Society</h1>
<p>Welcome to our Web page. Unfortunately,
it's still under construction.
We last worked on it on this date:</p>
<script LANGUAGE="JavaScript" type="text/javascript">
document.write(document.lastModified);
</script>
</body>
</html>
```

JavaScript's `document.write` statement, which you'll learn more about later, sends output as part of the Web document. In this case, it displays the modification date of the document.

> Notice that the `<script>` tag in Listing 1.2 includes the parameter `type="text/javascript"`. This specifies the scripting language to the browser. You can also specify a JavaScript version, as you'll learn later in this hour.

In this example, we placed the script within the body of the HTML document. There are actually four different places where you might use scripts:

- In the body of the page. In this case, the script's output is displayed as part of the HTML document when the browser loads the page.

- In the header of the page, between the `<head>` tags. Scripts in the header can't create output within the HTML document, but can be referred to by other scripts. The header is often used for functions—groups of JavaScript statements that can be used as a single unit. You will learn more about functions in Hour 3, "How JavaScript Programs Work."

- Within an HTML tag, such as `<body>` or `<form>`. This is called an *event handler* and allows the script to work with HTML elements. When using JavaScript in Event handlers, you don't need to use the `<script>` tag. You'll learn more about event handlers in Hour 3.

- In a separate file entirely. JavaScript supports the use of files with the `.js` extension containing scripts; these can be included by specifying a file in the `<script>` tag.

Using External JavaScript files

When you create more complicated scripts, you'll quickly find your HTML documents become large and confusing. To avoid this, you can use one or more external JavaScript files. These are files with the `.js` extension that contain JavaScript statements.

External scripts are supported by Netscape Navigator 3.0 or later and Internet Explorer 4.0 or later. To use an external script, you specify its filename in the `<script>` tag:

```
<script language="JavaScript" type="text/javascript" src="filename.js">
</script>
```

Since you'll be placing the JavaScript statements in a separate file, you don't need anything between the opening and closing `<script>` tags—in fact, anything between them will be ignored by the browser.

You can create the `.js` file using a text editor. It should contain one or more JavaScript commands, and only JavaScript—don't include `<script>` tags, other HTML tags, or HTML comments. Save the `.js` file in the same directory as the HTML documents that refer to it.

> External JavaScript files have a distinct advantage: you can link to the same `.js` file from two or more HTML documents. Since the browser stores this file in its cache, this can reduce the time it takes your Web pages to display.

Browsers and JavaScript

Like HTML, JavaScript requires a Web browser to be displayed, and different browsers may display it differently. Unlike HTML, the results of a browser incompatibility with JavaScript are more drastic: Rather than simply displaying your text incorrectly, the script may not execute at all, may display an error message, or may even crash the browser.

We'll take a quick look at the way different browsers—and different versions of the same browser—treat JavaScript in the following sections.

Netscape and Internet Explorer

Today's Web is dominated by two popular Web browsers: Netscape and Microsoft Internet Explorer. Netscape spent a few years being the more popular browser, but is now behind Internet Explorer in popularity; however, both are common enough that you should try to support them with your pages.

Although JavaScript 1.5, the latest version, is officially supported only by Netscape 6 and Internet Explorer 5 and 6, the majority of examples throughout this book will run on Netscape 4.5 or later or Internet Explorer 4.0 or later. Listings that require a more recent browser will be labeled.

Versions of JavaScript

The JavaScript language has evolved since its original release in Netscape 2.0. There have been several versions of JavaScript:

- JavaScript 1.0, the original version, is supported by Netscape 2.0 and Internet Explorer 3.0.

- JavaScript 1.1 is supported by Netscape 3.0 and mostly supported by Internet Explorer 4.0.

- JavaScript 1.2 is supported by Netscape 4.0, and partially supported by Internet Explorer 4.0.

- JavaScript 1.3 is supported by Netscape 4.5 and Internet Explorer 5.0.

- JavaScript 1.5 is supported by Netscape 6.0 and Internet Explorer 5.5 and later.

Each of these versions is an improvement over the previous version and includes a number of new features. With rare exception, browsers that support the new version will also support scripts written for earlier versions.

ECMA, the European Computer Manufacturing Association, has finalized the ECMA-262 specification for ECMAScript, a standardized version of JavaScript. JavaScript 1.3 follows the ECMA-262 standard, and JavaScript 1.5 follows ECMA-262 revision 3.

Another language you may hear of is JScript. This is how Microsoft refers to their implementation of JavaScript, which is generally compatible with the Netscape version.

Netscape is also working with ECMA on JavaScript 2.0, a future version that will correspond with the fourth edition of the ECMAScript standard. JavaScript 2.0 will improve upon earlier versions with a more modular approach, better object support, and features to make JavaScript useful as a general-purpose scripting language as well as a Web language.

Specifying JavaScript Versions

As mentioned earlier in this hour, you can specify a version of JavaScript in the
`<script>` tag. For example, this tag specifies JavaScript version 1.3:

`<script language="JavaScript1.3" type="text/javascript1.3">`

There are two ways of specifying the version number. The old method uses the `language`
attribute, and the new method recommended by the HTML 4.0 specification uses the
`type` attribute. To maintain compatibility with older browsers, you can use both attributes.

When you specify a version number, this allows your script to execute only if the
browser supports the version you specified or a later version.

When the `<script>` tag doesn't specify a version number, the browser assumes that the
script is compatible with JavaScript 1.0. Since the core of the JavaScript language is
unchanged since version 1.0, this is fine for most scripts.

> In most cases, you shouldn't specify a JavaScript version at all. This allows
> your script to run on all of the browsers that support JavaScript. You should
> only specify a particular version when your script uses features that are not
> available in earlier versions.

JavaScript Beyond the Browser

While JavaScript programs traditionally run within a Web browser, and Web-based
JavaScript is the focus of this book, JavaScript is becoming increasingly popular in other
applications. Here are a few examples:

- Macromedia Dreamweaver, used for Web applications and multimedia, can be
  extended with JavaScript.
- Several server-side versions of JavaScript are available. These run within a Web
  server rather than a browser.
- Microsoft's Windows Scripting Host (WSH) supports JScript, Microsoft's implementation of JavaScript, as a general-purpose scripting language for Windows.
  Unfortunately, the most popular applications developed for WSH so far have been
  email viruses.
- Microsoft's Common Language Runtime (CLR), part of the .NET framework, supports JavaScript.

Along with these examples, many of the changes in the upcoming JavaScript 2.0 are designed to make it more suitable as a general-purpose scripting language.

Alternatives to JavaScript

JavaScript is not the only language used on the Web, and in some cases, it may not be the right tool for the job. Other languages, such as Java, can do some things better than JavaScript. In the following sections, we'll look at a few other commonly used Web languages and their advantages.

Java

Java is a programming language developed by Sun Microsystems that can be used to create *applets*, or programs that execute within a Web page.

Java is a compiled language, but the compiler produces code for a *virtual machine* rather than a real computer. The virtual machine is a set of rules for bytecodes and their meanings, with capabilities that fit well into the scope of a Web browser.

The virtual machine code is then interpreted by a Web browser. This allows the same Java applet to execute the same way on PCs, Macintoshes, and UNIX machines, and on different browsers.

 Java is also a densely populated island in Indonesia and a slang term for coffee. This has resulted in a widespread invasion of coffee-related terms in computer literature.

At this point, we need to make one thing clear: Java is a fine language, but you won't be learning it in this book. Although their names and some of their commands are similar, JavaScript and Java are entirely different languages.

ActiveX

ActiveX is a specification developed by Microsoft that allows ordinary Windows programs to be run within a Web page. ActiveX programs can be written in languages such as Visual C++ and Visual Basic, and they are compiled before being placed on the Web server.

ActiveX applications, called *controls*, are downloaded and executed by the Web browser, like Java applets. Unlike Java applets, controls can be installed permanently when they are downloaded, eliminating the need to download them again.

ActiveX's main advantage is that it can do just about anything. This can also be a disadvantage: Several enterprising programmers have already used ActiveX to bring exciting new capabilities to Web pages, such as "the Web page that turns off your computer" and "the Web page that formats your disk drive. "

Fortunately, ActiveX includes a signature feature that identifies the source of the control and prevents controls from being modified. While this won't prevent a control from damaging your system, you can specify which sources of controls you trust.

ActiveX has two main disadvantages. First, it isn't as easy to program as a scripting language or Java. Second, ActiveX is proprietary: it works only in Microsoft Internet Explorer, and only under Windows platforms.

VBScript

VBScript, sometimes known as Visual Basic Scripting Edition, is Microsoft's answer to JavaScript. Just as JavaScript's syntax is loosely based on Java, VBScript's syntax is loosely based on Microsoft Visual Basic, a popular programming language for Windows machines.

Like JavaScript, VBScript is a simple scripting language, and you can include VBScript statements within an HTML document. To begin a VBScript script, you use the `<script LANGUAGE="VBScript">` tag.

VBScript can do many of the same things as JavaScript, and it even looks similar in some cases. It has two main advantages:

- For those who already know Visual Basic, it may be easier to learn than JavaScript.
- It is closely integrated with ActiveX, Microsoft's standard for Web-embedded applications.

VBScript's main disadvantage is that it is supported only by Microsoft Internet Explorer. JavaScript, on the other hand, is supported by Netscape, Internet Explorer, and several other browsers. JavaScript is a much more popular language, and you can see it in use all over the Web.

CGI and Server-Side Scripting

CGI (Common Gateway Interface) is not really a language, but a specification that allows programs to run on Web servers. CGI programs can be written in any number of languages, including Perl, C, and Visual Basic.

Along with traditional CGI, scripting languages such as Microsoft's Active Server Pages, Java Server Pages, Cold Fusion, and PHP are often used on Web servers. A server-side implementation of JavaScript is also available.

Server-side programs are heavily used on the Web. Any time you type information into a form and press a button to send it to a Web site, the data is processed by a server-side application.

The main difference between JavaScript and server-side languages is that JavaScript applications execute on the client (the Web browser) and server-side applications execute on the Web server. The main disadvantage of this approach is that, since the data must be sent to the Web server and back, response time may be slow.

On the other hand, CGI can do things JavaScript can't do. In particular, it can read and write files on the server and interact with other server components, such as databases. While a client-side JavaScript program can read information from a form and then manipulate it, it can't store the data on the Web server.

CGI and Server-side programming are outside the focus of this book. You can learn more about these technologies with other Sams books, including *Teach Yourself CGI Programming in 24 Hours*, *Teach Yourself Perl in 24 Hours*, and *Teach Yourself PHP in 24 Hours*. See Appendix A, "Other JavaScript Resources", for more sources of information.

Summary

During this hour, you've learned what Web scripting is and what JavaScript is. You've also learned how to insert a script into an HTML document or refer to an external JavaScript file, and how JavaScript differs from other Web languages.

If you're waiting for some real JavaScript code, look no further. The next hour, "Creating a Simple Script," guides you through the process of creating a working JavaScript application.

Q&A

Q If I plan to learn Java or CGI anyway, will I have any use for JavaScript?

A Certainly. JavaScript is the ideal tool for many applications, such as form validation. While Java and CGI have their uses, they can't do all that JavaScript can do.

Q Can a Web page include more than one set of `<script>` tags?

A Yes. In fact, the larger scripts in this book will often include two or more script sections. You can also include `<script>` tags that include JavaScript code and `<script>` tags that reference external JavaScript files in the same HTML file.

Q Can I make scripts that work on both Netscape and Internet Explorer?

A Yes, but it isn't always easy. Most JavaScript features are supported by both browsers, and if you carefully test your script on both browsers, you can make it work. For more complex scripts, you may need to use different sections of code for each browser. See Hour 14, "Creating Cross-Browser Scripts," for details.

Q What about supporting different versions of Netscape or Internet Explorer?

A If you don't specify a JavaScript version in the `<script>` tag, you can write simple scripts that will run in Netscape 2.0 and later or Internet Explorer 3.0 and later. In this case you will need to stick to the features of JavaScript 1.0 whenever possible.

Q What happens if a user's browser doesn't support JavaScript at all?

A You can use HTML comments to prevent older browsers from displaying JavaScript code. This is explained in Hour 2.

Quiz

Test your knowledge of the material covered in this hour by answering the following questions.

Questions

1. Why do JavaScript and Java have similar names?

    a. JavaScript is a stripped-down version of Java

    b. JavaScript's syntax is loosely based on Java's

    c. They both originated on the island of Java

2. When a user views a page containing a JavaScript program, which machine actually executes the script?

    a. The user's machine running a Web browser

    b. The Web server

    c. A central machine deep within Netscape's corporate offices

3. Which of the following languages is supported by both Microsoft Internet Explorer and Netscape?

    a. VBScript

    b. ActiveX

    c. JavaScript

Answers

1. b. Although they are different languages, JavaScript's syntax is loosely based on Java.

2. a. JavaScript programs execute on the Web browser. (There is actually a server-side version of JavaScript, but that's another story.)

3. c. JavaScript is supported by both Netscape and MSIE, although the implementations are not identical.

Exercises

If you want to learn a bit about JavaScript or check out the latest developments before you proceed with the next hour, perform these activities:

- Visit this book's Web site at `http://www.jsworkshop.com/` to check for news about JavaScript and updates to the scripts in this book.

- Visit Netscape's Developer Web site at `http://developer.netscape.com/tech/javascript/index.html` to view articles and news about JavaScript.

Hour 2

Creating a Simple Script

As you learned in Hour 1, "Understanding JavaScript," JavaScript is a script-ing language for Web pages. You can include JavaScript commands directly in the HTML document, and the script is executed when the page is viewed in a browser.

During this hour, you will create a simple script, edit it, and test it using a Web browser. Along the way you'll learn the basic tasks involved in creating and using scripts. We will cover the following topics:

- The software tools you will need to create and test scripts
- Beginning and ending scripts
- Formatting JavaScript statements
- How a script can display a result
- Including a script within a Web document
- Testing a script using Netscape
- Modifying a script
- Dealing with errors in scripts
- Hiding scripts from older browsers

Tools for Scripting

Unlike many programming languages, you won't need any special software to create JavaScript scripts. In fact, you probably already have everything you need.

The first thing you'll need to work with JavaScript is a *text editor*. JavaScript scripts are stored in simple text files, usually as part of HTML documents. Any editor that can store ASCII text files will work.

You can choose from a wide range of editors, from simple text editors to word processors. If you don't have a favorite editor already, a simple editor is most likely included with your computer. For Windows computers, the Notepad accessory will work just fine.

> If you use a word processor to create JavaScript programs, be sure you save the files as ASCII text rather than as word processing documents.

A variety of dedicated HTML editors are also available and will work with JavaScript. In fact, many include features specifically for JavaScript—for example, color-coding the various JavaScript statements to indicate their purposes, or even creating simple scripts automatically.

For Windows computers, here are a few recommended editors:

- **Homesite:** An excellent HTML editor that includes JavaScript support.
- **Microsoft Frontpage 2000:** Microsoft's visual HTML editor. The Script Builder component allows you to easily create simple scripts.
- **TextPad:** A powerful text editor that includes a number of features missing from Notepad.

The following editors are available for both Windows and Macintosh:

- **Macromedia Dreamweaver:** a visually-oriented editor that works with HTML, JavaScript and Macromedia's Flash plug-in.
- **Adobe GoLive:** A visual and HTML editor that also includes features for designing and organizing the structure of large sites.

Additionally for the Macintosh, BBEdit, BBEdit Lite, and Alpha are good HTML editors that you can use to create Web pages and scripts.

> Appendix B, "Tools for JavaScript Developers," includes Web addresses to download these and other HTML and JavaScript editors.

You'll need two other things to work with JavaScript: a Web browser and a computer to run it on. Since this book covers new features introduced up to JavaScript 1.5, I recommend that you use the latest version of Netscape or Microsoft Internet Explorer. See the Netscape or Microsoft Web site to download a copy:

```
http://www.netscape.com/
http://www.microsoft.com/
```

As a minimum, you should have Netscape 4.5 or later, or Internet Explorer 4.0 or later. Some of the advanced DHTML features covered beginning with Hour 18 will require Netscape 6.0 or later, or Internet Explorer 5.0 or later.

> If you plan on making your scripts available over the Internet, you'll also need a Web server, or access to one. However, you can use all of the JavaScript examples in this book directly from your computer's hard disk.

What Time is It?

One common and easy use for JavaScript is to display dates and times. Since JavaScript runs on the browser, the times it displays will be in the user's current time zone. However, you can also use JavaScript to calculate "universal" (UTC) time.

> UTC stands for the French equivalent of Universal Coordinated Time, and is the new name for the old GMT (Greenwich Mean Time) standard. This is the time at the Prime Meridian, near London, England.

As a basic introduction to JavaScript, you will now create a simple script that displays the current time and the UTC time within a Web page.

Beginning the Script

Your script, like most JavaScript programs, begins with the HTML `<script>` tag. As you learned in Hour 1, you use the `<script>` and `</script>` tags to enclose a script within the HTML document.

> Remember to include only valid JavaScript statements between the starting
> and ending <script> tags. If the browser finds anything but valid JavaScript
> statements within the <script> tags, it will display a JavaScript error mes-
> sage.

To begin creating the script, open your favorite text editor and type the beginning and
ending <script> tags, as shown below.

```
<script LANGUAGE="JavaScript" type="text/javascript">
</script>
```

Since this script does not use any of the new features of JavaScript 1.1 or later, you
won't need to specify a version number in the <script> tag. This script should work in
Netscape 2.0 and later or Internet Explorer 3.0 or later.

Adding JavaScript Statements

To complete your script, you will need to determine what the local and UTC times are,
and then display them to the browser. Fortunately all of the hard parts, such as converting
between dates, are built into the JavaScript interpreter.

Storing Data in Variables

To begin the script, you will use a *variable* to store the current date. You will learn more
about variables in Hour 4, "Using Functions and Variables." For now, think of them as
containers that can hold something—a number, or in this case, a date.

To start writing the script, add the following line after the first <script> tag. Be sure to
use the same combination of capital and lowercase letters in your version, since
JavaScript commands and variable names are case-sensitive.

```
now = new Date();
```

This statement creates a variable called now and stores the current date and time in it.
This statement and the others you will use in this script use JavaScript's built-in Date
object, which allows you to conveniently handle dates and times. You'll learn more about
working with dates in Hour 8, "Using Math and Date functions."

> Notice the semicolon at the end of the above statement. This tells the
> browser that it has reached the end of a statement. You can actually omit
> the semicolons, but we'll use them throughout this book for clarity.

Calculating the Results

Internally, JavaScript stores dates as the number of milliseconds since January 1, 1970. Fortunately, JavaScript includes a number of functions to convert dates and times in various ways, so you don't have to figure out how to convert milliseconds to day, date, and time.

To continue your script, add the following two statements before the final `</script>` tag:

```
localtime = now.toString();
utctime = now.toGMTString();
```

These statements create two new variables: `localtime`, containing the current time and date in a nice readable format, and `utctime`, containing the UTC equivalent.

> The `localtime` and `utctime` variables store a piece of text, such as "January 1, 2001 12:00 PM." In programming parlance, a piece of text is called a *string*. You will learn more about strings in Hour 5, "Using Strings and Arrays."

Creating Output

You now have two variables—`localtime` and `utctime`—which contain the results we want from our script. Of course, these variables don't do us much good unless we can see them. JavaScript includes a number of ways to display information, and one of the simplest is the `document.write` statement.

The `document.write` statement displays a text string, a number, or anything else you throw at it. Since your JavaScript program will be used within a Web page, the output will be displayed as part of the page. To display the result, add these statements before the final `</script>` tag:

```
document.write("<b>Local time:</b> " + localtime + "<br>");
document.write("<b>UTC time:</b> " + utctime);
```

These statements tell the browser to add some text to the Web page containing your script. The output will include some brief strings introducing the results, and the contents of the `localtime` and `utctime` variables.

Notice the HTML tags, such as `<b>`, within the quotation marks—since JavaScript's output appears within a Web page, it needs to be formatted using HTML. The `<br>` tag in the first line ensures that the two times will be displayed on separate lines.

Notice the plus signs (+) used between the text and variables in the above statements. In this case, it tells the browser to combine the values into one string of text. If you use the plus sign between two numbers, they are added together.

Adding the Script to a Web Page

You should now have a complete script that calculates a result and displays it. Your listing should match Listing 2.1.

LISTING 2.1 The complete Date and Time Script

```
<script language="JavaScript" type="text/javascript">
now = new Date();
localtime = now.toString();
utctime = now.toGMTString();
document.write("<b>Local time:</b> " + localtime + "<BR>");
document.write("<b>UTC time:</b> " + utctime);
</script>
```

To use your script, you'll need to add it to an HTML document. In its most basic form, the HTML document should include opening and closing <html> tags, <head> tags and <body> tags.

If you add these tags to the document containing your script along with a descriptive heading, you should end up with something like Listing 2.2.

LISTING 2.2 The Date and Time script in an HTML document

```
<html>
<head><title>Displaying Times and Dates</title></head>
<body>
<h1>Current Date and Time</h1>
<p>
<script language="JavaScript" type="text/javascript">
now = new Date();
localtime = now.toString();
utctime = now.toGMTString();
document.write("<b>Local time:</b> " + localtime + "<BR>");
document.write("<b>UTC time:</b> " + utctime);
</script>
</p>
</body>
</html>
```

Now that you have a complete HTML document, save it with the `.htm` or `.html`extension. (If you're using Windows 3.1, you'll need to use `.htm`; otherwise, `.html` is recommended.)

> Notepad and other Windows text editors may try to be helpful and add the `.txt` extension to your script. Be sure your saved file has the correct extension.

Testing the Script

To test your script, you simply need to load the HTML document you created in a Web browser. Start Netscape or Internet Explorer and select Open from the File menu. Click the Choose File or Browse button, and then find your HTML file. Once you've selected it, click the Open button to view the page.

If you typed the script correctly, your browser should display the result of the script, as shown in Figure 2.1. (Of course, your result won't be the same as mine, but it should be the same as the setting of your computer's clock.)

FIGURE 2.1

Netscape displays the results of the Date and Time script.

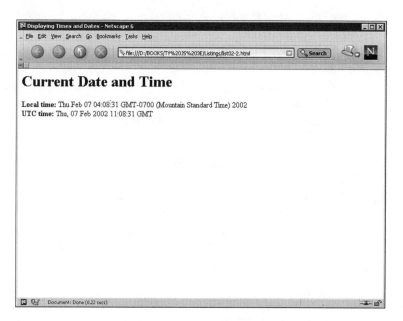

You can download the HTML document for this chapter from this book's
Web site, http://www.jsworkshop.com/. If the version you type doesn't
work, try downloading the online version.

Modifying the Script

While the current script does indeed display the current date and time, its display isn't
nearly as attractive as the clock on your wall or desk. To remedy that, you can use some
additional JavaScript features and a bit of HTML to display a large clock.

To display a large clock, we need the hours, minutes, and seconds in separate variables.
Once again, JavaScript has built-in functions to do most of the work:

```
hours = now.getHours();
mins = now.getMinutes();
secs = now.getSeconds();
```

These statements load the hours, mins, and secs variables with the components of the
time using JavaScript's built-in date functions.

Once the hours, minutes, and seconds are in separate variables, you can create docu-
ment.write statements to display them:

```
document.write("<font size='+5'>");
document.write(hours + ":" + mins + ":" + secs);
document.write("</font>");
```

The first statement displays an HTML <font> tag to display the clock in a large type-
face. The second statement displays the hours, mins, and secs variables, separated by
colons, and the third adds the closing </font> tag.

You can add the statements above to the original date and time script to add the large
clock display. Listing 2.3 shows the complete modified version of the script.

LISTING 2.3   The Date and Time script with large clock display

```
<html>
<head><title>Displaying Times and Dates</title></head>
<body>
<h1>Current Date and Time</h1>
<p>
<script language="JavaScript">
now = new Date();
localtime = now.toString();
utctime = now.toGMTString();
```

LISTING 2.3   Continued

```
document.write("<b>Local time:</b> " + localtime + "<BR>");
document.write("<b>UTC time:</b> " + utctime);
hours = now.getHours();
mins = now.getMinutes();
secs = now.getSeconds();
document.write("<font size='+5'>");
document.write(hours + ":" + mins + ":" + secs);
document.write("</font>");
</script>
</p>
</body>
</html>
```

Now that you have modified the script, save the HTML file and open the modified file in your browser. If you left the browser running, you can simply use the Reload button to load the new version of the script. Try it and verify that the same time is displayed in both the upper portion of the window and the new large clock. Figure 2.2 shows the results.

FIGURE 2.2

Internet Explorer displays the modified Date and Time script.

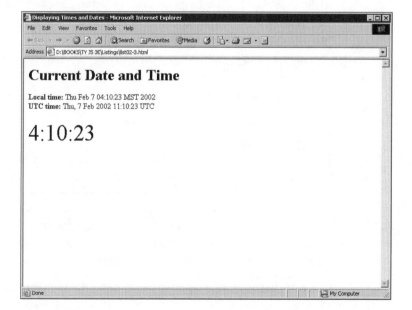

Dealing with JavaScript Errors

As you develop more complex JavaScript applications, you're going to run into errors from time to time. JavaScript errors are usually caused by mistyped JavaScript statements.

To see an example of a JavaScript error message, modify the statement you added in the previous section. We'll use a common error: omitting one of the parentheses. Change the last `document.write` statement to read:

```
document.write("</font>";
```

Save your HTML document again and load the document into the browser. Depending on the browser version you're using, one of two things will happen: Either an error message will be displayed, or the script will simply fail to execute.

If an error message is displayed, you're half way to fixing the problem by adding the missing parenthesis. If no error was displayed, you should configure your browser to display error messages so that you can diagnose future problems:

- In Netscape Navigator 4.5 or later, type `javascript:` into the browser's Location field to display the JavaScript console. In Netscape 6, you can also select Tasks, Tools, JavaScript Console from the menu. The console is shown in Figure 2.3, displaying the error message you created in this example.

- In Internet Explorer 4.0 or later, select Tools, then Internet Options. On the Advanced page, uncheck the box next to "Disable Script Debugging" and check the box next to "Display a notification about every script error."

> Notice the field at the bottom of the JavaScript console. This allows you to type a JavaScript statement, which will be executed immediately. This is a handy way to test JavaScript's features.

The error we get in this case is `missing ) after argument list` (Netscape) or `Expected ')'` (Internet Explorer), which turns out to be exactly the problem. Be warned, however, that error messages aren't always this enlightening.

While Internet Explorer displays error dialog boxes for each error, Netscape's JavaScript Console displays a single list of errors and allows you to test commands. For this reason, you may find it useful to install Netscape for debugging and testing JavaScript, even if Internet Explorer is your primary browser.

FIGURE 2.3

Netscape's JavaScript Console displays an error message.

As you develop larger JavaScript applications, finding and fixing errors becomes more important. You'll learn more about dealing with JavaScript errors in Hour 17, "Debugging JavaScript Applications."

Workshop: Hiding Scripts from Older Browsers

Since older browsers don't understand the `<script>` tag, they will not behave very well when they encounter a script in a Web page. In most cases, they will display the script in the middle of the page—probably not the effect you were looking for.

To avoid this, you can enclose the script within HTML comment tags. This tells older browsers to ignore the script completely. Newer browsers are smart enough to know that your script isn't really a comment.

HTML comments begin with the tag `<!--` and end with the `-->` tag. Listing 2.4 shows a simple example of a script with comments.

LISTING 2.4   Hiding a script from older browsers

```
<SCRIPT LANGUAGE="JavaScript">
  <!--
  document.write("Your browser supports JavaScript.");
  // -->
</SCRIPT>
```

This script includes the beginning and ending HTML comment tags. The `//` in the last line is a JavaScript comment; this prevents the HTML comment from being detected as a JavaScript error.

 This process of hiding scripts is not perfect. Certain characters within your script (particularly the greater than sign, >) may end the comment prematurely in some older browsers.

Summary

During this hour, you wrote a simple JavaScript program and tested it using a browser. You learned the tools you need to work with JavaScript—basically, an editor and a browser. You also learned how to modify and test scripts, and what happens when a JavaScript program runs into an error. Finally, you learned how to hide JavaScript from older browsers.

In the process of writing this script, you have used some of JavaScript's basic features: variables, the `document.write` statement, and functions for working with dates and times.

Now that you've learned a bit of JavaScript syntax, you're ready to learn more of the details. You'll get started in Hour 3, "How JavaScript Programs Work."

Q&A

Q If this is a book about JavaScript 1.5, why didn't we specify the JavaScript version number in the beginning `<script>` tag?

A Since this script doesn't use any features specific to JavaScript 1.5, it's best to include the lowest possible version number. If we used the tag `<script LANGUAGE="JavaScript1.5">`, the script would only run on Netscape 6.0 or later and Internet Explorer 5.5 or later. Since this script requires only JavaScript 1.0's basic features, we used the tag `<script LANGUAGE="JavaScript">`. With this tag, the script will run on Netscape 2.0, MSIE 3.0, and any other JavaScript-compatible browser.

Q When I try to run my script, the browser displays the actual script in the browser window instead of executing it. What did I do wrong?

A This is most likely caused by one of three errors. First, you may be missing the beginning or ending `<script>` tags. Check them, and verify that the first reads `<script LANGUAGE="JavaScript" type="text/javascript">`. Second, your file may have been saved with a `.txt` extension, causing the browser to treat it as a text file. Rename it to `.htm` or `.html` to fix the problem. Third, make sure your browser supports JavaScript, and that it is not disabled in the Preferences dialog.

Q Why are the `<b>` and `<br>` tags allowed in the statements to print the time? I thought HTML tags weren't allowed within the `<script>` tags.

A Since this particular tag is inside quotation marks, it's considered a valid part of the script. The script's output, including any HTML tags, is interpreted and displayed by the browser. You can use other HTML tags within quotation marks to add formatting, such as the `<font>` tags we added for the large clock display.

Q I can imagine a large script making a mess of my beautifully formatted HTML documents. Can I move the script to a separate file?

A Yes. You can separate the JavaScript statements into an external JavaScript file, as described in Hour 1.

Quiz

Test your knowledge of the basics of working with JavaScript by answering the following questions.

Questions

1. What software do you use to create and edit JavaScript programs?

    a. A browser

    b. A text editor

    c. A pencil and a piece of paper

2. What are variables used for in JavaScript programs?

    a. Storing numbers, dates, or other values

    b. Varying randomly

    c. Causing high-school Algebra flashbacks

3. What should appear at the very end of your JavaScript script?

 a. The `<script LANGUAGE="JavaScript">` tag

 b. The `</script>` tag

 c. The `END` statement

Answers

1. b. Any text editor can be used to create scripts. You can also use a word processor, if you're careful to save the document as a text file with the `.html` or `.htm` extension.

2. a. Variables are used to store numbers, dates, or other values.

3. b. Your script should end with the `</script>` tag.

Exercises

If you would like to gain a bit more practice working on the JavaScript features you learned in this hour, try these activities:

- Add HTML comments to the Date and Time script, as described in the Workshop section. Verify that the script still works in your browser.

- Add a millisecond field to the large clock. You can use the `getMilliseconds` function, which works just like `getSeconds` but returns milliseconds.

HOUR 3

How JavaScript Programs Work

Welcome to the end of Part I of this book. In the first couple of hours, you've learned what JavaScript is, created a simple script, and learned the variety of things JavaScript can do.

In this, the final hour of Part I, you'll learn a few basic concepts and script components that you'll use in just about every script you write. This will prepare you for the remaining hours of the book, in which you'll explore specific JavaScript functions and features.

Hour 3 covers the following topics:

- Organizing scripts using functions
- What objects are and how JavaScript uses them
- How JavaScript can respond to events
- An introduction to conditional statements and loops
- How browsers execute scripts in the proper order
- Adding comments to document your JavaScript code

Combining Tasks with Functions

In the basic scripts you've examined so far, you've seen many JavaScript statements that have a section in parentheses, like this:

```
document.write("Testing.");
```

This is an example of a *function*. Functions provide a simple way to handle a task, such as adding output to a Web page. JavaScript includes a wide variety of built-in functions, which you will learn about throughout this book. A statement that uses a function, as in the example above, is referred to as a *function call*.

Functions take parameters (the expression inside the parentheses) to tell them what to do. Additionally, a function can return a value to a waiting variable. For example, the following function call prompts the user for a response and stores it in the `text` variable:

```
text = prompt("Enter some text.")
```

You can also create your own functions. This is useful for two main reasons: First, you can separate logical portions of your script to make it easier to understand. Second, and more importantly, you can use the function several times or with different data to avoid repeating script statements.

> You will learn how to define, call, and return values from your own functions in Hour 4, "Using Functions and Variables."

Understanding Objects

In Hour 2, you learned that variables are containers that can store a number, a string of text, or another value. JavaScript also supports *objects*. Like variables, objects can store data —but they can store two or more pieces of data at once.

The items of data stored in an object are called the *properties* of the object. As an example, you could use objects to store information about people as in an address book. The properties of each person object might include a name, address, and telephone number.

JavaScript uses periods to separate object names and property names. For example, for a person object called Bob, the properties might include `Bob.address` and `Bob.phone`.

Objects can also include *methods*. These are functions that work with the object's data. For example, our person object for the address book might include a `display()` method to display the person's information. In JavaScript terminology, the statement `Bob.display()` would display Bob's details.

The document.write function we discussed earlier this hour is actually a method of the document object. You will learn more about this object in Hour 9, "Working with the Document Object Model."

Don't worry if this sounds confusing—you'll be exploring objects in much more detail later in this book. For now, you just need to know the basics. JavaScript supports three kinds of objects:

- *Built-in objects* are objects built into the JavaScript language. You've already encountered one of these, Date, in Hour 2, "Creating a Simple Script." Other built-in objects include Array and String, which you'll explore in Hour 5, "Using Strings and Arrays," and Math, which is explained in Hour 8, "Using Math and Date Functions."

- *Browser objects* are objects that represent various components of the browser and the current HTML document. For example, the alert() function you used earlier in this chapter is actually a method of the window object. You'll explore these in more detail in Hour 9, "Working with the Document Object Model."

- *Custom objects* are objects you create yourself. For example, you could create a person object, as in the examples in this section. You'll learn to use custom objects in Hour 15, "Creating Custom Objects."

Handling Events

As mentioned in Hour 1, not all scripts are located within <script> tags. You can also use scripts as *event handlers*. While this might sound like a complex programming term, it actually means exactly what it says: Event handlers are scripts that handle events.

In real life, an event is something that happens to you. For example, the things you write on your calendar are events: "Dentist appointment" or "Fred's Birthday." You also encounter unscheduled events in your life: for example, a traffic ticket, an IRS audit, or an unexpected visit from relatives.

Whether events are scheduled or unscheduled, you probably have normal ways of handling them. Your event handlers might include things like *When Fred's birthday arrives, send him a present* or *When relatives visit unexpectedly, turn out the lights and pretend nobody's home.*

Event handlers in JavaScript are similar: They tell the browser what to do when a certain event occurs. The events JavaScript deals with aren't as exciting as the ones you deal

3

with—they include such events as *When the mouse button clicks* and *When this page is finished loading*. Nevertheless, they're a very useful part of JavaScript.

Many JavaScript events (such as mouse clicks) are caused by the user. Rather than doing things in a set order, your script can respond to the user's actions. Other events don't involve the user directly—for example, an event is triggered when an HTML document finishes loading.

Event handlers are associated with particular browser objects, and you specify the event handler in the tag that defines the object. For example, images and text links have an event, onMouseOver, that happens when the mouse pointer moves over the object. Here is a typical HTML image tag with an event handler:

```
<img SRC="button.gif" onMouseOver="highlight();">
```

You specify the event handler as an attribute to the HTML tag and include the JavaScript statement to handle the event within the quotation marks. This is an ideal use for functions, since function names are short and to the point and can refer to a whole series of statements.

You'll learn more about event handlers in Hour 10, "Responding to Events."

Conditional Statements

While event handlers notify your script when something happens, you may want to check certain conditions yourself. For example, did the user enter a valid email address?

JavaScript supports *conditional statements*, which allow you to answer questions like this. A typical conditional uses the if statement, as in this example:

```
if (count==1) alert("The countdown has reached 1.");
```

This compares the variable count with the constant 1, and displays an alert message to the user if they are the same. You will use conditional statements like this in most of your scripts.

You'll learn more about conditionals in Hour 6, "Testing and Comparing Values."

Loops

Another useful feature of JavaScript—and most other programming languages—is the ability to create *loops*, or groups of statements that repeat a certain number of times. For example, these statements display the same alert 10 times, greatly annoying the user:

```
for (i=1;i<=10;i++) {
   Alert("Yes, it's yet another alert!");
}
```

The for statement is one of several statements JavaScript uses for loops. This is the sort of thing computers are supposed to be good at: performing repetitive tasks. You will use loops in many of your scripts, in much more useful ways than this example.

> Loops are covered in detail in Hour 7, "Repeating Yourself: Using Loops."

Which Script Runs First?

As you learned in Hour 1, you can actually have several scripts within a Web document: one or more sets of <script> tags, and any number of event handlers. With all of these scripts, you might wonder how the browser knows which to execute first. Fortunately, this is done in a logical fashion:

- Sets of <script> tags within the <head> section of an HTML document are handled first. Since these scripts cannot create output in the Web page, it's a good place to define functions for later use.

- Sets of <script> tags within the <body> section of the HTML document are executed after those in the <head> section, while the Web page loads and displays. If there is more than one script in the body, they are executed in order.

- Event handlers are executed when their events happen. For example, the onLoad event handler is executed when the body of a Web page loads. Since the <head> section is loaded before any events, you can define functions there and use them in event handlers.

Workshop: Using Comments

In Hour 2, you used HTML comments to hide your script from older browsers. JavaScript also includes its own type of comments. While these won't hide JavaScript from anyone or anything, they are useful for their intended purpose—commenting on your script.

Comments allow you to include documentation within your script. This will be useful if someone else tries to understand the script, or even if you try to understand it after a long break. To include comments in a JavaScript program, begin a line with two slashes, as in this example:

```
//this is a comment.
```

You can also begin a comment with two slashes in the middle of a line, which is useful for documenting a script. In this case, everything on the line after the slashes is treated as a comment and ignored by the browser. For example:

```
a = a + 1; // add one to the value of a
```

JavaScript also supports C-style comments, which begin with /* and end with */. These comments can extend across more than one line, as the following example demonstrates:

```
/*This script includes a variety
of features, including this comment. */
```

C-style comments are often used for *commenting out* sections of code. If you have some lines of JavaScript that you want to temporarily take out of the picture while you debug a script, you can add /* at the beginning of the section and */ at the end.

Since these comments are part of JavaScript syntax, they are only valid inside `<script>` tags or within an external JavaScript file.

Summary

During this hour, you've been introduced to several components of JavaScript programming and syntax: functions, objects, event handlers, conditions, and loops. You also learned how to use JavaScript comments to make your script easier to read.

You have now reached the end of Part I of this book and should have a general idea of what JavaScript's about. In Part II, you'll learn more about JavaScript's most important components: functions, variables, strings, arrays, conditions, and loops.

Q&A

Q I've heard the term *object-oriented* applied to languages such as C++ and Java. If JavaScript supports objects, is it an object-oriented language?

A Yes, although it might not fit some people's strict definitions. JavaScript objects do not support all of the features that languages such as C++ and Java support.

Q **Having several scripts that execute at different times seems confusing. Why would I want to use event handlers?**

A Event handlers are the ideal way (and in JavaScript, the only way) to handle gadgets within the Web page, such as buttons, check boxes, and text fields. It's actually more convenient to handle them this way. Rather than writing a script that sits and waits for a button to be pushed, you can simply create an event handler and let the browser do the waiting for you.

Quiz

Test your knowledge of the JavaScript concepts covered in this hour by answering the following questions.

Questions

1. A script that executes when the user clicks the mouse button is an example of what?

    a. An object

    b. An event handler

    c. An impossibility

2. Which of the following are capabilities of functions in JavaScript?

    a. Accept parameters

    b. Return a value

    c. Both of the above

3. Which of the following is executed first by a browser?

    a. A script in the <head> section

    b. A script in the <body> section

    c. An event handler for a button

Answers

1. b. A script that executes when the user clicks the mouse button is an event handler.

2. c. Functions can both accept parameters and return values.

3. a. Scripts defined in the <head> section of an HTML document are executed first by the browser.

Exercises

To further explore the JavaScript features you learned about in this hour, you can perform the following exercises:

- Examine the Date and Time script you created in Hour 2 and find any examples of functions and objects being used.

- Add JavaScript comments to the Date and Time script to make it more clear what each line does. Verify that the script still runs properly.

PART II
Learning JavaScript Basics

Hour

HOUR 4

Using Functions and Variables

Welcome to Part II of this book! In the next five hours, you will learn some specific scripting features and techniques that you will frequently use in JavaScript programs.

During this hour, you will focus on functions, variables, and expressions. Hour 4 covers the following topics:

- Declaring and calling functions
- Returning values from functions
- Naming and declaring variables
- Choosing whether to use local or global variables
- Assigning values to variables
- How to convert between different data types
- Using variables and literals in expressions
- Using variables to store data entered by the user

Using Functions

The scripts you've seen so far are simple lists of instructions. The browser begins with the first statement after the `<script>` tag and follows each instruction in order until it reaches the closing `<script>` tag (or encounters an error).

While this is a straightforward approach for short scripts, it can be confusing to read a longer script written in this fashion. To make it easier for you to organize your scripts, JavaScript supports functions, which you learned about in Hour 3, "How JavaScript Programs Work." In this section you will learn how to define and use functions.

Defining a Function

Functions are groups of JavaScript statements that can be treated as a single unit. To use a function, you must first define it. Here is a simple example of a function definition:

```
function Greet() {
    alert("Greetings.");
}
```

This defines a function that displays an alert message to the user. This begins with the `function` keyword. The function's name is `Greet`. Notice the parentheses after the function's name. As you'll learn next, the space between them is not always empty.

The first and last lines of the function definition include braces ({ and }). You use these to enclose all of the statements in the function. The browser uses the braces to determine where the function begins and ends.

Between the braces, this particular function contains a single line. This uses the built-in `alert` function, which displays an alert message. The message will contain the text "Greetings."

 Function names are case sensitive. If you define a function such as `Greet` with a capital letter, be sure you use the identical name when you call the function.

Now, about those parentheses. The current `Greet` function always does the same thing: Each time you use it, it displays the same message. While this avoids a bit of typing, it doesn't really provide much of an advantage.

To make your function more flexible, you can add *parameters*, also known as *arguments*. These are variables that are received by the function each time it is called.

For example, you can add a parameter called who that tells the function the name of the person to greet. Here is the modified Greet function:

```
function Greet(who) {
    alert("Greetings, " + who);
}
```

Of course, to use this function, you should include it in an HTML document. Traditionally, the best place for a function definition is within the <head> section of the document. Since the statements in the <head> section are executed first, this ensures that the function is defined before it is used.

Listing 4.1 shows the Greet function embedded in the header section of an HTML document.

Listing 4.1   The Greet function in an HTML document

```
<html>
<head>
<title>Functions</title>
<script LANGUAGE="JavaScript" type="text/javascript">
function Greet(who) {
    alert("Greetings," + who);
}
</script>
</head>
<body>
This is the body of the page.
</body>
</html>
```

4

 As usual, you can download the listings for this hour or view them online at this book's Web site: http://www.jsworkshop.com/.

Calling the Function

You have now defined a function and placed it in an HTML document. However, if you load Listing 4.1 into a browser, you'll notice that it does absolutely nothing. This is because the function is defined—ready to be used—but we haven't used it yet.

Making use of a function is referred to as *calling* the function. To call a function, use the function's name as a statement in a script. You will need to include the parentheses and the values for the function's parameters. For example, here's a statement that calls the Greet function:

```
Greet("Fred");
```

This tells the JavaScript interpreter to transfer control to the first statement in the Greet function. It also passes the parameter "Fred" to the function. This value will be assigned to the who variable inside the function.

 Functions can have more than one parameter. To define a function with multiple parameters, list a variable name for each parameter, separated by commas. To call the function, specify values for each parameter separated by commas.

Listing 4.2 shows a complete HTML document that includes the function definition and a second script in the body of the page that actually calls the function. To demonstrate the usefulness of functions, we'll call it twice to greet two different people.

LISTING 4.2   The complete function example

```
<html>
<head>
<title>Functions</title>
<script LANGUAGE="JavaScript" type="text/javascript">
function Greet(who) {
    alert("Greetings," + who);
}
</script>
</head>
<body>
<h1>Function Example</h1>
<p>Prepare to be greeted twice.</p>
<script LANGUAGE="JavaScript" type="text/javascript">
Greet("Fred");
Greet("Ethel");
</script>
</body>
</html>
```

This listing includes a second set of <script> tags in the body of the page. The second script includes two function calls to the Greet function, each with a different name.

Now that you have a script that actually does something, try loading it into a browser. You should see something like Figure 4.1 for Internet Explorer. Netscape's output is similar, except that you won't see the body of the page until after you acknowledge the two greeting dialogs.

FIGURE 4.1

The output of the Greeting example.

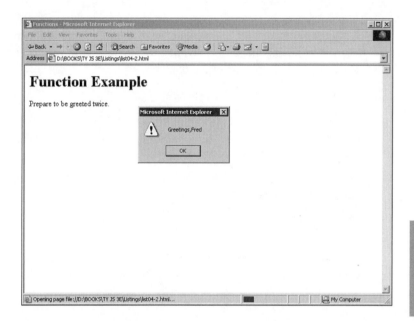

 Notice that the second alert message isn't displayed until you press the OK button on the first alert. This is because JavaScript processing is halted while alerts are displayed.

Returning a Value

While the function you just created displays a message to the user, functions can also return a value to the script that called them. This allows you to use functions to calculate values. As an example, you can create a function that averages four numbers.

Your function should begin with the function keyword, the function's name, and the parameters it accepts. We will use the variable names a, b, c, and d for the four numbers to average. Here is the first line of the function:

```
function Average(a,b,c,d) {
```

I've also included the opening brace ({) on the first line of the function. This is a common style, but you can also place the brace on the next line, or on a line by itself.

Next, the function needs to calculate the average of the four parameters. You can calculate this by adding them, then dividing by the number of parameters (in this case, 4). Thus, here is the next line of the function:

```
result = (a + b + c + d) / 4;
```

This statement creates a variable called `result` and calculates the result by adding the four numbers, then dividing by 4. (The parentheses are necessary to tell JavaScript to perform the addition before the division.)

To send this result back to the script that called the function, you use the `return` keyword. Here is the last part of the function:

```
return result;
}
```

Listing 4.3 shows the complete `Average` function in an HTML document. This HTML document also includes a small script in the `<body>` section that calls the `Average` function and displays the result.

LISTING 4.3   The Average function in an HTML document.

```
<html>
<head>
<title>Function Example</title>
<script LANGUAGE="JavaScript" type="text/javascript">
function Average(a,b,c,d) {
result = (a + b + c + d) / 4;
return result;
}
</script>
</head>
<body>
<p>The following is the result of the function call.</p>
<script LANGUAGE="JavaScript" type="text/javascript">
score = Average(3,4,5,6);
document.write("The average is: " + score);
</script>
</body>
</html>
```

You can use a variable with the function call, as shown in this listing. This statement averages the numbers 3, 4, 5, and 6 and stores the result in a variable called `score`:

```
score = Average(3,4,5,6);
```

> You can also use the function call directly in an expression. For example, you could use the `alert` statement to display the result of the function:
> `alert(Average(1,2,3,4)) .`

Understanding Expressions and Operators

In the definition of the `Average` function in the previous example, you used this statement to average the four numbers:

```
result = (a + b + c + d) / 4;
```

The portion of this statement to the right of the equal sign is called an *expression*: a combination of variables and values that the JavaScript interpreter can evaluate to a single value. The characters that are used to combine these values, such as + and /, are called *operators*.

> Along with variables and constant values, you can also use calls to functions that return results within an expression.

Using JavaScript Operators

You've already used some operators, such as the + sign (addition) and the / sign (division) in the `Average` function example. Table 4.1 lists some of the most important operators you can use in JavaScript expressions.

TABLE 4.1. Common JavaScript Operators

Operator	Description	Example
+	Concatenate (combine) strings	`message="this is" + " a test";`
+	Add	`result = 5 + 7;`
-	Subtract	`score = score - 1;`
*	Multiply	`total = quantity * price;`

TABLE 4.1.   Continued

Operator	Description	Example
/	Divide	`average = sum / 4;`
%	Modulo (remainder)	`remainder = sum % 4;`
++	Increment	`tries++;`
--	Decrement	`total--;`

You'll learn more about the increment and decrement operators later in this hour. There are also many other operators used in conditional statements—you'll learn about these in Hour 6, "Testing and Comparing Values."

Operator Precedence

When you use more than one operator in an expression, JavaScript uses rules of *operator precedence* to decide how to calculate the value. Table 4.1 above lists the operators from lowest to highest precedence, and operators with highest precedence are evaluated first. For example, consider this statement:

```
result = 4 + 5 * 3;
```

If you try to calculate this result, there are two ways to do it. You could multiply 5 * 3 first and then add 4 (result: 19) or add 4 + 5 first and then multiply by 3 (result: 27). JavaScript solves this dilemma by following the precedence rules: since multiplication has a higher precedence than addition, it first multiplies 5 * 3 and then adds 4, producing a result of 19.

> If you're familiar with any other programming languages, you'll find that the operators and precedence in JavaScript work, for the most part, the same way as those in C, C++, and Java.

Sometimes operator precedence doesn't produce the result you want. For example, consider this statement:

```
result = a + b + c + d / 4;
```

This is similar to the calculation in the Average function earlier this hour. However, since JavaScript gives division a higher precedence than addition, it will divide the d variable by 4 before adding the other numbers, producing an incorrect result.

You can control precedence by using parentheses. Here's the working statement from the Average function:

```
result = (a + b + c + d) / 4;
```

The parentheses ensure that the four variables are added first, and then the sum is divided by four.

> If you're unsure about operator precedence, you can use parentheses to make sure things work the way you expect and to make your script more readable.

Using Variables

Unless you skipped the first three hours of this book, you've already used a few variables. You probably can also figure out how to use a few more without any help. Nevertheless, there are some aspects of variables you haven't learned yet. We will now look at some of the details.

Choosing Variable Names

Variables are named containers that can store data (for example, a number, a text string, or an object). As you learned earlier in this book, each variable has a name. There are specific rules you must follow when choosing a variable name:

- Variable names can include letters of the alphabet, both upper- and lowercase. They can also include the digits 0–9 and the underscore (_) character.

- Variable names cannot include spaces or any other punctuation characters.

- The first character of the variable name must be either a letter or an underscore.

- Variable names are case-sensitive—totalnum, Totalnum, and TotalNum are separate variable names.

- There is no official limit on the length of variable names, but they must fit within one line. (And you must be able to type the same name twice to make use of the variable.)

Using these rules, the following are examples of valid variable names:

```
total_number_of_fish
LastInvoiceNumber
temp1
a
_var39
```

You can choose to use either friendly, easy-to-read names or completely cryptic ones. Do yourself a favor: use longer, friendly names whenever possible. While you might remember the difference between a, b, x, and x1 right now, you might not after a good night's sleep.

Using Local and Global Variables

Some computer languages require you to declare a variable before you use it. JavaScript includes the var keyword, which can be used to declare a variable. You can omit var in many cases; the variable is still declared the first time you assign a value to it.

To understand where to declare a variable, you will need to understand the concept of *scope*. A variable's scope is the area of the script in which that variable can be used. There are two types of variables:

- *Global variables* have the entire script (and other scripts in the same HTML document) as their scope. They can be used anywhere, even within functions.
- *Local variables* have a single function as their scope. They can be used only within the function they are created in.

To create a global variable, you declare it in the main script, outside any functions. You can use the var keyword to declare the variable, as in this example:

```
var students = 25;
```

This statement declares a variable called students and assigns it a value of 25. If this statement is used outside functions, it creates a global variable. The var keyword is optional in this case, so this statement is equivalent to the previous one:

```
students = 25;
```

Before you get in the habit of omitting the var keyword, be sure you understand exactly when it's required. It's actually a good idea to always use the var keyword—you'll avoid errors and make your script easier to read, and it won't usually cause any trouble.

For the most part, the variables you've used in earlier hours of this book have been global.

A local variable belongs to a particular function. Any variable you declare with the var keyword in a function is a local variable. Additionally, the variables in the function's parameter list are always local variables.

To create a local variable within a function, you must use the var keyword. This forces JavaScript to create a local variable, even if there is a global variable with the same name.

To better understand the types of variables and declarations better, look at Listing 4.4. This is a modified version of the Greet function example from earlier in this hour.

LISTING 4.4   A script using both local and global variables

```
<html>
<head>
<title>Local and Global Variables</title>
<script LANGUAGE="JavaScript" type="text/javascript">
var name1 = "Fred";
var name2 = "Ethel";
function Greet(who) {
alert("Greetings," + who);
    var name2 = "Barney";
}
</script>
</head>
<body>
<h1>Function Example: the Sequel</h1>
<p>Prepare to be greeted twice.</p>
<script LANGUAGE="JavaScript" type="text/javascript">
Greet(name1);
Greet(name2);
</script>
</body>
</html>
```

4

The script in Listing 4.4 uses the following variables:

- name1 and name2 are global variables defined in the header.
- who is a local variable created in the Greet function's parameter list.
- The Greet function creates a local variable called name2. Since the var keyword is used, this variable is local to the function and does not affect the global variable name2. (If it did, the name in the second greeting would change.)

If you think having two variables with the same name is confusing, you're right. To avoid this, it's best to use unique names for all variables.

Notice that the global variables are declared within the header of the HTML document. You can actually declare variables in any script in the document, but the header is a good place for global variables because it is executed first. If you attempt to use a variable before it is declared or assigned a value, it will contain the null value and may cause a browser error.

You should now understand the difference between local and global variables. If you're still a bit confused, don't worry—if you use the var keyword every time, you'll usually end up with the right type of variable.

Assigning Values to Variables

As you learned in Hour 2, "Creating a Simple Script," you can use the equal sign to assign a value to a variable. For example, this statement assigns the value 40 to the variable lines:

```
lines = 40;
```

You can use any expression to the right of the equal sign, including other variables. You have used this syntax earlier to add one to a variable:

```
lines = lines + 1;
```

Since incrementing or decrementing variables is quite common, JavaScript includes two types of shorthand for this syntax. The first is the += operator, which allows you to create the following shorter version of the above example:

```
lines += 1;
```

Similarly, you can subtract a number from a variable using the -= operator:

```
lines -= 1;
```

If you still think that's too much to type, JavaScript also includes the increment and decrement operators, ++ and --. This statement adds one to the value of lines:

```
lines++;
```

Similarly, this statement subtracts one from the value of lines:

```
lines--;
```

You can alternately use the ++ or -- operators before a variable name, as in ++lines. However, these are not identical. The difference is when the increment or decrement happens:

- If the operator is after the variable name, the increment or decrement happens *after* the current expression is evaluated.
- If the operator is before the variable name, the increment or decrement happens *before* the current expression is evaluated.

This difference is only an issue when you use the variable in an expression and increment or decrement it in the same statement. As an example, suppose you have assigned the lines variable the value 40. The following two statements have different effects:

```
alert(lines++);
```

```
alert(++lines);
```

The first statement displays an alert with the value 40, and then increments lines to 41. The second statement first increments lines to 41, then displays an alert with the value 41.

These operators are strictly for your convenience. If it makes more sense to you to stick to lines = lines + 1, do it—your script won't suffer.

4

Data Types in JavaScript

In some computer languages, you have to specify the type of data a variable will store: for example, a number or a string. In JavaScript, you don't need to specify a data type in most cases. However, you should know the types of data JavaScript can deal with.

These are the basic JavaScript data types:

- *Numbers*, such as 3, 25, or 1.4142138. JavaScript supports both integers and floating-point numbers.
- *Boolean*, or logical values. These can have one of two values: true or false. These are useful for indicating whether a certain condition is true.

You'll learn more about boolean values, and about using conditions in JavaScript, in Hour 6, "Testing and Comparing Values."

- *Strings*, such as `"I am a jelly doughnut"`. These consist of one or more characters of text. (Strictly speaking, these are string objects, which you'll learn about in Hour 5, "Using Strings and Arrays.")
- *The null value*, represented by the keyword `null`. This is the value of an undefined variable. For example, the statement `document.write(fig)` will result in this value (and an error message) if the variable `fig` has not been previously used or defined.

Although JavaScript keeps track of the data type currently stored in each variable, it doesn't restrict you from changing types midstream. For example, suppose you declared a variable by assigning it a value:

```
total = 31;
```

This statement declares a variable called `total` and assigns it the value of 31. This is a numeric variable. Now suppose you changed the value of `total`:

```
total = "albatross";
```

This assigns a string value to `total`. JavaScript will not display an error when this statement executes; it's perfectly valid, although it's probably not a very useful total.

> While this feature of JavaScript is convenient and powerful, it can also make it easy to make a mistake. For example, if the `total` variable was later used in a mathematical calculation, the result would be invalid—but JavaScript does not warn you that you've made this mistake.

Converting Between Data Types

JavaScript handles conversions between data types for you whenever it can. For example, you've already used statements like this:

```
document.write("The total is " + total);
```

This statement prints out a message such as "The total is 40." Since the `document.write` function works with strings, the JavaScript interpreter automatically converts any non-strings in the expression (in this case, the value of `total`) to strings before performing the function.

This works equally well with floating-point and boolean values. However, there are some situations where it won't work. For example, the following statement will work fine if the value of `total` is 40:

```
average = total / 3;
```

However, the total variable could also contain a string; in this case, the statement above would result in an error.

In some situations, you may end up with a string containing a number, and need to convert it to a regular numeric variable. JavaScript includes two functions for this purpose:

- parseInt() converts a string to an integer number.
- parseFloat() converts a string to a floating-point number.

Both of these functions will read a number from the beginning of the string, and return a numeric version. For example, these statements convert the string "30 angry polar bears" to a number:

```
stringvar = "30 angry polar bears";
numvar = parseInt(stringvar);
```

After these statements execute, the numvar variable contains the number 30. The non-numeric portion of the string is ignored.

These functions look for a number of the appropriate type at the beginning of the string. If a valid number is not found, the function will return the special value NaN, meaning *not a number.*

4

Workshop: Storing User Data in Variables

One common use of variables is to store information that comes from the user. As an example, you will now create a script that prompts the user for information and creates an HTML document containing that information.

In this script, we'll create a customized home page for the user. (It won't be a good one, but it will be customized.) You will use the prompt function to prompt for each piece of information. This function is similar to alert, but prompts the user for an entry.

To begin the script, you will prompt for a first name, a last name, and a title for the page. These statements prompt for three variables:

```
first = prompt("Enter your first name.");
last = prompt("Enter your last name.");
title = prompt("Enter a page title.");
```

You can now use the contents of the variables to customize the HTML document. Begin with the title the user entered:

```
document.write("<h1>" + title + "</h1>");
```

This statement adds the title to the page, enclosed in <h1> (heading 1) tags. Next, we'll make use of the first and last names to give the user credit:

```
document.write("<h2>By " + first + " " + last + "</h2>");
```

This begins with an <h2> tag, followed by the word "By", the first name, a space, the last name, and the closing </h2> tag.

To complete this script, add the usual <script> tags and an HTML framework. Listing 4.5 shows the final HTML document.

LISTING 4.5   A script to create a customized HTML document

```
<html>
<head>
<title>Customized home page</title>
</head>
<body>
<script LANGUAGE="JavaScript" type="text/javascript">
first = prompt("Enter your first name.");
last = prompt("Enter your last name.");
title = prompt("Enter a page title.");
document.write("<h1>" + title + "</h1>");
document.write("<h2>By " + first + " " + last + "</h2>");
</script>
<p>This page is under construction.</p>
</body>
</html>
```

To test this script, load the HTML document into a browser. You will be prompted for the three items, one at a time. After you have entered all three, the complete page is displayed. The final page should resemble Figure 4.2.

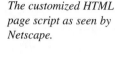

FIGURE 4.2

The customized HTML page script as seen by Netscape.

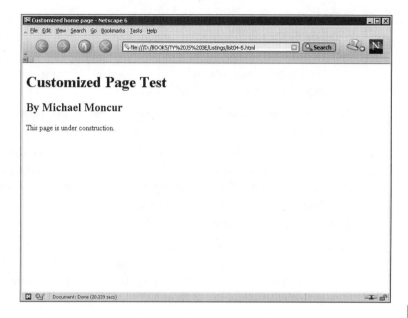

Summary

During this hour, you've focused on JavaScript functions, which combine several statements. You also learned more about variables and how JavaScript handles them. You've learned how to name variables, how to declare them, and the differences between local and global variables.

Finally, you also explored the data types supported by JavaScript and how to convert between them and created expressions using variables in literals. In the next hour, you'll move on to two more complicated types of variables: strings and arrays.

Q&A

Q Why does Netscape display the error message "missing semicolon before statement" when I try the function example?

A This is probably because you mistyped something. JavaScript is case-sensitive, so be sure you get the capitalization right. This specific error message will appear if you use the keyword Function instead of function.

Q **What is the importance of the var keyword? Should I always use it to declare variables?**

A You only need to use var to define a local variable in a function. However, if you're unsure at all, it's always safe to use var. Using it consistently will help you keep your scripts organized and error-free.

Q **Is there any reason I would want to use the var keyword to create a local variable with the same name as a global one?**

A Not on purpose. The main reason to use var is to avoid conflicts with global variables you may not know about. For example, you may add a global variable in the future, or you may add another script to the page that uses a similar variable name. This is more of an issue with large, complex scripts.

Q **What good are boolean variables?**

A Often in scripts you'll need a variable to indicate whether something has happened—for example, whether a phone number the user has entered is in the right format. Boolean variables are ideal for this; they're also useful in working with conditions, as you'll see in Hour 6.

Quiz

Test your knowledge of JavaScript variables and expressions by answering the following questions.

Questions

1. Which of the following is *not* a valid JavaScript variable name?

    a. `2names`

    b. `_first_and_last_names`

    c. `FirstAndLast`

2. If the statement var `fig=2` appears in a function, which type of variable does it declare?

    a. A global variable

    b. A local variable

    c. A constant variable

3. What will be the result of the JavaScript expression `31 + " angry polar bears"`?

   a. An error message

   b. 32

   c. "31 angry polar bears"

Answers

1. a. `2names` is an invalid JavaScript variable name since it begins with a number. The others are valid, although they're probably not ideal choices for names.

2. b. Since the variable is declared in a function, it is a local variable. The `var` keyword ensures that a local variable is created.

3. c. JavaScript converts the whole expression to the string "31 angry polar bears". (No offense to polar bears, who are seldom angry and rarely seen in groups this large.)

Exercises

If you would like to further explore the concepts you learned in this chapter, perform the following activities:

- Modify the `Greet` function to accept two parameters, `who1` and `who2`, and to include both names in a single greeting dialog. Modify Listing 4.2 to use a single function call to the new function.

- Modify Listing 4.4 by removing the `var` keyword before `name2` in the `Greet()` function. Are the greetings different than the original version? If they are, try to understand why.

- Add some additional customizable features to Listing 4.5. For example, you could prompt the user for a URL and include a link on the page.

4

Hour 5

Using Strings and Arrays

In Hour 4, "Using Functions and Variables," you used variables to store and work with numbers. Although you can do quite a bit with numbers, some of the most useful applications of JavaScript involve the use of strings (text) and arrays: groups of numbers, strings, or objects.

In this hour, you will learn to use strings and arrays in JavaScript. Hour 5 covers the following topics:

- How strings are stored in String objects
- Creating and using String objects
- Calculating the length of a string
- Working with parts of strings
- Finding a string within a larger string
- How arrays are stored in Array objects
- Creating and using arrays
- Working with string arrays
- Using strings to create scrolling messages

Using String Objects

You've already used several strings during the first few hours of this book. Strings store a group of text characters, and are named similarly to other variables. As a simple example, this statement assigns the string This is a test to a string variable called test:

```
test = "This is a test";
```

Creating a String Object

JavaScript stores strings as String objects. You usually don't need to worry about this, but it will explain some of the techniques for working with strings, which use methods (built-in functions) of the String object.

There are two ways to create a new String object. The first is the one you've already used, while the second uses official object syntax. The following two statements create the same string:

```
test = "This is a test";
test = new String("This is a test");
```

The second statement uses the new keyword, which you use to create objects. This tells the browser to create a new String object containing the text This is a test, and assigns it to the variable test.

> While you can create a string using object-oriented syntax, the standard JavaScript syntax is simpler, and there is no difference in the strings created by these two methods.

Assigning a Value

You can assign a value to a string in the same way as any other variable. Both of the examples in the previous section assigned an initial value to the string. You can also assign a value after the string has already been created. For example, the following statement replaces the contents of the test variable with a new string:

```
test = "This is only a test.";
```

You can also use the concatenation operator (+) to combine the values of two strings. Listing 5.1 shows a simple example of assigning and combining the values of strings.

LISTING 5.1   Assigning values to strings and combining them

```
<html>
<head>
<title>String Test</title>
</head>
<body>
<h1>String Test</h1>
<script LANGUAGE="JavaScript" type="text/javascript">;
test1 = "This is a test. ";
test2 = "This is only a test.";
both = test1 + test2;
alert(both);
</script>
</body>
</html>
```

This script assigns values to two string variables, test1 and test2, and then displays an alert with their combined value. If you load this HTML document in a browser, your output should resemble Figure 5.1.

FIGURE 5.1.

The output of the string example script.

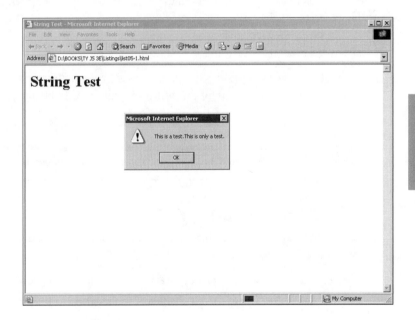

5

In addition to using the + operator to concatenate two strings, you can use the += operator to add text to a string. For example, this statement adds a period to the current contents of the string `sentence`:

```
sentence += ".";
```

 The plus sign (+) is also used to add numbers in JavaScript. The browser knows whether to use addition or concatenation based on the types of data you use with the plus sign. If you use it between a number and a string, the number is converted to a string and concatenated.

Calculating the String's Length

From time to time, you may find it useful to know how many characters a string variable contains. You can do this with the `length` property of `String` objects, which you can use with any string. To use this property, type the string's name followed by `.length`.

For example, `test.length` refers to the length of the `test` string. Here is an example of this property:

```
test = "This is a test.";
document.write(test.length);
```

The first statement assigns the string `This is a test` to the test variable. The second statement displays the length of the string—in this case, 15 characters.

 Remember that although `test` refers to a string variable, the value of `test.length` is a number and can be used in any numeric expression.

Converting the String's Case

Two methods of the `String` object allow you to convert the contents of a string to all uppercase or all lowercase:

- `toUpperCase()` converts all characters in the string to uppercase.
- `toLowerCase()` converts all characters in the string to lowercase.

For example, the following statement displays the value of the `test` string variable in lowercase:

```
document.write(test.toLowerCase());
```

Assuming that this variable contained the text `This Is A Test`, the result would be the following string:

```
this is a test
```

Note that the statement doesn't change the value of the `text` variable. These methods return the upper- or lowercase version of the string, but they don't change the string itself. If you want to change the string's value, you can use a statement like this:

```
test = test.toLowerCase();
```

 Note that the syntax for these methods is similar to the `length` property introduced earlier. The difference is that methods always use parentheses, while properties don't. The `toUpperCase` and `toLowerCase` methods do not take any parameters, but you still need to use the parentheses.

Working with Substrings

So far you've worked with entire strings. JavaScript also allows you to work with *substrings*, or portions of a string. You can use the `substring` method to retrieve a portion of a string, or the `charAt` method to get a single character. These are explained in the following sections.

Using Part of a String

The `substring` method returns a string consisting of a portion of the original string between two index values, which you must specify in parentheses. For example, the following statement displays the fourth through sixth characters of the `text` string:

```
document.write(text.substring(3,6));
```

At this point, you're probably wondering where the 3 and the 6 come from. There are three things you need to understand about the index parameters:

- Indexing starts with 0 for the first character of the string, so the fourth character is actually index 3.
- The second index is non-inclusive. A second index of 6 includes up to index 5 (the sixth character).
- You can specify the two indexes in either order. The smaller one will be assumed to be the first index. In the previous example, (6,3) would have produced the same result. Of course, there is rarely a reason to use the reverse order.

5

As another example, suppose you defined a string called `alpha` to hold the alphabet:

```
alpha = "ABCDEFGHIJKLMNOPQRSTUVWXYZ";
```

The following are examples of the `substring()` method using this string:

- `alpha.substring(0,4)` returns ABCD.
- `alpha.substring(10,12)` returns KL.
- `alpha.substring(12,10)` also returns KL. Because it's smaller, `10` is used as the first index.
- `alpha.substring(6,7)` returns G.
- `alpha.substring(24,26)` returns YZ.
- `alpha.substring(0,26)` returns the entire alphabet.
- `alpha.substring(6,6)` returns the `null` value, an empty string. This is true whenever the two index values are the same.

Getting a Single Character

The `charAt` method is a simple way to grab a single character from a string. You specify the character's index, or position, in parentheses. The indexes begin at 0 for the first character. Here are a few examples using the `alpha` string:

- `alpha.charAt(0)` returns A.
- `alpha.charAt(12)` returns M.
- `alpha.charAt(25)` returns Z.
- `alpha.charAt(27)` returns an empty string because there is no character at that position.

Finding a Substring

Another use for substrings is to find a string within another string. One way to do this is with the `indexOf` method. To use this method, add `indexOf` to the string you want to search, and specify the string to search for in the parentheses. This example searches for "this" in the `test` string:

```
loc = test.indexOf("this");
```

As with most JavaScript methods and property names, `indexOf` is case sensitive. Make sure you type it exactly as shown here when you use it in scripts.

The value returned in the `loc` variable is an index into the string, similar to the first index in the `substring` method. The first character of the string is index 0.

You can specify an optional second parameter to indicate the index value to begin the search. For example, this statement searches for the word `fish` in the `temp` string, starting with the 20th character:

```
location = temp.indexOf("fish",19);
```

> One use for the second parameter is to search for multiple occurrences of a string. After finding the first occurrence, you search starting with that location for the second one, and so on.

A second method, `lastIndexOf()`, works the same way, but finds the *last* occurrence of the string. It searches the string backwards, starting with the last character. For example, this statement finds the last occurrence of `Fred` in the `names` string:

```
location = names.lastIndexOf("Fred");
```

As with `indexOf()`, you can specify a location to search from as the second parameter. In this case, the string will be searched backward starting at that location.

Using Numeric Arrays

An array is a numbered group of data items that you can treat as a single unit. For example, you might use an array called `scores` to store several scores for a game. Arrays can contain strings, numbers, objects, or other types of data. Each item in an array is called an *element* of the array.

5

Creating a Numeric Array

Unlike most other types of JavaScript variables, you usually need to declare an array before you use it. The following example creates an array with four elements:

```
scores = new Array(4);
```

To assign a value to the array, you use an *index* in brackets. Indexes begin with 0, so the elements of the array in this example would be numbered 0 to 3. These statements assign values to the four elements of the array:

```
scores[0] = 39;
scores[1] = 40;
scores[2] = 100;
scores[3] = 49;
```

You can also declare an array and specify values for elements at the same time. This statement creates the same scores array in a single line:

```
scores = new Array(39,40,100,49);
```

In JavaScript 1.2 and later, you can also use a shorthand syntax to declare an array and specify its contents. The following statement is an alternate way to create the scores array:

```
scores = [39,40,100,49];
```

Remember to use parentheses when declaring an array with the new keyword, as in a=new Array(3,4,5), and use brackets when declaring an array without new, as in a=[3,4,5]. Otherwise you'll run into JavaScript errors.

Understanding Array Length

Like strings, arrays have a length property. This tells you the number of elements in the array. If you specified the length when creating the array, this value becomes the length property's value. For example, these statements would print the number 30:

```
scores = new Array(30);
document.write(scores.length);
```

You can declare an array without a specific length, and change the length later by assigning values to elements or changing the length property. For example, these statements create a new array and assign values to two elements:

```
test = new Array();
test[0]=21;
test[5]=22;
```

In this example, since the largest index number assigned so far is 5, the array has a length property of 6—remember, elements are numbered starting at zero.

Accessing Array Elements

You can read the contents of an array using the same notation you used when assigning values. For example, the following statements would display the values of the first three elements of the scores array:

```
scoredisp = "Scores: " + scores[0] + "," + scores[1] + "," + scores[2];
document.write(scoredisp);
```

> Looking at this example, you might imagine it would be inconvenient to display all of the elements of a large array. This is an ideal job for loops, which allow you to perform the same statements several times with different values. You'll learn all about loops in Hour 7, "Repeating Yourself: Using Loops."

Using String Arrays

So far, you've used arrays of numbers. JavaScript also allows you to use *string arrays*, or arrays of strings. This is a powerful feature that allows you to work with a large number of strings at the same time.

Creating a String Array

You declare a string array in the same way as a numeric array—in fact, JavaScript does not make a distinction between them:

```
names = new Array(30);
```

You can then assign string values to the array elements:

```
names[0] = "Henry J. Tillman";
names[1] = "Sherlock Holmes";
```

As with numeric arrays, you can also specify a string array's contents when you create it. Either of following statements would create the same string array as the above example:

```
names = new Array("Henry J. Tillman", "Sherlock Holmes");
names = ["Henry J. Tillman", "Sherlock Holmes"];
```

You can use string array elements anywhere you would use a string. You can even use the string methods introduced earlier. For example, the following statement prints the first five characters of the first element of the names array, resulting in Henry:

```
document.write(names[0].substring(0,5));
```

Splitting a String

JavaScript includes a string method called split, which splits a string into its component parts. To use this method, specify the string to split and a character to divide the parts:

```
test = "John Q. Public";
parts = test.split(" ");
```

In this example, the test string contains the name John Q. Public. The split method in the second statement splits the name string at each space, resulting in three strings.

5

These are stored in a string array called parts. After the example statements execute, the elements of parts contain the following:

- parts[0] = "John"
- parts[1] = "Q."
- parts[2] = "Public"

JavaScript also includes an array method, join, that performs the opposite function. This statement reassembles the parts array into a string:

```
fullname = parts.join(" ");
```

The value in the parentheses specifies a character to separate the parts of the array. In this case, a space is used, resulting in the final string John Q. Public. If you do not specify a character, commas are used.

Sorting a String Array

JavaScript also includes a sort method for arrays, which returns an alphabetically sorted version of the array. For example, the following statements initialize an array of four names and sort it:

```
names[0] = "Public, John Q.";
names[1] = "Tillman, Henry J.";
names[2] = "Bush, George W.";
names[3] = "Mouse, Mickey";
sortednames = names.sort();
```

The last statement sorts the names array and stores the result in a new array, sortednames.

Sorting a Numeric Array

Since the sort method sorts alphabetically, it won't work with a numeric array—at least not the way you'd expect. If an array contains the numbers 4, 10, 30, and 200, for example, it would sort them as 10, 200, 30, 4—not even close. Fortunately, there's a solution—you can specify a function in the sort method's parameters, and that function will be used to compare the numbers. The following code sorts a numeric array correctly:

```
function numcompare(a,b) {
    return a-b;
}
nums = new Array(30, 10, 200, 4);
sortednums = nums.sort(numcompare);
```

This example defines a simple function, numcompare, that subtracts the two numbers. Once you specify this function in the sort method, the array is sorted in the correct numeric order: 4, 10, 30, 200).

> JavaScript expects the comparison function to return a negative number if a belongs before b, zero if they are the same, or a positive number if a belongs after b. This is why a-b is all you need for the function to sort numerically.

Workshop: Displaying a Scrolling Message

One of the most common uses of JavaScript is to create a scrolling message in the browser's status line. You can create a scrolling message using the string methods you have learned in this hour.

To begin, you'll need to define the message to be scrolled. You will use a variable called msg to store the message. To begin the script, initialize the variable (feel free to choose your own text for the message):

```
msg = "This is an example of a scrolling message. Isn't it exciting?";
```

Next, add a spacer string to the beginning of msg. This will be displayed between the copies of the message to make it clear where one ends and the other begins. This statement adds the spacer to msg:

```
msg = "...     ..." + msg;
```

You'll need one more variable: a numeric variable to store the current position of the string. Call it pos and initialize it with 0:

```
pos = 0;
```

The actual scrolling will be done by a function called ScrollMessage. Here is the JavaScript code for this function:

```
function ScrollMessage() {
    window.status = msg.substring(pos, msg.length) + msg.substring(0, pos);
    pos++;
    if (pos > msg.length) pos = 0;
    window.setTimeout("ScrollMessage()",200);
}
```

5

The ScrollMessage function includes the following commands:

- The function keyword is used to begin the function.
- The window.status property is used to display a string in the status line. The string is composed of the portion of msg from pos to the end, followed by the portion of msg from the beginning to pos.
- Next, the pos variable is incremented using the pos++ shorthand.
- The if statement checks whether pos is larger than the length of msg. If it is, it resets it to 0. (You'll learn more about the if statement in the next hour.)
- The final statement of the function uses the window.setTimeout method, which allows you to set a statement to be executed after a time delay. In this case, it executes the ScrollMessage function again after .2 seconds.
- Finally, the closing bracket ends the function.

To complete the example, add the <script> tags and the HTML tags that make up a Web document. Listing 5.2 shows the complete scrolling message example.

Don't forget that you can download this listing from this book's Web site, http://www.jsworkshop.com/, rather than typing it in yourself.

LISTING 5.2   The complete scrolling message example

```
<html>
<head><title>Scrolling Message Example</title>
<script LANGUAGE="JavaScript" type="text/javascript">
msg = "This is an example of a scrolling message. Isn't it exciting?";
msg = "...          ..." + msg;pos = 0;
function ScrollMessage() {
   window.status = msg.substring(pos, msg.length) + msg.substring(0, pos);
   pos++;
   if (pos > msg.length) pos = 0;
   window.setTimeout("ScrollMessage()",200);
}
ScrollMessage();
</script>
</head>
<body>
<h1>Scrolling Message Example</h1>
```

LISTING 5.2   Continued

```
Look at the status line at the bottom of this page. (Don't
watch it too long, as it may be hypnotic.)
</body>
</html>
```

Figure 5.2 shows the output of the scrolling message program.

FIGURE 5.2.

The scrolling message example in action.

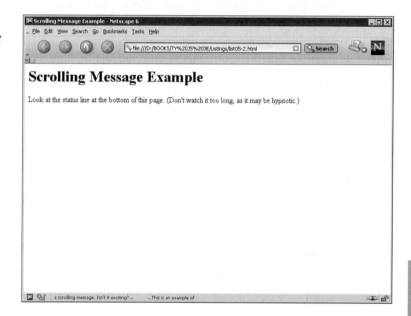

5

Summary

In this hour, you've learned how to store strings in JavaScript and how to work with portions of strings. You also learned how to use arrays and how to store numbers or strings in them.

You applied your knowledge of strings to create a scrolling message. In the next hour, you'll learn how to use the `if` statement and other JavaScript features to test the values of variables, including strings and arrays.

Q&A

Q Can I store other types of data in an array? For example, can I have an array of dates?

A Absolutely. JavaScript allows you to store any data type in an array.

Q What about two-dimensional arrays?

A These are arrays with two indexes (such as columns and rows). JavaScript does not directly support this type of arrays, but you can use objects to achieve the same effect. You will learn more about objects in Hour 15, "Creating Custom Objects."

Q If I assign values to array elements manually anyway, what is the advantage of using arrays?

A First of all, you can use a loop to work with the array elements, and use methods such as `join` and `sort` to work with the array. Arrays can also be used to store several lines of data from a form, as you'll see in Hour 12, "Getting Data with Forms."

Quiz

Test your knowledge of JavaScript strings and arrays by answering the following questions.

Questions

1. If the string `test` contains the value `The eagle has landed.`, what would be the value of `test.length`?

    a. `4`

    b. `21`

    c. `The`

2. Using the same example string, which of these statements would return the word `eagle`?

    a. `test.substring(4,9)`

    b. `test.substring(5,9)`

    c. `test.substring("eagle")`

3. What does the `join` method of an array do?

    a. Allows a new member to join the array.

    b. Combines the array with another array.

    c. Combines the array's elements into a string.

Answers

1. b. The length of the string is 21 characters.

2. a. The correct statement is `test.substring(4,9)`. Remember that the indexes start with `0`, and that the second index is non-inclusive.

3. c. The `join` method combines the array's elements into a string.

Exercises

You can further your knowledge of strings and arrays by performing these activities:

- Use Netscape's JavaScript console to create several strings and experiment with them. The console was introduced in Hour 2, "Creating a Simple Script." To use it, type `javascript:` in Netscape's Location field.

- Modify the scrolling message example to scroll the message in the opposite direction. (Hint: Since the `pos` variable controls what portion of the string is displayed, you need to make its value count downward instead of upward.)

5

HOUR 6

Testing and Comparing Values

Having survived Hours 4 and 5 of this book, you should now be familiar with creating and using variables of all sorts. In this hour, you'll learn how to make better use of variables by comparing, testing, and evaluating their values with the tools provided by JavaScript.

In Hour 6, you'll learn to use conditional statements in JavaScript. You will cover the following topics:

- Testing variables with the `if` statement
- Using various operators to compare values
- Using logical operators to combine conditions
- Using alternate conditions with `else`
- Creating expressions with conditional operators
- Testing for multiple conditions
- Evaluating data received from the user

The `if` Statement

One of the most important features of a computer language is the capability to test and compare values. This allows your scripts to behave differently based on the values of variables, or based on input from the user.

The `if` statement is the main conditional statement in JavaScript. This statement means much the same in JavaScript as it does in English—for example, here is a typical conditional statement in English:

If the phone rings, answer it.

This statement consists of two parts: a condition (*If the phone rings*) and an action (*answer it*). The `if` statement in JavaScript works much the same way. Here is an example of a basic `if` statement:

```
if (a == 1) window.alert("Found a 1!");
```

This statement includes a condition (if a equals 1) and an action (display a message). This statement checks the variable a and, if it has a value of 1, displays an alert message. Otherwise, it does nothing.

If you use an `if` statement like the preceding example, you can use a single statement as the action. You can also use multiple statements for the action by enclosing them in braces ({}), as shown here:

```
if (a == 1) {
   window.alert("Found a 1!");
   a = 0;
}
```

This block of statements checks the variable a once again. If it finds a value of 1, it displays a message and sets a back to 0.

Conditional Operators

While the action part of an `if` statement can include any of the JavaScript statements you've already learned (and any others, for that matter), the condition part of the statement uses its own syntax. This is called a *conditional expression*.

A conditional expression includes two values to be compared (in the preceding example, the values were a and 1). These values can be variables, constants, or even expressions in themselves.

Either side of the conditional expression can be a variable, a constant, or an expression. You can compare a variable and a value, or compare two variables. (You can compare two constants, but there's usually no reason to.)

Between the two values to be compared is a *conditional operator*. This operator tells JavaScript how to compare the two values. For instance, the == operator is used to test whether the two values are equal. A variety of conditional operators are available:

- == (is equal to)
- != (is not equal to)
- < (is less than)
- > (is greater than)
- >= (is greater than or equal to)
- <= (is less than or equal to)

Be sure not to confuse the equality operator (==) with the assignment operator (=), even though they both might be read as "equals." Remember to use = when *assigning* a value to a variable, and == when *comparing* values. Confusing these two is one of the most common mistakes in JavaScript programming.

Combining Conditions with Logical Operators

Often, you'll want to check a variable for more than one possible value, or check more than one variable at once. JavaScript includes *logical operators*, also known as boolean operators, for this purpose. For example, the following two statements check different conditions and use the same action:

```
if (phone == "") window.alert("error!");
if (email == "") window.alert("error!");
```

Using a logical operator, you can combine them into a single statement:

```
if (phone == "" || email == "") window.alert("Something's Missing!");
```

This statement uses the logical Or operator (||) to combine the conditions. Translated to English, this would be, "If the phone number is blank or the email address is blank, display an error message."

6

An additional logical operator is the And operator, &&. Consider this statement:

```
if (phone == "" && email == "") window.alert("Both are Missing!");
```

This statement uses && (And) instead of || (Or), so the error message will only be displayed if *both* the email address and phone number variables are blank. (In this particular case, Or is a better choice.)

> If the JavaScript interpreter discovers the answer to a conditional expression before reaching the end, it does not evaluate the rest of the condition. For example, if the first of two conditions separated by the && operator is false, the second is not evaluated. You can take advantage of this to improve the speed of your scripts.

The third logical operator is the exclamation mark (!), which means Not. It can be used to invert an expression—in other words, a true expression would become false, and a false one would become true. For example, here's a statement that uses the Not operator:

```
if (phone != "") alert("phone is OK");
```

In this case, the ! (Not) operator is used as part of the not-equal operator, !=. This operator inverts the condition, so the action of the if statement is executed only if the phone number variable is *not* blank.

> The logical operators are powerful, but it's easy to accidentally create an impossible condition with them. For example, the condition (a < 10 && a > 20) might look correct at first glance. However, if you read it out loud, you get "If a is less than 10 and a is greater than 20"—an impossibility in our universe. In this case, Or (||) should have been used.

The else Keyword

An additional feature of the if statement is the else keyword. Much like its English equivalent, else tells the JavaScript interpreter what to do if the condition isn't true. The following is a simple example of the else keyword in action:

```
if (a == 1) {
    alert("Found a 1!");
    a = 0;
}
else {
    alert("Incorrect value: " + a);
}
```

This is a modified version of the previous example. This displays a message and resets the variable a if the condition is met. If the condition is not met (if a is not 1), a different message is displayed.

> Like the `if` statement, `else` can be followed either by a single action statement or by a number of statements enclosed in braces.

Using Shorthand Conditional Expressions

In addition to the `if` statement, JavaScript provides a shorthand type of conditional expression that you can use to make quick decisions. This uses a peculiar syntax that is also found in other languages, such as C. A conditional expression looks like this:

```
variable = (condition) ? (true action) : (false action);
```

This assigns one of two values to the variable: one if the condition is true, and another if it is false. Here is an example of a conditional expression:

```
value = (a == 1) ? 1 : 0;
```

This statement may look confusing, but it is equivalent to the following `if` statement:

```
if (a == 1)
   value = 1;
else
   value = 0;
```

In other words, the value after the question mark (?) will be used if the condition is true, and the value after the colon (:) will be used if the condition is false. The colon represents the `else` portion of this statement and, like the `else` portion of the `if` statement, is optional.

These shorthand expressions can be used anywhere JavaScript expects a value. They provide an easy way to make simple decisions about values. As an example, here's an easy way to display a grammatically correct message about a variable:

```
document.write("Found " + counter + ((counter == 1) ? " word." : " words."));
```

This will print the message Found 1 word if the counter variable has a value of 1, and Found 2 words if its value is 2 or greater. This is one of the most common uses for a conditional expression.

6

Using Multiple Conditions with `switch`

Often, you'll use several `if` statements in a row to test for different conditions. Here is one example of this technique:

```
if (button=="next") window.location="next.html";
if (button=="previous") window.location="prev.html";
if (button=="home") window.location="home.html";
if (button=="back") window.location="menu.html";
```

Although this is a compact way of doing things, this method can get messy if each `if` statement has its own block of code with several statements. As an alternative, JavaScript includes the `switch` statement, which allows you to combine several tests of the same variable or expression into a single block of statements. The following shows the same example converted to use `switch`.

> The `switch` statement is included in JavaScript 1.2 and later. Be sure your browser supports this version before you try the examples. To ensure that scripts won't cause errors, specify the LANGUAGE="JavaScript1.2" parameter in the <script> tag.

```
switch(button) {
    case "next":
        window.location="next.html";
        break;
    case "previous":
        window.location="prev.html";
        break;
case "home":
        window.location="home.html";
        break;
case "back":
        window.location="menu.html";
        break;
default:
        window.alert("Wrong button.");
}
```

The `switch` statement has several components:

- The initial `switch` statement. This statement includes the value to test (in this case, `button`) in parentheses.
- Braces ({ and }) enclose the contents of the `switch` statement, similar to a function or an `if` statement.

- One or more `case` statements. Each of these statements specifies a value to compare with the value specified in the `switch` statement. If the values match, the statements after the `case` statement are executed. Otherwise, the next case is tried.

- The `break` statement is used to end each case. This skips to the end of the `switch`. If `break` is not included, statements in multiple cases might be executed whether they match or not.

- Optionally, the `default` case can be included and followed by one or more statements that are executed if none of the other cases were matched.

 You can use multiple statements after each `case` statement within the `switch` structure. You don't need to enclose them in braces. If the case matches, the JavaScript interpreter executes statements until it encounters a `break` or the next `case`.

Workshop: Evaluating a User Response

As a practical example of the `switch` statement, you can now create a Web page that asks the user a question, and then evaluates the user's response to determine what to do next. Specifically, you'll ask the user for a keyword that represents a Web page.

If the keyword matches one of those in your script, the user will be sent to the appropriate page. If the response doesn't match one of the predetermined keywords, the user will be sent to a default page.

Your script starts by prompting the user with the `prompt` function. To use this function, you include text that prompts the user as a parameter and assign the returned value to a variable. Here's the prompt statement:

```
where = prompt("Where do you want to go today?");
```

Next, use a `switch` statement and several `case` statements to evaluate the response:

```
switch (where) {
case "Netscape" :
        window.location="http://www.netscape.com/";
        break;
    case "Microsoft" :
        window.location="http://www.microsoft.com/";
        break;
case "Yahoo" :
        window.location="http://www.yahoo.com/";
        break;
```

6

Next, use the `default` statement to send the user to a default page (in this case, this book's site):

```
default :
        window.location="http://www.jsworkshop.com/";
}
```

Because this is the last statement in the `switch` structure, you don't need to use the `break` statement here. The final brace ends the `switch` statement.

Listing 6.1 shows the complete script embedded in a Web document. To test it, load the page. You should see a prompt, as shown in Figure 6.1. Next, enter one of the keywords. You should be sent to the appropriate page. If you specify an unknown keyword, you will be sent to the default page.

LISTING 6.1   The complete user response example

```html
<html>
<head><title>User Response Example</title>
</head>
<body>
<h1> User Response Example</h1>
Enter your destination.<br>
<script LANGUAGE="JavaScript1.2" type="text/javascript1.2">
where = prompt("Where do you want to go today?");
switch (where) {
case "Netscape" :
        window.location="http://www.netscape.com/";
        break;
    case "Microsoft" :
        window.location="http://www.microsoft.com/";
        break;
case "Yahoo" :
        window.location="http://www.yahoo.com/";
        break;
default :
        window.location="http://www.jsworkshop.com/";
}
</script>
</body>
</html>
```

As usual, you don't need to type in Listing 6.1 to try it—you can try it online or download the JavaScript code from this book's Web site at http://www.jsworkshop.com/.

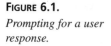

FIGURE 6.1.

Prompting for a user response.

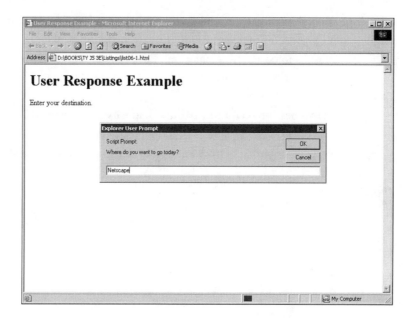

Summary

In this hour, you've learned to use JavaScript statements such as `if` and `else` to test and compare values. You've also learned a quick way to test values with the `?` operator, and used the `switch` statement to test for a number of different values. Finally, you've applied this knowledge by asking the user a question and testing the answer.

In the next hour, you'll learn another fundamental JavaScript programming tool, loops, which you can use to make JavaScript perform repetitive tasks without repetitive typing.

Q&A

Q What happens if I compare two items of different data types (for example, a number and a string) in a conditional expression?

A The JavaScript interpreter does its best to make the values a common format and compare them. In this case, it would convert them both to strings before comparing. In JavaScript 1.3 and later, you can use the special equality operator `===` to compare two values and their types—using this operator, the expression will be true only if the expressions have the same value *and* the same data type.

6

Q Why don't I get a friendly error message if I accidentally use = instead of ==?

A In some cases, this will result in an error. However, the incorrect version often appears to be a correct statement. For example, in the statement if (a=1), the variable a will be assigned the value 1. The if statement is considered true, and the value of a is lost.

Q Why does the script in Listing 6.1 specify JavaScript 1.2?

A The switch statement was added in JavaScript 1.2. Specifying that version prevents older browsers from attempting to execute the script and becoming confused.

Quiz

Test your knowledge of conditional statements in JavaScript by answering the following questions.

Questions

1. What does the statement if (fig==1) do?

    a. Assigns the variable fig the value 1.

    b. Displays an error message because the names of fruits cannot be used as variable names.

    c. Checks fig for a value of 1 and performs an action if it matches.

2. Which of the following operators means "is not equal to" in JavaScript?

    a. !

    b. !=

    c. <>

3. What does the switch statement do?

    a. Tests a variable for a number of different values.

    b. Turns a variable on or off.

    c. Makes ordinary if statements longer and more confusing.

Answers

1. c. This statement checks the fig variable and performs an action if its value is 1.

2. b. The != operator means *is not equal to*.

3. a. The switch statement can test the same variable or expression for a number of different values.

Exercises

If you want to explore the `if` statement and conditional expressions further, perform the following exercises:

- You might have noticed that the example in Listing 6.1 is case-sensitive. If you enter `netscape`, you won't be sent to the correct page. Modify the script to ignore case. (You can use the `toLowerCase` string method, described in Hour 5, "Using Strings and Arrays," and then compare the value with all-lowercase keywords.)

- Modify the script in Listing 6.1 so that if the keyword does not match one of the defined ones, the text the user entered will be used as a URL and loaded into the browser.

6

HOUR 7

Repeating Yourself: Using Loops

In the previous hour you learned about the `if` statement, one way to make JavaScript programs more powerful than simple sequential HTML documents. Loops are another powerful feature of JavaScript. In this hour, you'll learn how to use JavaScript's looping features to make the browser perform repetitive tasks for you.

Hour 7 covers the following topics:

- Performing repeated statements with the `for` loop
- Using `while` for a different type of loop
- Using `do...while` loops
- Creating infinite loops (and why you shouldn't)
- Escaping from a loop
- Continuing a loop
- Using `for...in` to loop through an array

Using for Loops

The for keyword is the first tool to consider for creating loops. A for loop typically uses a variable (called a *counter* or *index*) to keep track of how many times the loop has executed, and it stops when the counter reaches a certain number. A basic for statement looks like this:

```
for (var = 1; var < 10; var++) {
```

There are three parameters to the for loop, separated by semicolons:

- The first parameter (var = 1 in the example) specifies a variable and assigns an initial value to it. This is called the *initial expression* because it sets up the initial state for the loop.
- The second parameter (var < 10 in the example) is a condition that must remain true to keep the loop running. This is called the *condition* of the loop.
- The third parameter (var++ in the example) is a statement that executes with each iteration of the loop. This is called the *increment expression* because it is usually used to increment the counter.

After the three parameters are specified, a left brace ({) is used to signal the beginning of a block. A right brace (}) is used at the end of the block. All the statements between the braces will be executed with each iteration of the loop.

The parameters for a for loop may sound a bit confusing, but once you're used to it, you'll use for loops frequently. A simple example of this type of loop is shown below:

```
for (i=0; i<10; i++) {
   document.write("This is line " + i + "<br>");
}
```

These statements define a loop that uses the variable i, initializes it with the value of zero, and loops as long as the value of i is less than 10. The increment expression, i++, adds one to the value of i with each iteration of the loop.

When a loop includes only a single statement between the braces, as in this example, you can omit the braces if you wish. The following statement defines the same loop without braces:

```
for (i=0;i<10;i++)
   document.write("This is line " + i + "<br>");
```

It's a good style convention to use braces with all loops whether they contain one statement or many. This makes it easy to add statements to the loop later without causing syntax errors.

The loop in this example contains a document.write statement that will be repeatedly executed. To see just what this loop does, you can add it to a <script> section of an HTML document as shown in Listing 7.1.

As usual, you can download the listings presented in this hour from this book's Web site: http://www.jsworkshop.com/.

LISTING 7.1 A loop using the for keyword

```
<html>
<head>
<title>Using a for Loop</title>
</head>
<body>
<h1>"for" Loop Example</h1>
<p>The following is the output of the
<b>for</b> loop:</p>
<script language="JavaScript" type="text/javascript">
for (i=1;i<10;i++) {
   document.write("This is line " + i + "<br>");
}
</script>
</body>
</html>
```

This example displays a message with the loop's counter during each iteration. The output of Listing 7.1 is shown in Figure 7.1.

Notice that the loop was only executed nine times. This is because the conditional is i<10. When the counter (i) is incremented to 10, the expression is no longer true. If you need the loop to count to 10, you can change the conditional; either i<=10 or i<11 will work fine.

You might notice that the variable name i is often used as the counter in loops. This is a programming tradition that began with an ancient language called Forth. There's no need for you to follow this tradition, but it is a good idea to use one consistent variable for counters. (To learn more about Forth, see the Forth Interest Group's Web site at www.forth.org.)

7

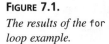

FIGURE 7.1.

The results of the for *loop example.*

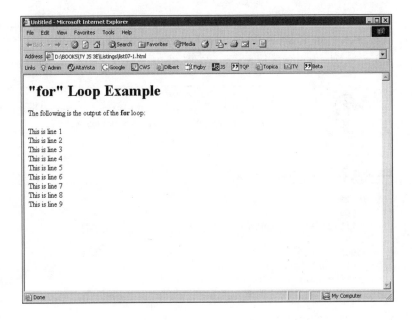

The structure of the for loop in JavaScript is based on Java, which in turn is based on C. Although it is traditionally used to count from one number to another, you can use just about any statement for the initialization, condition, and increment. However, there's usually a better way to do other types of loops with the while keyword, described in the next section.

Using while Loops

Another keyword for loops in JavaScript is while. Unlike for loops, while loops don't necessarily use a variable to count. Instead, they execute as long as a condition is true. In fact, if the condition starts out as false, the statements won't execute at all.

The while statement includes the condition in parentheses, and it is followed by a block of statements within braces, just like a for loop. Here is a simple while loop:

```
while (total < 10) {
n++;
total += values[n];
}
```

This loop uses a counter, n, to iterate through the values array. Rather than stopping at a certain count, however, it stops when the total of the values reaches 10.

You might have noticed that you could have done the same thing with a `for` loop:

```
for (n=0;total < 10; n++) {
total += values[n];
}
```

As a matter of fact, the `for` loop is nothing more than a special kind of `while` loop that handles an initialization and an increment for you. You can generally use `while` for any loop. However, it's best to choose whichever type of loop makes the most sense for the job, or that takes the least amount of typing.

Using do...while Loops

JavaScript 1.2 introduced a third type of loop: the `do...while` loop. This type of loop is similar to an ordinary `while` loop, with one difference: The condition is tested at the *end* of the loop rather than the beginning. Here is a typical `do...while` loop:

```
do {
n++;
total += values[n];
}
while (total < 10);
```

As you've probably noticed, this is basically an upside-down version of the `while` example above. There is one difference: With the `do` loop, the condition is tested at the end of the loop. This means that the statements in the loop will always be executed at least once, even if the condition is never true.

> As with the `for` and `while` loops, the `do` loop can include a single statement without braces, or a number of statements enclosed in braces.

Working with Loops

Although you can use simple `for` and `while` loops for straightforward tasks, there are some considerations you should make when using more complicated loops. In the next sections, we'll look at infinite loops and the `break` and `continue` statements, which give you more control over your loops.

7

Creating an Infinite Loop

The `for` and `while` loops give you quite a bit of control over the loop. In some cases, this can cause problems if you're not careful. For example, look at the following loop code:

```
while (i < 10) {
n++;
values[n] = 0;
}
```

There's a mistake in this example. The condition of the `while` loop refers to the `i` variable, but that variable doesn't actually change during the loop. This creates an *infinite loop*. The loop will continue executing until the user stops it, or until it generates an error of some kind.

Infinite loops can't always be stopped by the user, except by quitting the browser—and some loops can even prevent the browser from quitting, or cause a crash.

Obviously, infinite loops are something to avoid. They can also be difficult to spot because JavaScript won't give you an error that actually tells you there is an infinite loop. Thus, each time you create a loop in a script, you should be careful to make sure there's a way out.

Depending on the browser version in use, an infinite loop may even make the browser stop responding to the user. Be sure you provide an escape route from infinite loops, and save your script before you test it just in case.

Occasionally, you may want to create an infinite loop deliberately. This might include situations when you want your program to execute until the user stops it, or if you are providing an escape route with the `break` statement, which is introduced in the next section. Here's an easy way to create an infinite loop:

```
while (true) {
```

Because the value `true` is the conditional, this loop will always find its condition to be true.

Escaping from a Loop

There is one way out of an infinite loop. You can use the `break` statement during a loop to exit it immediately and continue with the first statement after the loop. Here is a simple example of the use of `break`:

```
while (true) {
n++;
if (values[n] == 1) break;
}
```

Although the `while` statement is set up as an infinite loop, the `if` statement checks the corresponding value of an array. If it finds a vale of 1, it exits the loop.

When the JavaScript interpreter encounters a `break` statement, it skips the rest of the loop and continues the script with the first statement after the right brace at the loop's end. You can use the `break` statement in any type of loop, whether infinite or not. This provides an easy way to exit if an error occurs, or if another condition is met.

Continuing a Loop

One more statement is available to help you control the execution of statements in a loop. The `continue` statement skips the rest of the loop but, unlike `break`, it continues with the next iteration of the loop. Here is a simple example:

```
for (i=1; i<21; i++) {
   if (score[i]==0) continue;
   document.write("Student number ",i, " Score: ", score[i], "\n");
}
```

This script uses a `for` loop to print out scores for 20 students, stored in the `score` array. The `if` statement is used to check for scores with a value of `0`. The script assumes that a score of `0` means that the student didn't take the test, so it continues the loop without printing that score.

Using for…in loops

A third type of loop is available in JavaScript. The `for…in` loop is not as flexible as an ordinary `for` or `while` loop. Instead, it is specifically designed to perform an operation on each property of an object.

For example, the `navigator` object contains properties that describe the user's browser, as you'll learn in Hour 14, "Creating Cross-Browser Scripts." You can use `for…in` to display this object's properties:

```
for (i in navigator) {
document.write("property: " + i);
document.write(" value: " + navigator[i] + "<br>");
}
```

Like an ordinary `for` loop, this type of loop uses an index variable (`i` in the example). For each iteration of the loop, the variable is set to the next property of the object. This makes it easy when you need to check or modify each of an object's properties.

7

Workshop: Working with Arrays and Loops

To apply your knowledge of loops, you will now create a script that deals with arrays using loops. As you progress through this script, try to imagine how difficult it would be without JavaScript's looping features.

This simple script will prompt the user for a series of names. After all of the names have been entered, it will display the list of names in a numbered list. To begin the script, initialize some variables:

```
names = new Array();
i = 0;
```

The names array will store the names the user enters. You don't know how many names will be entered, so you don't need to specify a dimension for the array. The i variable will be used as a counter in the loops.

Next, use the prompt statement to prompt the user for a series of names. Use a loop to repeat the prompt for each name. You want the user to enter at least one name, so a do loop is ideal:

```
do {
    next = prompt("Enter the Next Name", "");
    if (next > " ") names[i] = next;
    i = i + 1;
    }
    while (next > " ");
```

> If you're interested in making your scripts as short as possible, remember that you could use the increment (++) operator to combine the i = i + 1 statement with the previous statement.

This loop prompts for a string called next. If a name was entered and isn't blank, it's stored as the next entry in the names array. The i counter is then incremented. The loop repeats until the user doesn't enter a name or clicks Cancel in the prompt dialog.

Next, your script can display the number of names that were entered:

```
document.write("<h2>" + (names.length) + " names entered.</h2>");
```

This statement displays the length property of the names array, surrounded by level 2 header tags for emphasis.

Next, the script should display all the names in the order they were entered. Because the names are in an array, the for...in loop is a good choice:

```
document.write("<ol>");
for (i in names) {
    document.write("<li>" + names[i] + "<br>");
}
document.write("</ol>");
```

Here you have a for...in loop that loops through the names array, assigning the counter i to each index in turn. The script then prints the name with a <li> tag as an item in an ordered list. Before and after the loop, the script prints beginning and ending <ol> tags.

You now have everything you need for a working script. Listing 7.2 shows a complete version of the script, including the usual HTML and <script> tags.

LISTING 7.2   A script to prompt for names and display them

```
<html>
<head>
<title>Loops Example</title>
</head>
<body>
<h1>Loop Example</h1>
<p>Enter a series of names. I will then
display them in a nifty numbered list.</p>
<script LANGUAGE="JavaScript1.2" type="text/javascript1.2">
names = new Array();
i = 0;
do {
    next = window.prompt("Enter the Next Name", "");
    if (next > " ") names[i] = next;
    i = i + 1;
    }
    while (next > " ");
document.write("<h2>" + (names.length) + " names entered.</h2>");
document.write("<ol>");
for (i in names) {
    document.write("<li>" + names[i] + "<br>");
}
document.write("</ol>");
</script>
</body>
</html>
```

When you load this document into a browser, you'll be prompted for a name. Enter several names, and then click Cancel to indicate that you're finished. Figure 7.2 shows what the final results should look like in a browser.

FIGURE 7.2.

The output of the names example, as shown by Netscape.

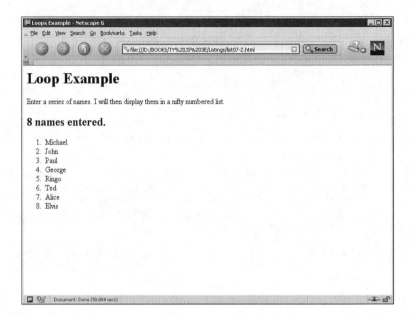

Summary

In Hour 7, you have learned to use the `for`, `while`, and `do` statements to make various kinds of loops. You also learned about the `for…in` loop for arrays and objects, and created a simple application using loops and arrays.

Q&A

Q **It seems like I could use a `for` loop to replace any of the other loop methods (`while`, `do`, and so on). Why so many choices?**

A You're right. In most cases a `for` loop would work, and you can do all your loops that way if you want. For that matter, you could use `while` to replace a `for` loop. You can use whichever looping method makes the most sense for your application.

Q **I want to support JavaScript 1.1 for older browsers. Is there an alternative to the `do…while` loop?**

A Yes. Use a `while` statement to create an infinite loop, as shown in this hour, and then use an `if` statement at the end of the loop to check the condition. If the condition is met, use the `break` statement to end the loop.

Q Entering names in repeated prompt dialogs is annoying. Is there an easier way to ask the user for many pieces of information?

A The ideal way to do this is to use a form. You'll learn all about forms in Hour 12, "Getting Data with Forms."

Quiz

Test your knowledge of JavaScript loops by answering the following questions.

Questions

1. Which type of JavaScript loop checks the condition at the *end* of the loop?

   a. `for`

   b. `while`

   c. `do…while`

2. Within a loop, what does the `break` statement do?

   a. Breaks the user's computer.

   b. Starts the loop over.

   c. Escapes the loop entirely.

3. The statement `while (3==3)` is an example of:

   a. A typographical error.

   b. An infinite loop.

   c. An illegal JavaScript statement.

Answers

1. c. The `do…while` loop uses a condition at the end of the loop.

2. c. The `break` statement escapes the loop.

3. b. This statement creates an infinite loop.

Exercises

To further your knowledge of JavaScript and loops, perform the following exercises:

- Modify Listing 7.2 to sort the names in alphabetical order before displaying them. You can use the `sort` method of the Array object, described in Hour 5, "Using Strings and Arrays."

- Modify Listing 7.2 to prompt for exactly 10 names. What happens if you click the Cancel button instead of entering a name?

7

HOUR **8**

Using Math and Date Functions

You've nearly reached the end of Part II! In Hour 8, you'll learn the basics of objects in JavaScript and the details of using the Math and Date objects. This hour covers the following topics:

- What JavaScript objects are and how to use them
- How to access an object's properties
- Using an object's methods
- Using with to work with objects
- Using the Math object's methods
- Using the Date object to work with dates
- Creating an application using JavaScript math functions

What Is an Object?

As you know from earlier hours of this book, *objects* allow you to combine several kinds of data (properties) and functions to act on the data (methods) into a single, convenient package. In this hour, you'll learn more about the built-in `Math` and `Date` objects—but first, here's a quick overview of the way objects work in JavaScript.

Creating Objects

Each object has a special function, called a *constructor*, that's used to create objects. For example, JavaScript includes a built-in function called `String` to create `String` objects. That's why you can create a string variable like this:

```
myname=new String("Figby");
```

The `new` keyword tells JavaScript to create a new object—or in technical terms, a new *instance* of the `String` object. This particular instance will have the value `Figby` and will be stored in the variable `myname`.

You can use the same basic syntax to create `String` objects, `Date` objects, `Array` objects, and even your own custom objects. (The `Math` object is an exception, which you'll learn about later in this hour.)

 If you're dying to create some custom objects right away, you should probably get some sleep. If you're serious, you can skip to Hour 15, "Creating Custom Objects."

Object Properties and Values

Each object can have one or more *properties*, or attributes. Each property is basically a variable in itself, and is contained within the object. Each property can be assigned a value. You can use properties to store any type of data a variable can store.

You've already used a few object properties, such as the `length` property of strings and arrays. To refer to a property, you use the object's name, a period, and the property's name. For example, the length of the `names` array is referred to with this property:

```
names.length
```

Object properties can even contain objects themselves. For example, each of an array's elements is a special type of property, named with an index value. If the `names` array contains strings, it is an array of `String` objects. Here is the syntax for the length of the first element of `names`:

```
names[1].length
```

Understanding Methods

As you learned in Hour 4, "Using Functions and Variables," functions are combinations of statements that can be executed as a single unit. Methods are functions that are stored as properties of an object.

You've already used methods. For example, you've used the `write` method of the `document` object to write content to a Web page. Here is an example:

```
document.write("Hello there.");
```

Like ordinary functions, methods can optionally return a value. For example, this statement rounds a number using the `round` method of the `Math` object, which you'll learn more about later, and stores the result in the variable `final`:

```
final = Math.round(num);
```

Using the `with` Keyword

The `with` keyword is one you haven't seen before. You can use it to make JavaScript programming easier—or at least easier to type.

The `with` keyword specifies an object, and it is followed by a block of statements enclosed in braces. For each statement in the block, any properties you mention without specifying an object are assumed to be for that object.

As an example, suppose you have a string called `lastname`. You can use `with` to perform string operations on it without specifying the name of the string every time:

```
with (lastname) {
   window.alert("length of last name: " + length);
   toUpperCase();
}
```

In this example, the `length` property and the `toUpperCase` method refer to the `lastname` string, although it is only specified once with the `with` keyword.

Obviously, the `with` keyword only saves a bit of typing in situations like this. However, you will find it very useful when you're dealing with an object throughout a large procedure, or when you are using a built-in object, such as the `Math` object.

The `Math` Object

The `Math` object is a built-in JavaScript object that includes math constants and functions. You don't need to create a `Math` object; it exists automatically in any JavaScript program. The `Math` object's properties represent mathematical constants, and its methods are mathematical functions.

> Because you may use the `Math` object's properties and methods throughout an entire group of statements, you may find it useful to use the `with` keyword, introduced earlier in this hour, to specify the `Math` object for those statements.

Rounding and Truncating

Three of the most useful methods of the `Math` object allow you to round decimal values up and down:

- `Math.ceil()` rounds a number up to the next integer.
- `Math.floor()` rounds a number down to the next integer.
- `Math.round()` rounds a number to the nearest integer.

All of these take the number to be rounded as their single parameter. You might notice one thing missing: the capability to round to a decimal place, such as for dollar amounts. Fortunately, you can easily simulate this. Here is a simple function that rounds numbers to two decimal places:

```
function round(num) {
    return Math.round(num * 100) / 100;
}
```

This function multiplies the value by 100 to move the decimal, and then rounds the number to the nearest integer. Finally, the value is divided by 100 to restore the decimal to its original position.

Generating Random Numbers

One of the most commonly used methods of the `Math` object is the `Math.random()` method, which generates a random number. This method doesn't require any parameters. The number it returns is a random decimal number between zero and one.

You'll usually want a random number between one and a value. You can do this with a general-purpose random number function. The following is a function that generates random numbers between one and the parameter you send it:

8

```
function rand(num) {
    return Math.floor(Math.random() * num) + 1;
}
```

This function multiplies a random number by the value specified in the num parameter, and then converts it to an integer between 1 and the number by using the Math.floor() method.

Working with Dates

The Date object is a built-in JavaScript object that enables you to conveniently work with dates and times. You can create a Date object anytime you need to store a date, and use the Date object's methods to work with the date.

You encountered one example of a Date object in Hour 2, "Creating a Simple Script," with the time/date script. The Date object has no properties. To set or obtain values from a Date object, you must use the methods described in the next section.

JavaScript dates are stored as the number of milliseconds since midnight, January 1, 1970. This date is called the *epoch*. Dates before 1970 weren't allowed in early versions, but are now represented by negative numbers.

Creating a Date Object

You can create a Date object using the new keyword. You can also optionally specify the date to store in the object when you create it. You can use any of the following formats:

```
birthday = new Date();
birthday = new Date("June 20, 2003 08:00:00");
birthday = new Date(6, 20, 2003);
birthday = new Date(6, 20, 2003, 8, 0, 0);
```

You can choose any of these formats, depending on which values you wish to set. If you use no parameters, as in the first example, the current date is stored in the object. You can then set the values using the set methods, described in the next section.

Setting Date Values

A variety of set methods enable you to set components of a Date object to values:

- setDate() sets the day of the month.
- setMonth() sets the month. JavaScript numbers the months from 0 to 11, starting with January (0).

- `setFullYear()` sets the year.
- `setTime()` sets the time (and the date) by specifying the number of milliseconds since January 1, 1970.
- `setHours()`, `setMinutes()`, and `setSeconds()` set the time.

As an example, the following statement sets the year of a `Date` object called `holiday` to 2003:

```
holiday.setFullYear(2003);
```

Getting Date Values

You can use the `get` methods to get values from a `Date` object. This is the only way to obtain these values, because they are not available as properties. Here are the available `get` methods for dates:

- `getDate()` gets the day of the month.
- `getMonth()` gets the month.
- `getFullYear()` gets the year.
- `getTime()` gets the time (and the date) as the number of milliseconds since January 1, 1970.
- `getHours()`, `getMinutes()`, `getSeconds()`, and `getMilliseconds()` get the components of the time.

> Along with `setFullYear` and `getFullYear`, which require four-digit years, JavaScript includes `setYear` and `getYear` methods, which use two-digit year values. You should always use the four-digit version to avoid Year 2000 issues.

Working with Time Zones

Finally, a few functions are available to help your `Date` objects work with local time values and time zones:

- `getTimeZoneOffset()` gives you the local time zone's offset from GMT (Greenwich Mean Time, also known as UTC). In this case, *local* refers to the location of the browser. (Of course, this only works if the user has set their system clock accurately.)

- `toUTCString()` converts the date object's time value to text, using UTC. This method was introduced in JavaScript 1.2 to replace the `toGMTString` method, which still works but should be avoided.

- `toLocalString()` converts the date object's time value to text, using local time.

Along with these basic functions, JavaScript 1.2 and later include UTC versions of several of the functions described above. These are identical to the regular commands, but work with UTC instead of local time:

- `getUTCDate()` gets the day of the month in UTC time.

- `getUTCDay()` gets the day of the week in UTC time.

- `getUTCFullYear()` gets the four-digit year in UTC time.

- `getUTCMonth()` returns the month of the year in UTC time.

- `getUTCHours()`, `getUTCMinutes()`, `getUTCSeconds()`, and `getUTCMilliseconds()` return the components of the time in UTC.

- `setUTCDate()`, `setUTCFullYear()`, `setUTCMonth()`, `setUTCHours()`, `setUTCMinutes()`, `setUTCSeconds()` and `setUTCMilliseconds()` set the time in UTC.

Converting Between Date Formats

Two special methods of the `Date` object allow you to convert between date formats. Instead of using these methods with a `Date` object you created, you use them with the built-in object `Date` itself. These include the following:

- `Date.parse()` converts a date string, such as `June 20, 1996` to a `Date` object (number of milliseconds since 1/1/1970).

- `Date.UTC()` does the opposite. It converts a `Date` object value (number of milliseconds) to a UTC (GMT) time.

Workshop: Working with the `Math` Object

The `Math.random` method, discussed earlier in this hour, generates a random number between `0` and `1`. However, it's very difficult for a computer to generate a truly random number. (It's also hard for a human being to do so—that's why dice were invented.)

Today's computers do reasonably well at generating random numbers, but just how good is JavaScript's `Math.random` function? One way to test it is to generate many random numbers and calculate the average of all of them.

In theory, the average should be somewhere near .5, halfway between 0 and 1. The more random values you generate, the closer the average should get to this middle ground.

As an example of the use of the Math object, you can create a script that tests JavaScript's random number function. To do this, you'll generate 5,000 random numbers and calculate their average.

 Rather than typing it in, you can download and try this hour's example at this book's Web site: http://www.jsworkshop.com/.

In case you skipped Hour 7, "Repeating Yourself: Using Loops," and are getting out your calculator, don't worry—you'll use a loop to generate the random numbers. You'll be surprised how fast JavaScript can do this.

To begin your script, you will initialize a variable called total. This variable will store a running total of all of the random values, so it's important that it starts at 0:

```
total = 0;
```

Next, begin a loop that will execute 5,000 times. Use a for loop because you want it to execute a fixed number of times:

```
for (i=1; i<=5000; i++) {
```

Within the loop, you will need to create a random number and add its value to total. Here are the statements that do this and continue with the next iteration of the loop:

```
    num = Math.random();
    total += num;
}
```

Depending on the speed of your computer, it might take a few minutes to generate those 5,000 random numbers. Just to be sure something's happening, the script will update the status line to tell the user how many numbers have been generated so far and the current total:

```
window.status = "Generated " + i + " numbers. Current total: " + total;
```

The final part of your script will calculate the average by dividing total by 5,000. Your script can also round the average to three decimal places, using the trick you learned earlier in this hour:

```
average = total / 5000;
average = Math.round(average * 1000) / 1000;
document.write("<H2>Average of 5000 numbers: " + average + "</H2>");
```

If you're using a particularly slow computer (say, less than 60 MHz), you may want to consider changing the three instances of the number 5000 to a lower number. Or you can go out to lunch while the script executes.

To test this script and see just how random those numbers are, combine the complete script with an HTML document and <script> tags. Listing 8.1 shows the complete random number testing script.

LISTING 8.1   A script to test JavaScript's random number function

```
<html>
<head>
<title>Math Example</title>
</head>
<body>
<h1>Math Example</h1>
<p>How random are JavaScript's random numbers?
Let's generate 5000 of them and find out.</p>
<script LANGUAGE="JavaScript" type="text/javascript">
total = 0;
for (i=1; i<=5000; i++) {
    num = Math.random();
    total += num;
    window.status = "Generated " + i + " numbers.";
}
average = total / 5000;
average = Math.round(average * 1000) / 1000;
document.write("<H2>Average of 5000 numbers: " + average + "</H2>");
</script>
</body>
</html>
```

To test the script, load the HTML document into a browser. The status line will immediately begin counting up to 5,000. After a short delay, you should see a result. If it's close to .5, the numbers are reasonably random. My result was .502, as shown in Figure 8.1.

The average you've used here is called an *arithmetic mean*. This type of average isn't a perfect way to test randomness. Actually, all it tests is the distribution of the numbers above and below .5. For example, if the numbers turned out to be 2,500 .4's and 2,500 .6's, the average would be a perfect .5—but they wouldn't be very random numbers. (Thankfully, JavaScript's random numbers don't have this problem.)

FIGURE 8.1.

The random number testing script in action.

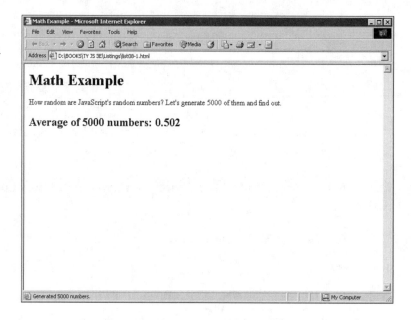

Summary

In this hour, you learned the fundamentals of JavaScript objects, which you'll use throughout this book. You also learned some specifics about the Math and Date objects, and learned more than you ever wanted to know about random numbers.

You've reached the end of Part II, which covered some basic building blocks of JavaScript programs. In Part III, you'll learn about the most useful objects in JavaScript: the Document Object Model, which contains objects that refer to various parts of the browser window and HTML document. This begins in Hour 9, "Working with the Document Object Model."

Q&A

Q Can one of an object's properties be another object?

A Absolutely. In this case, the second object is called a *child object*. You'll encounter quite a few parent and child objects, such as window.location, in Hour 9.

Q **You mentioned that the properties of the Math object are constants. What are they?**

A They include a wide variety of mathematical constants, such as Math.PI and Math.E. A wide variety of more esoteric constants are included. There are also some methods of the Math object that weren't discussed here, such as the trigonometric functions. For details, see the JavaScript quick reference in Appendix D.

Q **I tried the random number example in Listing 8.1, and I'm surprised it takes more than a few seconds to add a few numbers together—aren't computers supposed to be really good at that sort of thing?**

A Actually, the slowest part of the loop in the example script is the command that updates the status line. If you remove this command, the script will execute much faster—but you won't be able to watch its progress.

Quiz

Test your knowledge of JavaScript's built-in Math and Date objects by answering the following questions.

Questions

1. Which of the following objects *cannot* be used with the new keyword?

   a. Date

   b. Math

   c. String

2. How does JavaScript store dates in a Date object?

   a. The number of milliseconds since January 1, 1970.

   b. The number of days since January 1, 1900.

   c. The number of seconds since Netscape's public stock offering.

3. What is the range of random numbers generated by the Math.random function?

   a. Between 1 and 100.

   b. Between 1 and the number of milliseconds since January 1, 1970.

   c. Between 0 and 1.

Answers

1. b. The Math object is static; you can't create a Math object.

2. a. Dates are stored as the number of milliseconds since January 1, 1970.

3. c. JavaScript's random numbers are between 0 and 1.

Exercises

If you want to spend more time working with the Math and Date objects in JavaScript, perform the following activities:

- Modify the random number script in Listing 8.1 to prompt the user for the number of random numbers to generate.

- Modify the random number script to run three times, calculating a total of 15,000 random numbers, and display separate totals for each set of 5,000. (You'll need to use another for loop that encloses most of the script.)

PART III

The Document Object Model (DOM)

Hour

HOUR 9

Working with the Document Object Model

You've arrived at Part III of this book. (If you've been reading nonstop, it's been eight hours, so you might want to get some sleep before you continue.) In this part, you'll explore some of the most important objects used with JavaScript.

In Hour 8, "Using Math and Date Functions," you learned about JavaScript's support for objects, which allow you to store data in all sorts of interesting ways. However, the objects you'll use the most are those in the Document Object Model (DOM), which let your scripts manipulate Web pages, windows, and documents.

In this hour, you will explore this hierarchy of objects. Hour 9 covers the following topics:

- How to access the various objects in the DOM
- Working with windows using the window object
- Working with Web documents with the document object

- Using objects for links and anchors
- Using the `location` object to work with URLs
- Getting information about the browser with the `navigator` object
- Creating JavaScript-based Back and Forward buttons

Understanding the Document Object Model

One advantage that JavaScript has over basic HTML is that scripts can manipulate the Web document and its contents. Your script can load a new page into the browser, work with parts of the browser window and document, open new windows, and even modify text within the page dynamically.

To work with the browser and documents, JavaScript uses a hierarchy of parent and child objects called the Document Object Model, or DOM. These objects are organized into a tree-like structure, and represent all of the content and components of a Web document.

Like other objects you've explored, the objects in the DOM have *properties*, which describe the Web page or document, and *methods*, which allow you to work with parts of the Web page.

When you refer to an object, you use the parent object name followed by the child object name or names, separated by periods. For example, JavaScript stores objects to represent images in a document as children of the `document` object. The following refers to the `image9` object, a child of the `document` object, which is a child of the `window` object:

```
window.document.image9
```

The `window` object is the parent object for all the objects we will be looking at in this hour. Figure 9.1 shows this section of the DOM object hierarchy and a variety of its objects.

FIGURE 9.1.

The JavaScript browser object hierarchy.

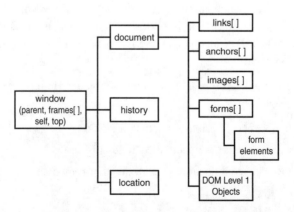

This diagram only includes the basic browser objects that will be covered in this hour. These are actually a small part of the Document Object Model, which you'll learn more about starting with Hour 18, "Working with Style Sheets."

9

History of the DOM

Starting with the introduction of JavaScript 1.0 in Netscape 2.0, JavaScript has included objects to represent parts of a Web document and other browser features. However, there was never a true standard. While both Netscape and Microsoft Internet Explorer included many of the same objects, there was no guarantee that the same objects would work the same way in both browsers, let alone in less common browsers.

The bad news is that there are still differences between the browsers—but here's the good news. Since the release of Netscape 3.0 and Internet Explorer 4.0, all the basic objects (those covered in this hour) are supported in much the same way in both browsers, and new DOM standards are supported by the latest versions of Netscape and Internet Explorer.

While all this standardization doesn't change how the objects described in this hour work, you'll be thankful for it as you move into the advanced features of the DOM later in this book.

DOM Levels

The W3C (World-Wide Web Consortium) has recently developed the DOM level 1 standard. This standard defines not only basic objects, but an entire set of objects that encompass all parts of an HTML document. A level 2 DOM standard is also under development.

The basic object hierarchy described in this hour is informally referred to as DOM level 0, and the objects are included in the DOM level 1 standard. You'll learn how to use the full set of Level 1 DOM objects in Part V of this book.

The Level 1 and Level 2 DOM objects allow you to modify a Web page in real time after it has loaded. This is called dynamic HTML (DHTML) and you'll learn more about it in Part V.

Using window Objects

At the top of the browser object hierarchy is the window object, which represents a browser window. You've already used a few methods and properties of the window object:

- You used the window.status property to change the contents of the browser's status line.
- The window.alert, window.confirm, and window.prompt methods display message dialogs to the user.

There can be several window objects at a time, each representing an open browser window. Frames are also represented by window objects. You'll learn more about windows and frames in Hour 11, "Using Windows and Frames."

> Layers, which allow you to include, modify, and position dynamic content within a Web document, are also similar to window objects. These are explained in Hour 19, "Using Dynamic HTML (DHTML)."

Working with Web Documents

The document object represents a Web document, or page. Web documents are displayed within browser windows, so it shouldn't surprise you to learn that the document object is a child of the window object.

Because the window object always represents the current window (the one containing the script), you can use window.document to refer to the current document. You can also simply refer to document, which automatically refers to the current window.

> You've already used the document.write method to display text within a Web document. The examples in earlier hours only used a single window and document, so it was unnecessary to use window.document.write—but this longer syntax would have worked equally well.

If multiple windows or frames are in use, there might be several window objects, each with its own document object. To use one of these document objects, you use the name of the window and the name of the document.

In the following sections, you will look at some of the properties and methods of the document object that will be useful in your scripting.

Getting Information About the Document

Several properties of the document object include information about the current document in general:

- document.URL specifies the document's URL. This is a simple text field. You can't change this property. If you need to send the user to a different location, use the window.location object, described later in this hour.

- document.title lists the title of the current page, defined by the HTML <title> tag.

- document.referrer is the URL of the page the user was viewing prior to the current page—usually, the page with a link to the current page.

- document.lastModified is the date the document was last modified. This date is sent from the server along with the page.

- document.bgColor and document.fgColor are the background and foreground (text) colors for the document, corresponding to the BGCOLOR and TEXT attributes of the <body> tag.

- document.linkColor, document.alinkColor, and document.vlinkColor are the colors for links within the document. These correspond to the LINK, ALINK, and VLINK attributes of the <body> tag.

- document.cookie allows you to read or set a cookie for the document. See Hour 24, "JavaScript Tips and Tricks", for information about cookies.

As an example of a document property, Listing 9.1 shows a short HTML document that displays its last modified date using JavaScript.

LISTING 9.1 Displaying the last modified date

```
<html><head><title>Test Document</title></head>
<body>
<p>This page was last modified on:
<script language="JavaScript" type="text/javascript">
document.write(document.lastModified);
</script>
</p><br>
</html>
```

This can tell the user when the page was last changed. If you use JavaScript, you don't have to remember to update the date each time you modify the page. (You could also use the script to always print the current date, but that would be cheating.)

You might find that the `document.lastModified` property doesn't work on your Web pages. The date is received from the Web server, and some servers do not maintain modification dates correctly.

Writing Text in a Document

The simplest `document` object methods are also the ones you will use most often. In fact, you've used one of them already. The `document.write` method prints text as part of the HTML page in a document window. This statement is used whenever you need to include output in a Web page.

An alternative statement, `document.writeln`, also prints text, but it also includes a new-line (\n) character at the end. This is handy when you want your text to be the last thing on the line.

Bear in mind that the newline character is ignored by HTML, except inside the `<pre>` container. You will need to use the `<br>` tag if you want an actual line break.

You can use these methods only within the body of the Web page, so they will be executed when the page loads. You can't use these methods to add to a page that has already loaded without reloading it. You can write new content for a document, however, as the next section explains.

You can also directly modify the text of a Web page on newer browsers using the features of the new DOM. You'll learn these techniques in Hour 20, "Using Advanced DOM Features."

The `document.write` method can be used within a `<script>` tag in the body of an HTML document. You can also use it in a function, provided you include a call to the function within the body of the document.

Clearing and Rewriting Documents

The `document` object includes `open` and `close` methods. These methods don't actually open and close new documents or windows. Instead, the `open` method opens a *stream*, which clears the document and allows you to create a new one with the `write` or `writeln` methods.

When you use the `document.open` method, the current document is cleared. Any data already displayed in the document is erased, and you can begin writing new content to the document.

The data you write after the `document.open` isn't actually displayed until you close the stream with the `document.close` method. You can use this to ensure that blocks of `write` commands execute at the same time.

9

> If you use the `document.open` method on the current window, your script—part of the current document—will be cleared, and will stop executing. For this reason, these methods are best used with separate windows and frames. You'll learn about this in Hour 11.

You can optionally specify a MIME document type in the `document.open` command. This enables you to create a document of any type, including images and documents used by plug-in applications. You'll learn about plug-ins in detail in Hour 16, "Working with Sounds and Plug-Ins."

> MIME stands for *Multipurpose Internet Mail Extensions*. It's an Internet standard for document types. Web servers send a MIME type to the browser with documents to tell the browser how to display them. Typical browser documents are HTML (MIME type `text/html`) and text (MIME type `text/plain`).

Using Links and Anchors

Another child of the `document` object is the `link` object. Actually, there can be multiple `link` objects in a document. Each one includes information about a link to another location or an anchor.

> Anchors are named places in an HTML document that can be jumped to directly. You define them with a tag like this: `<a name="part2">`. You can then link to them: `<a HREF="#part2">`.

You can access link objects with the links array. Each member of the array is one of the link objects in the current page. A property of the array, document.links.length, indicates the number of links in the page.

Each link object (or member of the links array) has a list of properties defining the URL. The href property contains the entire URL, and other properties define portions of it. These are the same properties as the location object, defined later in this hour.

You can refer to a property by indicating the link number and property name. For example, the following statement assigns the entire URL of the first link to the variable link1:

```
link1 = links[0].href;
```

The anchor objects are also children of the document object. Each anchor object represents an anchor in the current document—a particular location that can be jumped to directly.

Like links, you can access anchors with an array, anchors. Each element of this array is an anchor object. The document.anchors.length property gives you the number of elements in the anchors array.

Accessing Browser History

The history object is another child (property) of the window object. This object holds information about the URLs that have been visited before and after the current one, and it includes methods to go to previous or next locations.

The history object has one property you can access:

- history.length keeps track of the length of the history list—in other words, the number of different locations that the user has visited.

The history object has current, previous, and next properties that store URLs of documents in the history list. However, for security reasons, these objects are not normally accessible in today's browsers.

The history object has three methods you can use to move through the history list:

- history.go() opens a URL from the history list. To use this method, specify a positive or negative number in parentheses. For example, history.go(-2) is equivalent to pressing the Back button twice.

- `history.back()` loads the previous URL in the history list—equivalent to pressing the Back button.
- `history.forward()` loads the next URL in the history list, if available. This is equivalent to pressing the Forward button.

You'll use these methods in the Workshop at the end of this hour.

Working with the `location` Object

9

A third child of the `window` object is the `location` object. This object stores information about the current URL stored in the window. For example, the following statement loads a URL into the current window:

```
window.location.href="http://www.starlingtech.com";
```

The `href` property used in this statement contains the entire URL of the window's current location. You can also access portions of the URL with various properties of the `location` object. To explain these properties, consider the following URL:

```
http://www.jsworkshop.com:80/test.cgi?lines=1#anchor
```

The following properties represent parts of the URL:

- `location.protocol` is the protocol part of the URL (`http:` in the example).
- `location.hostname` is the host name of the URL (`www.jsworkshop.com` in the example).
- `location.port` is the port number of the URL (`80` in the example).
- `location.pathname` is the filename part of the URL (`test.cgi` in the example).
- `location.search` is the query portion of the URL, if any (`lines=1` in the example). Queries are used mostly by CGI scripts.
- `location.hash` is the anchor name used in the URL, if any (`#anchor` in the example).

The `link` object, introduced earlier this hour, also includes this list of properties for accessing portions of the URL.

Although the `location.href` property usually contains the same URL as the `document.URL` property described earlier in this hour, you can't change the `document.URL` property. Always use `location.href` to load a new page.

The location object has two methods:

- location.reload() reloads the current document. This is the same as the Reload button on the browser's toolbar. If you optionally include the true parameter, it will ignore the browser's cache and force a reload whether the document has changed or not.

- location.replace() replaces the current location with a new one. This is similar to setting the location object's properties yourself. The difference is that the replace method does not affect the browser's history. In other words, the Back button can't be used to go to the previous location. This is useful for splash screens or temporary pages that it would be useless to return to.

Reading Information about the Browser

The navigator object isn't part of the browser object hierarchy, but it is another useful object for scripting. This object contains information about the browser version. You can use this object to find out which browser and computer platform the user is running, and your script can change its behavior to match that browser.

> The navigator object is named after Netscape Navigator, which was the only browser that supported JavaScript when the language first appeared in Navigator 2.0. Despite its Netscape-specific name, this object is now supported in Microsoft Internet Explorer.

Browser-specific scripting can be complicated, and you'll learn more about the navigator object in Hour 14, "Creating Cross-Browser Scripts."

Workshop: Creating Back and Forward Buttons

One common use for the back and forward methods of the history object is to add your own Back and Forward buttons to a Web document. This can improve the user interface of your pages.

As an example of the use of the history object, you will now create a script that displays Back and Forward buttons and uses these methods to navigate the browser.

You will use graphic images for the Back and Forward buttons. You can use the images from this book's Web site or make your own images to match the other graphics on your page.

> Visit this book's Web site to download the listings for this hour and the graphics for the Back and Forward buttons: http://www.jsworkshop.com/.

9

Here's the part of the script that will handle the Back button:

```
<a HREF="javascript:history.back();">
  <img BORDER = 0 SRC="left.gif">
</a>
```

This uses a javascript: URL to execute a command when the user clicks on a link. In this case, the link is the left-arrow image. The script for the Forward button is nearly identical:

```
<a HREF="javascript:history.forward();">
  <img BORDER = 0 SRC="right.gif">
</a>
```

With these out of the way, you just need to build the rest of an HTML document. Listing 9.2 shows the complete HTML document, and Figure 9.2 shows a browser's display of the document. After you load this document into a browser, visit other URLs and make sure the Back and Forward buttons work.

LISTING 9.2   A Web page that uses JavaScript to include Back and Forward buttons

```
<html>
<head><title>Graphic Back and Forward Buttons</title>
</head>
<body>
<h1>Graphical Back and Forward Buttons</h1>
<hr>
<p>This page allows you to go back or forward to pages in the history list.
These should be equivalent to the back and forward arrow buttons in the
browser's toolbar.</p>
<hr>
<a HREF="javascript:history.back();">
  <IMG BORDER = 0 SRC="left.gif">
</a>
<a HREF="javascript:history.forward();">
  <IMG BORDER = 0 SRC="right.gif">
```

LISTING 9.2   Continued

```
</a>
<hr>
</body>
</html>
```

FIGURE 9.2.

The Back and Forward buttons in Internet Explorer.

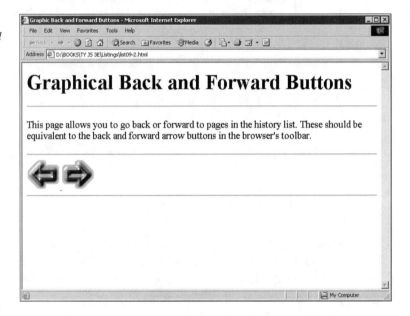

 This script is an example of how much JavaScript can do with very little scripting. In fact, Listing 9.2 doesn't use any <script> tags at all, and only two JavaScript commands.

Summary

In this hour, you've learned about the Document Object Model (DOM), JavaScript's hierarchy of Web page objects. You've learned how you can use the document object to work with documents, and used the history and location objects to control the current URL displayed in the browser.

You should now be comfortable working with a variety of objects in JavaScript. In the next hour, you'll learn the event handlers that work with each of the objects in the DOM.

Q&A

Q I can use `history` and `document` instead of `window.history` and `window.document`. Can I leave out the `window` object in other cases?

A Yes. For example, you can use `alert` instead of `window.alert` to display a message. The `window` object contains the current script, so it's treated as a default object. However, be warned that you shouldn't omit the `window` object's name when you're using frames, layers, or multiple windows, or in an event handler.

Q I used the `document.lastModified` method to display a modification date for my page, but it displays a date in 1970, or a date that I know is incorrect. What's wrong?

A This function depends on the server sending the last modified date of the document to the browser. Some Web servers don't do this properly, or require specific file attributes in order for this to work.

Q Can I change history entries, or prevent the user from using the Back and Forward buttons?

A You can't change the history entries. You can't prevent the use of the Back and Forward buttons, but you can use the `location.replace()` method to load a series of pages that don't appear in the history. However, the Back button will still take the user to the page they visited before yours.

Quiz

Questions

1. Which of the following objects can be used to load a new URL into the browser window?

    a. `document.url`

    b. `window.location`

    c. `window.url`

2. What information is stored by the `navigator` object?

    a. The current browser and version.

    b. The user's name, phone number, and hair color.

    c. The previous and next page in the navigation history.

3. Which of the following describes the W3C DOM specification for the objects described in this hour?

   a. `DOM level 0`

   b. `DOM level 1`

   c. `DOM level 2`

Answers

1. b. The `window.location` object can be used to send the browser to a new URL.

2. a. The `navigator` object can tell you the current browser version.

3. a. The objects described in this hour fall under the informal DOM level 0 specification.

Exercises

To gain more experience working with browser objects in JavaScript, perform the following exercises:

- Modify the Back and Forward example in Listing 9.2 to include a Reload button along with the Back and Forward buttons. (This button would trigger the `location.reload()` method.)

- Modify the Back and Forward example to display the current number of history entries.

HOUR **10**

Responding to Events

In your experience with JavaScript so far, most of the scripts you've written have executed in a calm, orderly fashion, moving from the first statement to the last.

In this hour, you'll learn to use the wide variety of event handlers supported by JavaScript. Rather than executing in order, scripts using event handlers can interact directly with the user. You'll use event handlers in just about every script you write in the rest of this book.

Hour 10 covers the following topics:

- How event handlers work
- How event handlers relate to objects
- Creating an event handler
- Testing an event handler
- Detecting mouse actions
- Detecting keyboard actions
- Intercepting events with a special handler
- Adding friendly link descriptions to a Web page

Understanding Event Handlers

As you learned in Hour 3, "How JavaScript Programs Work," JavaScript programs don't have to execute in order. They can also detect *events* and react to them. Events are things that happen to the browser—the user clicking a button, the mouse pointer moving, or a Web page or image loading from the server.

A wide variety of events allow your scripts to respond to the mouse, the keyboard, and other circumstances. Events are the key method JavaScript uses to make Web documents interactive.

The script that you use to detect and respond to an event is called an *event handler*. Event handlers are among the most powerful features of JavaScript. Luckily, they're also among the easiest features to learn and use—often, a useful event handler requires only a single statement.

Objects and Events

As you learned in Hour 9, "Working with the Document Object Model," JavaScript uses a set of objects to store information about the various parts of a Web page—buttons, links, images, windows, and so on. An event can often happen in more than one place (for example, the user could click any one of the links on the page), so each event is associated with an object.

Each event has a name. For example, the onMouseOver event occurs when the mouse pointer moves over an object on the page. When the pointer moves over a particular link, the onMouseOver event is sent to that link's event handler, if it has one.

To define an event handler, you add the word on to the beginning of the event's name. For example, the onMouseOver event handler is called when the mouse moves over a link. To define the event handler, you add it to that particular link's <a> HTML tag.

> Notice the strange capitalization on the onMouseOver keyword. This is the standard notation for event handlers. The on is always lowercase, and each word in the event name is capitalized.

Creating an Event Handler

You don't need the <script> tag to define an event handler. Instead, you add an event handler attribute to an individual HTML tag. For example, here is a link that includes an onMouseOver event handler:

```
<a href="http://www.jsworkshop.com/"
   onMouseOver="window.alert('You moved over the link.');">
Click here</a>
```

Note that this is all one <a> tag, although it's split into multiple lines. This specifies a statement to be used as the onMouseOver event handler for the link. This statement displays an alert message when the mouse moves over the link.

> The previous example uses single quotation marks to surround the text. This is necessary in an event handler because double quotation marks are used to surround the event handler itself. (You can also use single quotation marks to surround the event handler and double quotes within the script statements.)

You can use JavaScript statements like the previous one in an event handler, but if you need more than one statement, it's a good idea to use a function instead. Just define the function in the header of the document, and then call the function as the event handler like this:

```
<a href="#bottom" onMouseOver="DoIt();">Move the mouse over this link.</a>
```

This example calls a function called DoIt() when the user moves the mouse over the link. Using a function is convenient because you can use longer, more readable JavaScript routines as event handlers. You'll use a longer function to handle events in the "Workshop: Adding Link Descriptions to a Web Page" section of this hour.

> For simple event handlers, you can use two statements if you separate them with a semicolon. However, in most cases it's easier to use a function to perform the statements.

Changing Event Handlers with JavaScript

Rather than specifying an event handler in an HTML document, you can use JavaScript to assign a function as an event handler. This allows you to set event handlers conditionally, turn them on and off, and change the function that handles an event dynamically.

To define an event handler in this way, you first define a function, then assign the function as an event handler. Event handlers are stored as properties of the document object or another object that can receive an event. For example, these statements define a function called `mousealert`, then assign it as the `onMouseDown` event handler for the document:

```
function mousealert() {
alert ("You clicked the mouse!");
}
document.onmousedown = mousealert;
```

Using the event Object

When an event occurs, you may need to know more about the event—for example, for a keyboard event, you need to know which key was pressed. JavaScript includes an event object that provides this information.

To use the `event` object, you can pass it on to your event handler function. For example, this statement defines an `onKeyPress` event that passes the `event` object to a function:

```
<body onKeyPress="getkey(event);">
```

You can then define your function to accept the event as a parameter:

```
function getkey(e) {
...
}
```

Unfortunately, while both Internet Explorer and Netscape support the `event` object, they support different properties. One property that is the same in both browsers is `event.type`, the type of event. This is simply the name of the event, such as `mouseover` for an `onMouseOver` event, and `keypress` for an `onKeyPress` event. The following sections list some additional useful properties for each browser.

Internet Explorer event Properties

The following are some of the commonly used properties of the `event` object for Internet Explorer 4.0 and later:

- `event.button`: The mouse button that was pressed. This value is 1 for the left button and usually 2 for the right button.
- `event.clientX`: The x-coordinate (column, in pixels) where the event occurred.
- `event.clientY`: The y-coordinate (row, in pixels) where the event occurred.
- `event.altkey`: A flag that indicates whether the ALT key was pressed during the event.
- `event.ctrlkey`: Indicates whether the CTRL key was pressed.
- `event.shiftkey`: Indicates whether the SHIFT key was pressed.

- `event.keyCode`: The key code (in Unicode) for the key that was pressed.
- `event.srcElement`: The object where the element occurred.

Netscape `event` Properties

The following are some of the commonly used properties of the `event` object for Netscape 4.0 and later:

- `event.modifiers`: Indicates which modifier keys (`SHIFT`, `CTRL`, `ALT`, etc.) were held down during the event. This value is an integer that combines binary values representing the different keys.
- `event.pageX`: The x-coordinate of the event within the Web page.
- `event.pageY`: The y-coordinate of the event within the Web page.
- `event.which`: The keycode for keyboard events (in Unicode), or the button that was pressed for mouse events (1 for the left button, 3 for the right.)
- `event.target`: The object where the element occurred.

> The `event.pageX` and `event.pageY` properties are based on the top-left corner of the element where the event occurred, not always the exact position of the mouse pointer.

Using Mouse Events

JavaScript includes a number of event handlers for detecting mouse actions. Your script can detect the movement of the mouse pointer and when a button is clicked, released, or both.

Over and Out

You've already seen the first and most common event handler, `onMouseOver`. This handler is called when the mouse pointer moves over a link or other object.

The `onMouseOut` handler is the opposite—it is called when the mouse pointer moves out of the object's border. Unless something strange happens, this always happens some time after the `onMouseOver` event is called.

This handler is particularly useful if your script has made a change when the pointer moved over the object—for example, displaying a message in the status line or changing an image. You can use an `onMouseOut` handler to undo the action when the pointer moves away.

You'll use both onMouseOver and onMouseOut handlers in the "Workshop: Adding Link Descriptions to a Web Page" section at the end of this hour.

> One of the most common uses for the onMouseOver and onMouseOut event handlers is to create *rollovers*—images that change when the mouse moves over them. You'll learn how to create these in Hour 13, "Using Graphics and Animation."

Using the onMouseMove event

The onMouseMove event occurs any time the mouse pointer moves. As you might imagine, this happens quite often—the event can trigger hundreds of times as the mouse pointer moves across a page.

Because of the large number of generated events, browsers don't support the onMouseMove event by default. To enable it for a page, you need to use *event capturing*. This is similar to the dynamic events technique you learned earlier in this hour, but requires an extra step for Netscape browsers.

The basic syntax to support this event, for both browsers, is to set a function as the onMouseMove handler for the document or another object. For example, this statement sets the onMouseMove handler for the document to a function called MoveHere, which must be defined in the same page:

```
document.onMouseMove=MoveHere;
```

Additionally, Netscape requires that you specifically enable the event using the document.captureEvents method:

```
document.captureEvents(Event.MOUSEMOVE);
```

Ups and Downs

You can also use events to detect when the mouse button is clicked. The basic event handler for this is onClick. This event handler is called when the mouse button is clicked while positioned over the appropriate object.

> The object in this case can be a link. It can also be a form element. You'll learn more about forms in Hour 12, "Getting Data with Forms."

For example, you can use the following event handler to display an alert when a link is clicked:

```
<a href="http://www.jsworkshop.com/"
onClick="alert('You are about to leave this site.');">Click Here</a>
```

In this case, the onClick event handler runs before the linked page is loaded into the browser. This is useful for making links conditional or displaying a disclaimer before launching the linked page.

If your onClick event handler returns the false value, the link will not be followed. For example, the following is a link that displays a confirmation dialog. If you click Cancel, the link is not followed; if you click OK, the new page is loaded:

```
<a href="http://www.jsworkshop.com/"
onClick="return(window.confirm('Are you sure?'));">
Click Here</a>
```

This example uses the return statement to enclose the event handler. This ensures that the false value that is returned when the user clicks Cancel is returned from the event handler, which prevents the link from being followed.

The onDblClick event handler is similar, but is only used if the user double-clicks on an object. Because links usually require only a single click, you could use this to make a link do two different things depending on the number of clicks. (Needless to say, this could be confusing.) You can also detect double-clicks on images and other objects.

To give you even more control of what happens when the mouse button is pressed, two more events are included:

- onMouseDown is used when the user presses the mouse button.
- onMouseUp is used when the user releases the mouse button.

These two events are the two halves of a mouse click. If you want to detect an entire click, use onClick. Use onMouseUp and onMouseDown to detect just one or the other.

To detect which mouse button is pressed, you can use the which property of the event object. This property is assigned the value 1 for the left button, or 3 for the right button. This property is assigned for onClick, onDblClick, onMouseUp, and onMouseDown events.

For example, this script creates an onMouseDown event handler that displays an alert indicating which button was pressed.

```
function mousealert(e) {
whichone = (e.which == 1) ? "Left" : "Right";
message = "You clicked the " + whichone + " button.";
alert(message);
}
document.onmousedown = mousealert;
```

10

Using Keyboard Events

Prior to the release of Netscape 4.0, JavaScript programs couldn't detect keyboard actions—just mouse actions. This made it difficult to create some types of programs in JavaScript. For example, games were difficult to play using Go Left and Go Right buttons.

Thankfully, JavaScript 1.2 and later can detect keyboard actions. The main event handler for this purpose is onKeyPress, which occurs when a key is pressed and released, or held down. As with mouse buttons, you can detect the down and up parts of the keypress with the onKeyDown and onKeyUp event handlers.

Of course, you may find it useful to know which key the user pressed. You can find this out with the event object, which is sent to your event handler when the event occurs. In Netscape, the event.which property stores the ASCII character code for the key that was pressed. In Internet Explorer, event.keyCode serves the same purpose.

> ASCII (American Standard Code for Information Interchange) is the standard numeric code used by most computers to represent characters. It assigns the numbers 0–128 to various characters—for example, the capital letters A through Z are ASCII values 65 to 90.

Displaying Typed Characters

If you'd rather deal with actual characters than key codes, you can use the fromCharCode string method to convert them. This method converts a numeric ASCII code to its corresponding string character. For example, the following statement converts Netscape's event.which property to a character and stores it in the key variable:

```
Key = String.fromCharCode(event.which);
```

Since Internet Explorer and Netscape have different ways of returning the key code, displaying keys browser-independently is a bit harder. However, you can create a script that displays keys for either browser. The following function will display each key in the status line:

```
function DisplayKey(e) {
    if (e.keyCode) keycode=e.keyCode;
        else keycode=e.which;
    character=String.fromCharCode(keycode);
    window.status += character;
}
```

The DisplayKey function receives the event object from the event handler and stores it in the variable e. It checks whether the e.keyCode property exists, and stores it in the keycode variable if present. Otherwise, it assumes the browser is Netscape and assigns keycode to the e.which property.

The remaining lines of the function convert the key code to a character and add it to the window.status property, which displays it in the browser's status line. Listing 10.1 shows a complete example using this function.

10

LISTING 10.1   Displaying typed characters

```
<html>
<head>
<title>Displaying Keypresses</title>
<script language="javascript" type="text/javascript">
    function DisplayKey(e) {
        if (e.keyCode) keycode=e.keyCode;
            else keycode=e.which;
        character=String.fromCharCode(keycode);
        window.status += character;
    }
</script>
</head>
<body onKeyPress="DisplayKey(event);">
<h1>Displaying Typed Characters</h1>
<p>This document includes a simple script that displays the keys
you type in the status line. Type a few keys and try it. </p>
</body>
</html>
```

When you load this example into either Netscape or Internet Explorer, you can type and see the characters you've typed in the status line. Figure 10.1 shows this example in action in Netscape.

FIGURE **10.1.**

Netscape displays the keypress example.

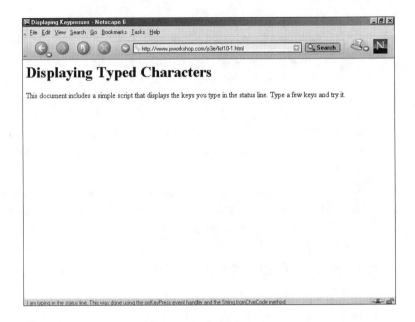

Using the `onLoad` and `onUnload` Events

Another event you'll use frequently is `onLoad`. This event occurs when the current page (including all of its images) finishes loading from the server.

The `onLoad` event is related to the `document` object, and to define it you use an event handler in the `<body>` tag. For example, the following is a `<body>` tag that uses a simple event handler to display an alert when the page finishes loading:

```
<body onLoad="alert('Loading complete.');">
```

> Since the `onLoad` event occurs after the HTML document has finished loading and displaying, you cannot use the `document.write` or `document.open` statements within an `onLoad` event handler. This would overwrite the current document.

In JavaScript 1.1 and later, images can also have an `onLoad` event handler. When you define an `onLoad` event handler for an `<img>` tag, it is triggered as soon as the specified image has completely loaded.

You can also specify an onUnload event for the <body> tag. This event will be triggered whenever the browser unloads the current document—this occurs when another page is loaded or when the browser window is closed.

Workshop: Adding Link Descriptions to a Web Page

One of the most common uses for an event handler is to display a message on the status line when the user moves the mouse over a link. For example, moving the mouse over the Order Form link might display a message like "Order a product or check an order's status" on the status line.

Status line descriptions like these are typically displayed with the onMouseOver event handler. You will now create a script that displays messages in this manner and clears the message using the onMouseOut event handler. You'll use functions to simplify the process.

When you use this technique, your status line message will replace the URL that is usually displayed there. Make sure your description is at least as useful as the URL. All too often, Web designers use this technique to display a redundant message: For example, a link labeled "Order Form" displays the description "Goes to the Order Form."

To begin the script, you will define a function to display a message on the status line. Although you don't need to use a function, it makes your job a bit easier. For example, a link with an event handler that displays a message on the status line might look like this:

```
<a href="order.html"
    onMouseOver="window.status='Order a product'; return true;">
Order Form</a>
```

In this example, the return true statement is necessary to prevent the status message from being overwritten immediately by the URL display. As you can see, this makes the <a> tag complicated—and there isn't even a way to clear the message.

Using a function simplifies the link tags slightly. More importantly, it will make it easy to add other features (such as graphics) at a later time. You will call the describe function to display a message. Here is the definition for this function:

```
<script LANGUAGE="JavaScript" type="text/javascript">
function describe(text) {
    window.status = text;
    return true;
}
</script>
```

This function accepts a parameter called text. The contents of this variable are placed on the status line. Because the function returns a true value, the status line will continue to display this message until it is cleared. To clear the message, you can create a small function, clearstatus, to call using the onMouseOut handler:

```
function clearstatus() {
    window.status="";
}
```

Last but not least, your HTML document needs to include the actual links, with the appropriate event handlers to call these two functions. Listing 10.2 shows the complete HTML document with three typical links.

LISTING 10.2   The complete descriptive links example

```
<html>
<head>
<title>Descriptive Links</title>
<script LANGUAGE="JavaScript" type="text/javascript">
function describe(text) {
    window.status = text;
    return true;
}
function clearstatus() {
    window.status="";
}
</script>
</head>
<body>
<h1>Descriptive Links</h1>
<p>Move the mouse pointer over one of
these links to view a description:</p>
<ul>
<li><a HREF="order.html"
    onMouseOver="describe('Order a product'); return true;"
    onMouseOut="clearstatus();">
Order Form</a>
<li><a HREF="email.html"
```

LISTING 10.2 Continued

```
    onMouseOver="describe('Send us a message'); return true;"
    onMouseOut="clearstatus();">
Email</a>
<li><A HREF="complain.html"
    onMouseOver="describe('Insult us, our products, or our families'); return
true;"
    onMouseOut="clearstatus();">
Complaint Department</a>
</ul>
</body>
</html>
```

In this example, the functions are defined in the header portion of the document. Each link includes `onMouseOver` and `onMouseOut` event handlers to call the two status line functions.

To test the script, load it into a browser; this script should work on any JavaScript-capable browser. Internet Explorer's display of the example is shown in Figure 10.2.

As usual, you can download the listings for this chapter from this book's Web site: http://www.jsworkshop.com/js3/.

FIGURE 10.2.
Internet Explorer's display of the descriptive links example.

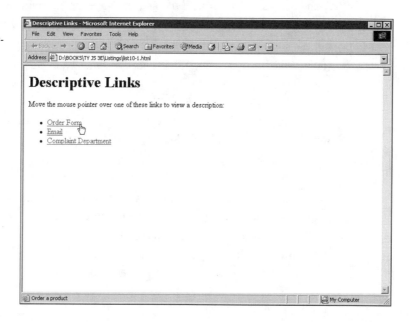

Summary

In this hour, you've learned to use events to detect mouse actions, keyboard actions, and other events, such as the loading of the page. You can use event handlers to perform a simple JavaScript statement when an event occurs, or to call a more complicated function.

JavaScript includes a variety of other events. Many of these are related to forms, which you'll learn more about in Hour 12. Another useful event is onError, which you can use to prevent error messages from displaying. This event is described in Hour 17, "Debugging JavaScript Applications."

In the next hour, you'll continue learning about the objects in the DOM. Specifically, Hour 12 looks at the objects associated with Web forms and how they work with JavaScript.

Q&A

Q I noticed that the `<img>` tag in HTML can't have `onMouseOver` or `onClick` event handlers in some browsers. How can my scripts respond when the mouse moves over an image?

A The easiest way to do this is to make the image a link by surrounding it with an `<a>` tag. You can include the `BORDER=0` attribute to prevent the blue link border from being displayed around the image. You'll see an example of this in Hour 13.

Q My image rollovers using `onMouseOver` work perfectly in Internet Explorer, but not in Netscape. Why?

A Re-read the previous answer, and check whether you've used an `onMouseOver` event for an `<img>` tag. This is supported by Internet Explorer and Netscape 6, but not by earlier versions of Netscape.

Q What happens if I define both `onKeyDown` and `onKeyPress` event handlers? Will they both be called when a key is pressed?

A The `onKeyDown` event handler is called first. If it returns `true`, the `onKeyPress` event is called. Otherwise, no keypress event is generated.

Q When I use the `onLoad` event, my event handler sometimes executes before the page is done loading, or before some of the graphics. Is there a better way?

A This is a bug in some older versions of JavaScript. One solution is to add a slight delay to your script using the `setTimeout` method. You'll learn how to use this method in Hour 11, "Using Windows and Frames."

Q When I try the descriptive links example in Netscape 6.2, the descriptions don't display. Why not?

A At this writing, the latest version of Netscape 6 fails to display the descriptions if your link includes the `HREF` attribute. One way around this is to use an `onClick` event handler instead, as in `<a onClick="location.href='newpage.html';">`. This works, but Netscape doesn't display it in the correct link color.

Quiz

Test your knowledge of event handlers in JavaScript by answering the following questions.

Questions

10

1. Which of the following is the correct event handler to detect a mouse click on a link?

   a. `onMouseUp`

   b. `onLink`

   c. `onClick`

2. When does the `onLoad` event handler for the `<body>` tag execute?

   a. When an image is finished loading.

   b. When the entire page is finished loading.

   c. When the user attempts to load another page.

3. Which of the following `event` object properties indicates which key was pressed for an `onKeyPress` event in Internet Explorer?

   a. `event.which`

   b. `event.keyCode`

   c. `event.onKeyPress`

Answers

1. c. The event handler for a mouse click is `onClick`.

2. b. The `<body>` tag's `onLoad` handler executes when the page and all its images are finished loading.

3. b. In Internet Explorer, the `event.keyCode` property stores the character code for each keypress.

Exercises

To gain more experience using event handlers in JavaScript, try the following exercises:

- Add several additional links to the document in Listing 10.2. Include event handlers that display a unique description for each link.

- Modify Listing 10.2 to display a default welcome message in the status line whenever a description isn't being displayed. (Hint: You'll need to include a statement to display the welcome message when the page loads. You'll also need to change the clearstatus function to restore the welcome message.)

Hour **11**

Using Windows and Frames

You should now have a basic understanding of the objects in the level 0 DOM, and the events that can be used with each object.

In this hour, you'll learn more about some of the most useful objects in the level 0 DOM—browser windows and frames—and how JavaScript can work with them. Hour 11 covers the following topics:

- The window object hierarchy
- Creating new windows with JavaScript
- Delaying your script's actions with timeouts
- Displaying alerts, confirmations, and prompts
- Using JavaScript to work with frames
- Creating a JavaScript-based navigation frame

Controlling Windows with Objects

In Hour 9, "Working with the Document Object Model," you learned that you can use DOM objects to represent various parts of the browser window and the current HTML document. You also learned that the history, document, and location objects are all children of the window object.

In this hour, you'll take a closer look at the window object itself. As you've probably guessed by now, this means you'll be dealing with browser windows. A variation of the window object also allows you to work with frames, as you'll see later in this hour.

The window object always refers to the current window (the one containing the script). The self keyword is also a synonym for the current window. As you'll learn in the next section, you can have more than one window on the screen at the same time, and can refer to them with different names.

Creating a New Window

One of the most convenient uses for the window object is to create a new window. You can do this to display a document—for example, the instructions for a game—without clearing the current window. You can also create windows for specific purposes, such as navigation windows.

You can create a new browser window with the window.open() method. A typical statement to open a new window looks like this:

```
WinObj=window.open("URL", "WindowName", "Feature List");
```

The following are the components of the window.open() statement:

- The WinObj variable is used to store the new window object. You can access methods and properties of the new object by using this name.

- The first parameter of the window.open() method is a URL, which will be loaded into the new window. If it's left blank, no Web page will be loaded.

- The second parameter specifies a window name (here, WindowName). This is assigned to the window object's name property and is used to refer to the window.

- The third parameter is a list of optional features, separated by commas. You can customize the new window by choosing whether to include the toolbar, status line, and other features. This enables you to create a variety of "floating" windows, which may look nothing like a typical browser window.

The features available in the third parameter of the window.open() method include width and height, to set the size of the window, and several features that can be set to either yes (1) or no (0): `toolbar`, `location`, `directories`, `status`, `menubar`, `scrollbars`, and `resizable`. You can list only the features you want to change from the default. This example creates a small window with no toolbar or status line:

```
SmallWin = window.open("","small","width=100,height=120,toolbar=0,status=0");
```

> You can also manipulate the current window in a variety of ways from a signed script, which has the user's permission to gain greater control over the browser. See Appendix A, "Other Javascript Resources," for a list of Web sites with information about signed scripts and other advanced features.

Opening and Closing Windows

Of course, you can close windows as well. The `window.close()` method closes a window. Netscape doesn't allow you to close the main browser window without the user's permission; its main purpose is for closing windows you have created. For example, this statement closes a window called `updatewindow`:

```
updatewindow.close();
```

As another example, Listing 11.1 shows an HTML document that enables you to open a new window by pressing a button. (I have specified a very small size for the second window so you can tell them apart.) You can then press another button to close the new window. The third button attempts to close the current window. Netscape allows this, but asks for confirmation first.

LISTING 11.1 An HTML document that uses JavaScript to enable you to create and close windows

```
<html>
<head><title>Create a New Window</title>
</head>
<body>
<h1>Create a New Window</h1>
<hr>
<p>Use the buttons below to test opening and closing windows in JavaScript.</p>
<hr>
<form NAME="winform">
<input TYPE="button" VALUE="Open New Window"
onClick="NewWin=window.open('','NewWin',
'toolbar=no,status=no,width=200,height=100'); ">
<p><input TYPE="button" VALUE="Close New Window"
onClick="NewWin.close();" ></p>
<p><input TYPE="button" VALUE="Close Main Window"
onClick="window.close();"></p>
```

11

LISTING 11.1 Continued

```
</form>
<br><p>Have fun!</p>
<hr>
</body>
</html>
```

This example uses event handlers to do its work, one for each of the buttons. Figure 11.1 shows Netscape's display of this page, with the small new window on top.

FIGURE 11.1.

A new browser window opened with JavaScript.

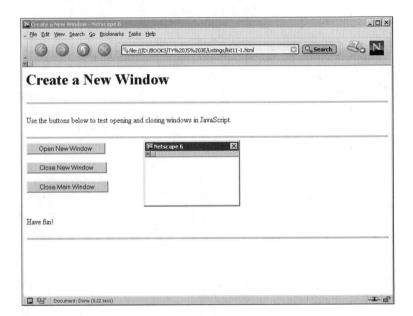

Moving and Resizing Windows

New to JavaScript 1.2 is the ability to move or resize windows. While Netscape 4 placed some restrictions on this, Netscape 6 and Internet Explorer 5 and later allow you to move and resize any window freely. You can do this using the following methods for any `window` object:

- `window.moveTo()` moves the window to a new position. The parameters specify the x (column) and y (row) position.
- `window.moveBy()` moves the window relative to its current position. The x and y parameters can be positive or negative, and are added to the current values to reach the new position.

- `window.resizeTo()`resizes the window to the width and height specified as parameters.

- `window.resizeBy()` resizes the window relative to its current size. The parameters are used to modify the current width and height.

As an example, Listing 11.2 shows an HTML document with a simple script that allows you to resize or move the main window.

LISTING 11.2 Moving and resizing the current window

```
<html>
<head>
<title>Moving and resizing windows</title>
<script language="javascript1.2" type="text/javascript1.2">
   function DoIt() {
       if (document.form1.w.value && document.form1.h.value)
           self.resizeTo(document.form1.w.value, document.form1.h.value);
       if (document.form1.x.value && document.form1.y.value)
           self.moveTo(document.form1.x.value, document.form1.y.value);
   }
</script>
</head>
<body>
<h1>Moving and Resizing Windows</h1>
<form name="form1">
<b>Width:</b> <input type="text" name="w"><br>
<b>Height:</b> <input type="text" name="h"><br>
<b>X-position:</b> <input type="text" name="x"><br>
<b>Y-position:</b> <input type="text" name="y"><br>
<input type="button" value="Change Window" onClick="DoIt();">
</form>
</body>
</html>
```

11

In this example, the `DoIt` function is called as an event handler when you click the Change Window button. This function checks if you have specified width and height values. If you have, it uses the `self.resizeTo()` method to resize the current window. Similarly, if you have specified x and y values, it uses `self.moveTo()` to move the window.

While developers have wanted a way to move or resize windows for a long time, this is one of those JavaScript features you should think twice before using. These methods are best used for resizing or moving pop-up windows your script has generated—not as a way to force the user to use your preferred window size.

Using Timeouts

Sometimes the hardest thing to get a script to do is to do nothing at all—for a specific amount of time. Fortunately, JavaScript includes a built-in function to do this. The `window.setTimeout` method allows you to specify a time delay and a command that will execute after the delay passes.

> Timeouts don't actually make the browser stop what it's doing. Although the statement you specify in the `setTimeout` method won't be executed until the delay passes, the browser will continue to do other things while it waits (for example, acting on event handlers).

You begin a timeout with a call to the `setTimeout()` method, which has two parameters. The first is a JavaScript statement, or group of statements, enclosed in quotes. The second parameter is the time to wait in milliseconds (thousandths of seconds). For example, the following statement displays an alert dialog box after 10 seconds:

```
ident=window.setTimeout("alert('Time's up!')",10000);
```

> Like event handlers, timeouts use a JavaScript statement within quotation marks. Make sure that you use a single quote (apostrophe) on each side of each string within the statement, as shown in the preceding example.

A variable (`ident` in this example) stores an identifier for the timeout. This enables you to set multiple timeouts, each with its own identifier. Before a timeout has elapsed, you can stop it with the `clearTimeout()` method, specifying the identifier of the timeout to stop:

```
window.clearTimeout(ident);
```

Updating a Page with Timeouts

Normally, a timeout only happens once because the statement you specify in the `setTimeout` statement is only executed once. But often, you'll want your statement to execute over and over. For example, your script may be updating a clock or countdown and need to execute once per second.

You can make a timeout repeat by issuing the `setTimeout()` method call again in the function called by the timeout. Listing 11.3 shows an HTML document that demonstrates a repeating timeout.

LISTING 11.3 Using timeouts to update a page every two seconds

```
<html>
<head><title>Timeout Example</title>
<script language="javascript" type="text/javascript">
var counter = 0;
// call Update function in 2 seconds after first load
ID=window.setTimeout("Update();",2000);
function Update() {
   counter++;
   window.status="The counter is now at " + counter;
   document.form1.input1.value="The counter is now at " + counter;
// set another timeout for the next count
   ID=window.setTimeout("Update();",2000);
}
</script>
</head>
<body>
<h1>Timeout Example</h1>
<hr><p>
The text value below and the status line are being updated every two seconds.
Press the RESET button to restart the count, or the STOP button to stop it.
</p><hr>
<form NAME="form1">
<input TYPE="text" NAME="input1" SIZE="40"><br>
<input TYPE="button" VALUE="RESET" onClick="counter = 0;"><br>
<input TYPE="button" VALUE="STOP" onClick="window.clearTimeout(ID);">
</form>
<hr>
</body>
</html>
```

This program displays a message in the status line and in a text field every two seconds, including a counter that increments each time. You can use the Reset button to start the count over and the Stop button to stop the counting.

This script calls the `setTimeout()` method when the page loads, and again at each update. The `Update()` function performs the update, adding one to the counter and setting the next timeout. The Reset button sets the counter to zero, and the Stop button demonstrates the `clearTimeout()` method. Figure 11.2 shows Internet Explorer's display of the timeout example after the counter has been running for a while.

11

FIGURE 11.2.

The output of the time-out example.

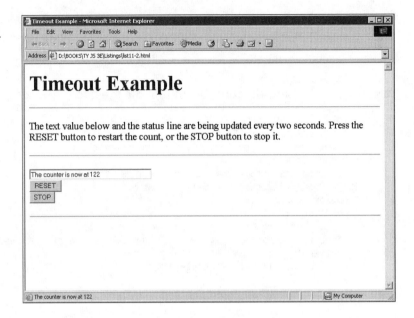

This example and the next one use buttons, which are a simple example of what you can do with HTML forms and JavaScript. You'll learn much more about forms in Hour 12, "Getting Data with Forms."

Displaying Dialog Boxes

The window object includes three methods that are useful for displaying messages and interacting with the user. You've already used these in some of your scripts. Here's a summary:

- The alert method displays an alert dialog box, shown in Figure 11.3. This dialog box simply gives the user a message.

- The confirm method displays a confirmation dialog box. This displays a message and includes OK and Cancel buttons. This method returns true if OK is pressed and false if Cancel is pressed. A confirmation is displayed in Figure 11.4.

- The prompt method displays a message and prompts the user for input. It returns the text entered by the user.

FIGURE 11.3.

A JavaScript alert dialog box displays a message.

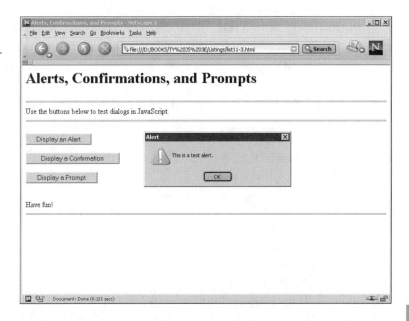

FIGURE 11.4.

A JavaScript confirm dialog box asks for confirmation.

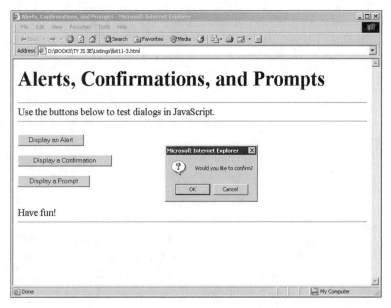

11

Creating a Script to Display Dialog Boxes

As a further illustration of these types of dialog boxes, Listing 11.4 shows an HTML document that uses buttons and event handlers to enable you to test dialog boxes.

LISTING 11.4 An HTML document that uses JavaScript to display alerts, confirmations, and prompts

```
<html>
<head><title>Alerts, Confirmations, and Prompts</title>
</head>
<body>
<h1>Alerts, Confirmations, and Prompts</h1>
<hr>
Use the buttons below to test dialogs in JavaScript.
<hr>
<form NAME="winform">
<p><input TYPE="button" VALUE="Display an Alert"
onClick="window.alert('This is a test alert.');  "></p>
<p><input TYPE="button" VALUE="Display a Confirmation"
onClick="temp = window.confirm('Would you like to confirm?');
window.status=(temp)?'confirm: true':'confirm: false'; "></p>
<P><input TYPE="button" VALUE="Display a Prompt"
onClick="var temp = window.prompt('Enter some Text:','This is the default
value');
window.status=temp;  "></p>
</form>
<br>Have fun!
<hr>
</body>
</html>
```

This document displays three buttons, and each one uses an event handler to display one of the dialog boxes. Let's take a detailed look at each one:

- The alert dialog box is displayed when you click on the first button.

- The confirmation dialog box is displayed when you click the second button, and displays a message in the status line indicating whether true or false was returned. The returned value is stored in the temp variable.

- The third button displays the prompt dialog box. Notice that the prompt method accepts a second parameter, which is used to set a default value for the entry. The value you enter is stored in the temp variable and displayed on the status line. Notice that if you press the Cancel button in the prompt dialog box, the null value is returned.

Figure 11.5 shows the script in Listing 11.4 in action. The prompt dialog box is currently displayed and shows the default value, and the status line still displays the result of a previous confirmation dialog box.

FIGURE 11.5.

The dialog box example's output, including a prompt dialog box.

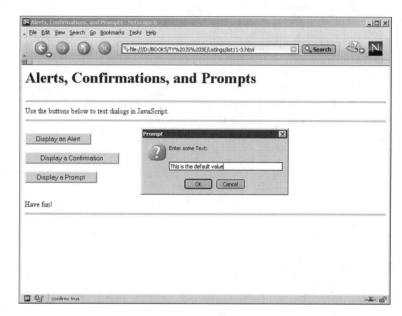

Working with Frames

Some browsers (including the latest Netscape and Microsoft browsers) support *frames*, which enable you to divide the browser window into multiple panes. Each frame can contain a separate URL or the output of a script.

Using JavaScript Objects for Frames

When a window contains multiple frames, each frame is represented in JavaScript by a frame object. This object is equivalent to a window object, but it is used for dealing with that frame. The frame object's name is the same as the NAME attribute you give it in the <frame> tag.

Remember the window and self keywords, which refer to the current window? When you are using frames, these keywords refer to the current frame instead. Another keyword, parent, enables you to refer to the main window.

Each frame object in a window is a child of the `parent` window object. Suppose you define a set of frames using the HTML below:

```
<frameset ROWS="*,*" COLS="*,*">
<frame NAME="topleft" SRC="topleft.htm">
<frame NAME="topright" SRC="topright.htm">
<frame NAME="bottomleft" SRC="botleft.htm">
<frame NAME="bottomright" SRC="botright.htm">
</frameset>
```

This simply divides the window into quarters. If you have a JavaScript program in the `topleft.htm` file, it would refer to the other windows as `parent.topright`, `parent.bottomleft`, and so on. The keywords `window` and `self` would refer to the `topleft` frame.

> If you use nested framesets, things are a bit more complicated. `window` still represents the current frame, `parent` represents the frameset containing the current frame, and `top` represents the main frameset that contains all the others.

The `frames` Array

Rather than referring to frames in a document by name, you can use the `frames` array. This array stores information about each of the frames in the document. The frames are indexed starting with zero and beginning with the first `<frame>` tag in the frameset document.

For example, you could refer to the frames defined in the previous example using array references:

- `parent.frames[0]` is equivalent to the `topleft` frame.
- `parent.frames[1]` is equivalent to the `topright` frame.
- `parent.frames[2]` is equivalent to the `bottomleft` frame.
- `parent.frames[3]` is equivalent to the `bottomright` frame.

You can refer to a frame using either method interchangeably, and depending on your application, you should use the most convenient method. For example, a document with 10 frames would probably be easier to use by number, but a simple two-frame document is easier to use if the frames have meaningful names.

Workshop: Creating a Navigation Frame

A common use for frames is to display a navigation frame along the side or top of a page. Using frame objects, you can create a navigation frame that controls the document in another frame.

To begin, you'll need a document to define the frameset. This is the simple part. Listing 11.5 defines a frameset with frames on the left and right.

LISTING 11.5   An HTML document to divide the window into two frames

```
<html>
<head>
<title>Frame Navigation Example</title>
</head>
<frameset COLS="*,*">
<frame NAME="left" SRC="left.html">
<frame NAME="right" SRC="about:blank">
</frameset>
</html>
```

Next, you will need the document for the left-hand frame, which will act as the navigation frame. Listing 11.6 shows the HTML document for this frame.

LISTING 11.6   The HTML document for the navigation frame

```
<html>
<head>
<title>Navigation Frame</title>
</head>
<body>
<p>
Follow one of these links
to load a page into the right-hand
frame:
</p>
<ul>
<li><a HREF="#"
onClick="parent.right.location='order.html';
        window.location='ordernav.html';">
Order form</a>
<li><a HREF="#"
onClick="parent.right.location='email.html';
        window.location='emailnav.html';">
```

11

LISTING 11.6   Continued

```
Email</a>
<li><a HREF="#"
onClick="parent.right.location='sales.html';
         window.location='salesnav.html';">
Sales Dept.</a>
<li><a HREF="#"
onClick="parent.right.location='link.html';">
Other Links</a>
</ul>
</body>
</html>
```

This listing looks complicated, but it actually uses two simple JavaScript statements to do its job. These statements are repeated for each of the links, with a slight variation. Here's one example:

```
onClick="parent.right.location='email.html';
         window.location='emailnav.html';">
```

These statements are an event handler that loads a document into the right-hand frame, and also loads a new document into the navigation frame. Because the current script is itself in a frame, you need to use the parent keyword before the name of the other frame's object.

 If you're only loading one document when the user clicks on a link, you can use the TARGET attribute of the <a> tag and avoid JavaScript. However, using JavaScript allows you to update two frames at once, as seen in this example.

To test this script, make sure that you've saved Listing 11.6 as left.html, and then load Listing 11.5 into the browser. Try one of the links. (You can download a complete set of HTML documents for this example from this book's Web site, www.jsworkshop.com.) Figure 11.6 shows Internet Explorer's display of this example.

FIGURE 11.6.

The frame example as displayed by Internet Explorer.

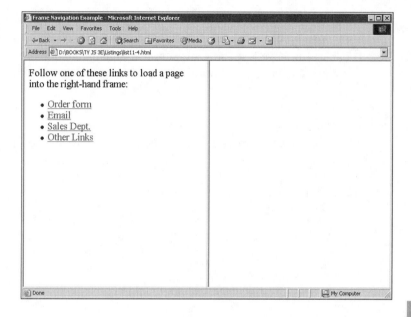

Summary

In this hour, you've learned how to use the `window` object to work with browser windows, and used its properties and methods to set timeouts and display dialog boxes. You've also learned how JavaScript can work with framed documents.

In the next hour, you'll move on to another unexplored area of the JavaScript object hierarchy—the `form` object. You'll learn how to use forms to create some of the most useful applications of JavaScript.

Q&A

Q When a script is running in a window created by another script, how can it refer back to the original window?

A JavaScript 1.1 and later include the `window.opener` property, which lets you refer to the window that opened the current window.

Q I've heard about layers, which are similar to frames, but more versatile, and are supported in the latest browsers. Can I use them with JavaScript?

A Yes. You'll learn how to use layers with JavaScript in Hour 19, "Using Dynamic HTML (DHTML)."

11

Q How can I update two frames at once when the user clicks on a single link?

A You can do this by using an event handler, as in Listing 11.6, and including two statements to load different frames. To simplify things, you can also create a function that loads both frames and then call the function from the event handler.

Quiz

Test your knowledge of JavaScript windows and frames by answering the following questions.

Questions

1. Which of the following methods displays a dialog box with OK and Cancel buttons, and waits for a response?

    a. `window.alert`

    b. `window.confirm`

    c. `window.prompt`

2. What does the `window.setTimeout` method do?

    a. Executes a JavaScript statement after a delay.

    b. Locks up the browser for the specified amount of time.

    c. Sets the amount of time before the browser exits automatically.

3. You're working with a document that contains three frames with the names `first`, `second`, and `third`. If a script in the second frame needs to refer to the first frame, what is the correct syntax?

    a. `window.first`

    b. `parent.first`

    c. `frames.first`

Answers

1. b. The `window.confirm` method displays a dialog box with OK and Cancel buttons.

2. a. The `window.setTimeout` method executes a JavaScript statement after a delay.

3. b. The script in the second frame would use `parent.first` to refer to the first frame.

Exercises

If you want to study the window object and its properties and methods further, perform these exercises:

- Return to the date/time script you created in Hour 2, "Creating a Simple Script." This script only displays the date and time once when the page is loaded. Using timeouts, you can modify the script to reload automatically every second or two and display a "live" clock. (Use the location.reload method, described in Hour 9.)

- Modify the examples in Listings 11.5 and 11.6 to use three frames instead of two. For each link in the left frame, use the script to load new documents into both the middle and right frames.

11

HOUR 12

Getting Data with Forms

In this hour you'll explore one of the most powerful uses for JavaScript: working with HTML forms. You can use JavaScript to make a form more interactive, validate data the user enters, and enter data based on other data.

This hour covers the following topics:

- Understanding HTML forms
- Creating a form
- Using the form object to work with forms
- How form elements are represented by JavaScript
- Getting data from a form
- Sending form results by email
- How JavaScript can work with CGI forms
- Validating a form with JavaScript

The Basics of HTML Forms

Forms are among the most useful features of the HTML language. As you'll learn during this hour, adding JavaScript to forms can make them more interactive and provide a number of useful features. The first step in creating an interactive form is to create the HTML form itself.

Defining a Form

An HTML form begins with the `<form>` tag. This tag indicates that a form is beginning, and it enables form elements to be used. The `<form>` tag includes three parameters:

- NAME is simply a name for the form. You can use forms without giving them names, but you'll need to assign a name to a form in order to easily use it with JavaScript.

- METHOD is either GET or POST; these are the two ways the data can be sent to the server.

- ACTION is the CGI script that the form data will be sent to when submitted. You can also use the `mailto:` action to send the form's results to an email address, as described later in this hour.

For example, here is a `<form>` tag for a form named Order. This form uses the GET method and sends its data to a CGI script called `order.cgi` in the same directory as the Web page itself:

```
<form NAME="Order" METHOD="GET" ACTION="order.cgi">
```

For a form that will be processed entirely by JavaScript (such as a calculator or interactive game), the METHOD and ACTION attributes are not needed. You can use a simple `<form>` tag that names the form:

```
<form NAME="calcform">
```

The `<form>` tag is followed by one or more form elements. These are the data fields in the form, such as text fields, buttons, and check boxes. In the next section, you'll learn how JavaScript assigns objects to each of the form elements.

Using the `form` Object with JavaScript

Each form in your HTML page is represented in JavaScript by a `form` object, which has the same name as the NAME attribute in the `<form>` tag you used to define it.

Alternately, you can use the `forms` array to refer to forms. This array includes an item for each form element, indexed starting with 0. For example, if the first form in a document has the name `form1`, you can refer to it in one of two ways:

```
document.form1
document.forms[0]
```

The `form` Object's Properties

Along with the elements, each `form` object also has a list of properties, most of which are defined by the corresponding `<form>` tag. You can also set these from within JavaScript. They include the following:

- `action` is the form's `ACTION` attribute, or the program to which the form data will be submitted.

- `encoding` is the `MIME` type of the form, specified with the `ENCTYPE` attribute. In most cases, this is not needed.

- `length` is the number of elements in the form. You cannot change this property.

- `method` is the method used to submit the form, either `GET` or `POST`.

- `target` specifies the window in which the result of the form (from the CGI script) will be displayed. Normally, this is done in the main window, replacing the form itself.

Submitting and Resetting Forms

The `form` object has two methods, `submit` and `reset`. You can use these methods to submit the data or reset the form yourself, without requiring the user to press a button. One reason for this is to submit the form when the user clicks an image or performs another action that would not usually submit the form.

> If you use the `submit` method to send data to a server or by email, Netscape will prompt the user to verify that she wants to submit the information. There's no way to do this behind the user's back.

Detecting Form Events

The `form` object has two event handlers, `onSubmit` and `onReset`. You can specify a group of JavaScript statements or a function call for these events within the `<form>` tag that defines the form.

12

If you specify a statement or function for the onSubmit event, the statement is called before the data is submitted to the CGI script. You can prevent the submission from happening by returning a value of false from the onSubmit event handler. If the statement returns true, the data will be submitted. In the same fashion, you can prevent a Reset button from working with an onReset event handler.

Scripting Form Elements

The most important property of the form object is the elements array, which contains an object for each of the form elements. You can refer to an element by its own name or by its index in the array. For example, the following two expressions both refer to the first element in the order form, the name1 text field:

```
document.order.elements[0]
```

```
document.order.name1
```

> Both forms and elements can be referred to by their own names or as indices in the forms and elements arrays. For clarity, the examples in this hour use individual form and element names rather than array references. You'll also find it easier to use names in your own scripts.

If you do refer to forms and elements as arrays, you can use the length property to determine the number of objects in the array: document.forms.length is the number of forms in a document, and document.form1.elements.length is the number of elements in the form1 form.

Text Fields

Probably the most commonly used form elements are text fields. You can use them to prompt for a name, address, or any information. With JavaScript, you can display text in the field automatically. The following is an example of a simple text field:

```
<input TYPE="TEXT" NAME="text1" VALUE="hello" SIZE="30">
```

This defines a text field called text1. The field is given a default value of "hello" and allows up to 30 characters to be entered. JavaScript treats this field as a text object with the name text1.

Text fields are the simplest to work with in JavaScript. Each `text` object has the following properties:

- `name` is the name given to the field. This is also used as the object name.
- `defaultValue` is the default value and corresponds to the VALUE attribute. This is a read-only property.
- `value` is the current value. This starts out the same as the default value, but can be changed, either by the user or by JavaScript functions.

When you work with text fields, most of the time you will use the `value` attribute to read the value the user has entered or to change the value. For example, the following statement changes the value of a text field called `username` in the `order` form to "John Q. User":

```
document.order.username.value = "John Q. User"
```

Text Areas

Text areas are defined with their own tag, `<textarea>`, and are represented by the `textarea` object. There is one major difference between a text area and a text field: Text areas allow the user to enter more than just one line of information. Here is an example of a text area definition:

```
<textarea NAME="text1" ROWS="2" COLS="70">
This is the content of the TEXTAREA tag.
</textarea>
```

This HTML defines a text area called `text1`, with two rows and 70 columns available for text. In JavaScript, this would be represented by a text area object called `text1` under the `form` object.

The text between the opening and closing `<textarea>` tags is used as the initial value for the text area. You can include line breaks within the default value.

Working with Text in Forms

The `text` and `textarea` objects also have a few methods you can use:

- `focus()` sets the focus to the field. This positions the cursor in the field and makes it the current field.
- `blur()` is the opposite; it removes the focus from the field.
- `select()` selects the text in the field, just as a user can do with the mouse. All of the text is selected; there is no way to select part of the text.

12

You can also use event handlers to detect when the value of a text field changes. The text and textarea objects support the following event handlers:

- The onFocus event happens when the text field gains focus.
- The onBlur event happens when the text field loses focus.
- The onChange event happens when the user changes the text in the field and then moves out of it.
- The onSelect event happens when the user selects some or all of the text in the field. Unfortunately, there's no way to tell exactly which part of the text was selected. (If the text is selected with the select() method described above, this event is not triggered.)

If used, these event handlers should be included in the <input> tag declaration. For example, the following is a text field including an onChange event that displays an alert:

```
<input TYPE="TEXT" NAME="text1" onChange="window.alert('Changed.');">
```

Buttons

The final type of form element is a button. Buttons use the <input> tag and can use one of three different types:

- type=SUBMIT is a submit button. This button causes the data in the form fields to be sent to the CGI script.
- type=RESET is a reset button. This button sets all the form fields back to their default value, or blank.
- type=BUTTON is a generic button. This button performs no action on its own, but you can assign it one using a JavaScript event handler.

All three types of buttons include a NAME attribute to identify the button and a VALUE that indicates the text to display on the button's face. A few buttons were used in the examples in Hour 11, "Using Windows and Frames." As another example, the following defines a Submit button with the name sub1 and the value "Click Here":

```
<input TYPE="SUBMIT" NAME="sub1" VALUE="Click Here">
```

If the user presses a Submit or Reset button, you can detect it with the onSubmit or onReset event handlers, described earlier in this hour. For generic buttons, you can use an onClick event handler.

Check Boxes

A check box is a form element that looks like a small box. Clicking on the check box switches between the checked and unchecked states, which is useful for indicating Yes or

No choices in your forms. You can use the `<input>` tag to define a check box. Here is a simple example:

```
<input TYPE="CHECKBOX" NAME="check1" VALUE="Yes" CHECKED>
```

Again, this gives a name to the form element. The `VALUE` attribute assigns a meaning to the check box; this is a value that is returned to the server if the box is checked. The default value is "on." The `CHECKED` attribute can be included to make the box checked by default.

A check box is simple: it has only two states. Nevertheless, the `checkbox` object in JavaScript has four different properties:

- `name` is the name of the check box, and also the object name.
- `value` is the "true" value for the check box—usually `on`. This value is used by the server to indicate that the check box was checked. In JavaScript, you should use the `checked` property instead.
- `defaultChecked` is the default status of the check box, assigned by the `CHECKED` attribute.
- `checked` is the current value. This is a boolean value: `true` for checked and `false` for unchecked.

To manipulate the check box or use its value, you use the `checked` attribute. For example, this statement turns on a check box called `same` in the `order` form:

```
document.order.same.checked = true;
```

The check box has a single method, `click()`. This method simulates a click on the box. It also has a single event, `onClick`, which occurs whenever the check box is clicked. This happens whether the box was turned on or off, so you'll need to examine the `checked` property to see what happened.

Radio Buttons

Another element for decisions is the radio button, using the `<input>` tag's `RADIO` type. Radio buttons are also known as option buttons. These are similar to check boxes, but they exist in groups and only one button can be checked in each group. They are used for a multiple-choice or "one of many" input. Here's an example of a group of radio buttons:

```
<input TYPE="RADIO" NAME="radio1" VALUE="Option1" CHECKED> Option 1
<input TYPE="RADIO" NAME="radio1" VALUE="Option2"> Option 2
<input TYPE="RADIO" NAME="radio1" VALUE="Option3"> Option 3
```

These statements define a group of three radio buttons. The `NAME` attribute is the same for all three (which is what makes them a group). The `VALUE` attribute is the value passed to

12

a script or CGI program to indicate which button is selected—be sure you assign a different value to each button.

 Radio buttons are named for their similarity to the buttons on old pushbutton radios. Those buttons used a mechanical arrangement so that when you pushed one button in, the others popped out.

As for scripting, radio buttons are similar to check boxes, except that an entire group of them shares a single name and a single object. You can refer to the following properties of the radio object:

- name is the name common to the radio buttons.
- length is the number of radio buttons in the group.

To access the individual buttons, you treat the radio object as an array. The buttons are indexed, starting with 0. Each individual button has the following properties:

- value is the value assigned to the button. (This is used by the server.)
- defaultChecked indicates the value of the CHECKED attribute and the default state of the button.
- checked is the current state.

For example, you can check the first radio button in the radio1 group on the form1 form with this statement:

```
document.form1.radio1[0].checked = true;
```

However, if you do this, be sure you set the other values to false as needed. This is not done automatically. You can use the click method to do both of these in one step.

Like a check box, radio buttons have a click() method and an onClick event handler. Each radio button can have a separate statement for this event.

Drop-Down Lists

A final form element is also useful for multiple-choice selections. The <select> HTML tag is used to define a *selection list*, or a drop-down list of text items. The following is an example of a selection list:

```
<select NAME="select1" SIZE=40>
<option VALUE="choice1" SELECTED>This is the first choice.
<option VALUE="choice2">This is the second choice.
<option VALUE="choice3">This is the third choice.
</select>
```

Each of the <option> tags defines one of the possible choices. The VALUE attribute is the name that is returned to the program, and the text outside the <option> tag is displayed as the text of the option.

An optional attribute to the <select> tag, MULTIPLE, can be specified to allow multiple items to be selected. Browsers usually display a single-selection <select> as a drop-down list and a multiple-selection list as a scrollable list.

The object for selection lists is the select object. The object itself has the following properties:

- name is the name of the selection list.
- length is the number of options in the list.
- options is the array of options. Each selectable option has an entry in this array.
- selectedIndex returns the index value of the currently selected item. You can use this to check the value easily. In a multiple-selection list, this indicates the first selected item.

The options array has a single property of its own, length, which indicates the number of selections. In addition, each item in the options array has the following properties:

- index is the index into the array.
- defaultSelected indicates the state of the SELECTED attribute.
- selected is the current state of the option. Setting this property to true selects the option. You can select multiple options if the MULTIPLE attribute is included in the <select> tag.
- name is the value of the NAME attribute. This is used by the server.
- text is the text that is displayed in the option. In Netscape 3.0 or later, you can change this value.

The select object has two methods—blur() and focus()—which perform the same purposes as the corresponding methods for text objects. The event handlers are onBlur, onFocus, and onChange, also similar to other objects.

12

 You can change selection lists dynamically—for example, choosing a product in one list could control which options are available in another list. You can also add and delete options from the list.

Reading the value of a selected item is a two-step process. You first use the `selectedIndex` property, then use the `value` property to find the value of the selected choice. Here's an example:

```
ind = document.navform.choice.selectedIndex;
val = document.navform.choice.options[ind].value;
```

This uses the `ind` variable to store the selected index, then assigns the `val` variable to the value of the selected choice. You'll see an example script that uses this technique in Hour 21, "Improving a Web Page with JavaScript."

Displaying Data from a Form

As a simple example of using forms, Listing 12.1 shows a form with name, address, and phone number fields, as well as a JavaScript function that displays the data from the form in a pop-up window.

LISTING 12.1 A form that displays data in a pop-up window

```
<html>
<head>
<title>Form Example</title>
<script LANGUAGE="JavaScript" type="text/javascript">
function display() {
    DispWin = window.open('','NewWin',
'toolbar=no,status=no,width=300,height=200')
    message = "<ul><li><b>NAME: </b>" + document.form1.yourname.value;
    message += "<li><b>ADDRESS: </b>" + document.form1.address.value;
    message += "<li><b>PHONE: </b>" + document.form1.phone.value + "</ul>";
    DispWin.document.write(message);
}
</script>
</head>
<body>
<h1>Form Example</h1>
Enter the following information. When you press the Display button,
the data you entered will be displayed in a pop-up window.
<form name="form1">
<p><b>Name:</b> <input TYPE="TEXT" SIZE="20" NAME="yourname">
</p>
<p><b>Address:</b> <input TYPE="TEXT" SIZE="30" NAME="address">
</p>
<p><b>Phone: </b> <input TYPE="TEXT" SIZE="15" NAME="phone">
</p>
<p><input TYPE="BUTTON" VALUE="Display" onClick="display();"></p>
</form>
</body>
</html>
```

Here is a breakdown of how this HTML document and script work:

- The <script> section in the document's header defines a function called display that opens a new window (as described in Hour 11) and displays the information from the form.

- The <form> tag begins the form. Because this form is handled entirely by JavaScript, no form action or method is needed.

- The <input> tags define the form's three fields: yourname, address, and phone. The last <input> tag defines the Display button, which is set to run the display function.

> As usual, you can download the listings for this chapter from this book's Web site: http://www.jsworkshop.com/.

Figure 12.1 shows this form in action. The Display button has been pressed, and the pop-up window shows the results.

FIGURE 12.1.

Displaying data from a form in a pop-up window.

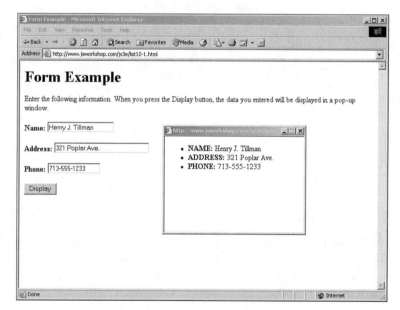

12

Sending Form Results by Email

One easy way to use a form is to send the results by email. You can do this without using any JavaScript, although you could use JavaScript to validate the information entered (as you'll learn later in this hour).

To send a form's results by email, you use the mailto: action in the form's ACTION attribute. Listing 12.2 is a modified version of the name and address form from Listing 12.1 that sends the results by email.

LISTING 12.2   Sending a form's results by email

```
<html>
<head>
<title>Form Example</title>
</head>
<body>
<h1>Form Example</h1>
Enter the following information. When you press the Submit button,
the data you entered will be sent by email.
<form name="form1" action="mailto:user@host.com"
  enctype="text/plain" method="POST">
<p><b>Name:</b> <input TYPE="TEXT" SIZE="20" NAME="yourname">
</p>
<p><b>Address:</b> <input TYPE="TEXT" SIZE="30" NAME="address">
</p>
<p><b>Phone: </b> <input TYPE="TEXT" SIZE="15" NAME="phone">
</p>
<p><input TYPE="SUBMIT" VALUE="Submit"></p>
</form>
</body>
</html>
```

To use this form, change user@host.com to your email address. Notice the enctype=text/plain attribute in the <form> tag. This ensures that the information in the email message will be in a readable format.

While this provides a quick and dirty way of retrieving data from a form, the disadvantage of this technique is that it is highly browser-dependent. Whether it will work for each user of your page depends on the configuration of their browser and their email client.

For a more reliable way of sending form results, you can use a CGI form-to-email gateway. Several free CGI scripts and services are available. You'll find links to them on this book's Web site: http://www.jsworkshop.com/.

Workshop: Validating a Form

JavaScript's single most useful purpose is probably validating forms. This means using a script to verify that the information entered is valid—for example, that no fields are blank and that the data is in the right format.

You can use JavaScript to validate a form whether it's submitted by email or to a CGI script, or is simply used by a script. Listing 12.3 is a version of the name and address form that includes validation.

LISTING 12.3 A form with a validation script

```
<html>
<head>
<title>Form Example</title>
<script LANGUAGE="JavaScript" type="text/javascript">
function validate() {
    if (document.form1.yourname.value.length < 1) {
        alert("Please enter your full name.");
        return false;
    }
    if (document.form1.address.value.length < 3) {
        alert("Please enter your address.");
        return false;
    }
    if (document.form1.phone.value.length < 3) {
        alert("Please enter your phone number.");
        return false;
    }
    return true;
}
</script>
</head>
<body>
<h1>Form Example</h1>
<p>Enter the following information. When you press the Submit button,
the data you entered will be validated, then sent by email.</p>
<form name="form1" action="mailto:user@host.com" enctype="text/plain"
 method="POST" onSubmit="return validate();">
<p><b>Name:</b> <input TYPE="TEXT" SIZE="20" NAME="yourname">
</p>
<p><b>Address:</b> <input TYPE="TEXT" SIZE="30" NAME="address">
</p>
<p><b>Phone: </b> <input TYPE="TEXT" SIZE="15" NAME="phone">
</p>
<p><input TYPE="SUBMIT" VALUE="Submit"></p>
</form>
</body>
</html>
```

12

This form uses a function called `validate` to check the data in each of the form fields. Each `if` statement in this function checks a field's length. If the field is long enough to be valid, the form can be submitted; otherwise, the submission is stopped and an alert message is displayed.

This form is set up to send its results by email, as in listing 12.2—if you wish to use this feature, be sure to read the information about email forms earlier in this hour and change `user@host.com` to your desired email address.

The `<form>` tag uses an `onSubmit` event handler to call the `validate` function. The `return` keyword ensures that the value returned by `validate` will determine whether the form is submitted.

You can also use the `onChange` event handler in each form field to call a validation routine. This allows the field to be validated before the Submit button is pressed.

Figure 12.2 shows this script in action, as displayed by Netscape. The form has been filled out except for the name, and a dialog box indicates that the name needs to be entered.

FIGURE 12.2.

The form validation example in action.

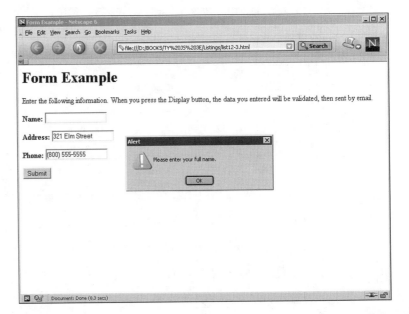

Summary

During this hour, you've learned all about HTML forms and how they can be used with JavaScript. You learned about the form object and the objects for the various form elements, and used them in several example scripts.

You also learned how to submit a form by email, and how to use JavaScript to validate a form before it is submitted.

While JavaScript allows you to create such businesslike things as forms, it also has uses that are a bit more fun. In the next hour, you'll learn how to use JavaScript to work with graphics and create simple animations.

Q&A

Q If I use JavaScript to add validation and other features to my form, can users with non-JavaScript browsers still use the form?

A Yes, if you're careful. Be sure to use a Submit button rather than the submit action. Also, the CGI script may receive nonvalidated data, so be sure to include validation in the CGI script. Non-JavaScript users will be able to use the form, but won't receive instant feedback about their errors.

Q Can I add new form elements "on the fly" or change them—for example, change a text box into a password field?

A No. The form elements are set by the HTML code. There are ways to work around this, such as updating the form in a separate frame or layer.

Q Is there any way to create a large number of text fields without dealing with different names for all of them?

A Yes. If you use the same name for several elements in the form, their objects will form an array. For example, if you defined 20 text fields with the name member, you could refer to them as member[0] through member[19]. This also works with other types of form elements.

Q Why doesn't JavaScript recognize my form elements when I use a table to lay them out?

A Some versions of JavaScript do not deal well with forms or scripts within tables when <table> tags are nested. For now, the only solution is to avoid using nested tables.

12

Q **Is there a way to place the cursor on a particular field when the form is loaded, or after my validation routine displays an error message?**

A Yes. You can use the field's `focus()` method to send the cursor there. To do this when the page loads, you can use the `onLoad` method in the `<body>` tag. However, there is no way to place the cursor in a particular position within the field.

Quiz

Test your knowledge of JavaScript's form objects by answering the following questions.

Questions

1. Which of these attributes of a `<form>` tag determines where the data will be sent?

   a. `ACTION`

   b. `METHOD`

   c. `NAME`

2. Where do you place the `onSubmit` event handler to validate a form?

   a. In the `<body>` tag.

   b. In the `<form>` tag.

   c. In the `<input>` tag for the Submit button.

3. What can JavaScript do with forms that a CGI script can't?

   a. Cause all sorts of problems.

   b. Give the user instant feedback about errors.

   c. Submit the data to a server.

Answers

1. a. The `ACTION` attribute determines where the data is sent.

2. b. You place the `onSubmit` event handler in the `<form>` tag.

3. b. JavaScript can validate a form and let the user know about errors immediately, without waiting for a response from a server. (If you use server-side JavaScript, you can also submit the data to the server, but that's another story.)

Exercises

If you want to study the form objects further, perform these exercises:

- Change the validate function in Listing 12.3 so that after a message is displayed indicating that a field is wrong, the cursor is moved to that field. (Use the focus method for the appropriate form element.)

- Add a text field to the form in Listing 12.3 for an email address. Add a feature to the validate function that verifies that the email address is at least five characters and that it contains the @ symbol.

12

HOUR 13

Using Graphics and Animation

One of the most challenging—and rewarding—uses of a programming language is creating graphic applications and games. In this hour, you'll look at some techniques you can use for graphic pages—or to add excitement to any Web page.

Of course, JavaScript is a relatively simple language and this is a relatively simple book, so you won't be learning how to write your own version of Quake in JavaScript. Nevertheless, JavaScript can perform some useful features with graphics, and can even do simple animations.

In this hour, you'll learn how to use graphics and animation in JavaScript. You will cover the following topics:

- Using image maps with JavaScript
- How JavaScript uses objects to represent images
- Creating rollover images
- Pre-loading images into the cache
- Creating a simple JavaScript animation

Using Image Maps with JavaScript

Image maps are a popular way to provide navigation for a site. They're images that are divided into a number of "hot spots," or areas that act as links. Using JavaScript, you can perform script commands when an area of the image is clicked.

There are two types of image maps: client-side and server-side. Client-side maps define the linked areas of the image within the HTML document, and thus can be used with JavaScript. Server-side maps require a separate map definition file, and are handled by Web servers.

As an example of using a client-side image map with JavaScript, let's create a simple image map menu for a fictional company. (The company's name isn't important, but it's obviously not a graphic design company.)

To create a client-side map, you need to do three things:

- Use your favorite graphics application to create the actual graphic as a GIF or JPEG image.
- Create a MAP definition that describes areas in the image.
- Include the image map in the document, using the USEMAP attribute to point to the map definition.

As usual, you can download all of the graphics and HTML files for this hour's listings from this book's Web site: http://www.jsworkshop.com/.

Listing 13.1 shows the example client-side image map definition.

LISTING 13.1 Using a client-side image map with JavaScript

```
<html>
<head>
<title>Image Map Example</title>
<script LANGUAGE="JavaScript" type="text/javascript">
function update(t) {
    document.form1.text1.value = t;
}
</script>
```

LISTING 13.1 Continued

```
</head>
<body>
<map NAME="map1">
<area SHAPE=RECT COORDS="14,15,151,87" onClick="update('service');"
onMouseOver="window.status='Service Department'; return true;">
<area SHAPE=RECT COORDS="162,16,283,85" onClick="update('sales');"
onMouseOver="window.status='Sales Department'; return true;">
<area SHAPE=RECT COORDS="294,15,388,87" onClick="update('info');"
onMouseOver="window.status='Information'; return true;">
<area SHAPE=RECT COORDS="13,98,79,178" onClick="update('email');"
onMouseOver="window.status='Email Us'; return true;">
<area SHAPE=RECT COORDS="92,97,223,177" onClick="update('products');"
onMouseOver="window.status='Products'; return true;">
<area SHAPE=RECT COORDS="235,98,388,177" onClick="update('our staff');"
onMouseOver="window.status='Our Staff'; return true;">
<area SHAPE=default onClick="update('No item selected.');"
onMouseOver="window.status='Please select an item.'; return true;">
</map>
<h1>Client-Side Image Map Example</h1>
<hr>
The image map below uses JavaScript functions in each of its areas. Moving over
an area will display information about it in the status line. Clicking on an
area
places the name of the area in the text field below the image map.
<hr>
<img SRC="imagemap.gif" USEMAP="#map1">
<hr>
<FORM NAME="form1">
<b>Clicked Item:</b>
<input TYPE="text" NAME="text1" VALUE="Please select an item.">
</form>
<hr>
</body>
</html>
```

This script uses the onMouseOver and onClick event handlers to perform its functions. Rather than link to an actual page, clicking on the areas will display a message in a text field (see Figure 13.1). In addition, the onMouseOver event handlers display a description in the status line for each area.

Recent browsers won't display status line descriptions for an image map when the HREF attribute is included for the links. This is why the example uses onClick. For image maps with links, you can use the onClick event handler with location.href to load the pages and avoid this problem.

13

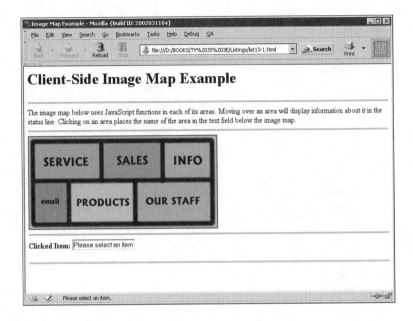

Figure 13.1.

An image map in JavaScript.

This program uses a single JavaScript function called update(), which simply places an item in the text field form1.text1. The text is sent directly by the link in each area definition.

Using Dynamic Images in JavaScript

One of the most useful features of JavaScript is the capability to dynamically change images. This means you can create images that "magically" change, which could be used for clocks, image rollovers (images that change when you move the mouse over them), or even simple animations.

The images in a Web page are reflected in an array, just like form elements. By modifying the properties of the array items, you can replace the image with a different one. This enables you to create dynamically changing content on the page without even using frames or layers.

This technique isn't perfect for all applications. Before you get started, note the following limitations:

- You can only change existing images in the page with this technique—you can't add new ones or remove an image entirely.

- You can replace an image with a larger or smaller image, but this may not look good because the text won't be reformatted to match.

- Any image you use will have to be loaded from the server. This makes this technique impractical for complicated animations or large images.

> Dynamic images are part of JavaScript 1.1, supported in Netscape 3.0 and later, as well as Internet Explorer 4.0 and later.

Working with the `images` Array

You can change images dynamically by using the `images` array. This array contains an item for each of the images defined on the page. Each image can also have a name. In the object hierarchy, each `image` object is a child of the `document` object.

Each `image` object has the following properties:

- `border` represents the `BORDER` attribute of the `<IMG>` tag. This defines whether a border is drawn around a linked image.

- `complete` is a flag that tells you whether the image has been completely loaded. This is a Boolean value (true or false).

- `height` and `width` reflect the corresponding image attributes. This is for information only; you can't change an image's size dynamically.

- `hspace` and `vspace` represent the corresponding image attributes, which define the image's placement on the page. Again, this is a read-only attribute.

- `name` is the image's name. You can define this with the `NAME` attribute in the image definition.

- `lowsrc` is the value of the `LOWSRC` attribute. This is a Netscape-specific attribute that enables you to specify a low-resolution image to be loaded before the "real" image.

- `src` is the image's source, or URL. You can change this value to change images dynamically.

For most purposes, the `src` attribute is the only one you'll use. However, you can also change the `lowsrc` attribute. This defines a low-resolution image to load first and will be used only when you change the `src` attribute.

13

The image object has no methods. It does have three event handlers you can use:

- The onLoad event occurs when the image finishes loading. (Since the onLoad event for the entire document is triggered when all images have finished loading, it's usually a better choice.)
- The onAbort event occurs if the user aborts the page before the image is loaded.
- The onError event occurs if the image file is not found or corrupt.

Preloading Images

Although you can't add an image to the page dynamically, you can create an independent image object. This enables you to specify an image that will be loaded and placed in the cache, but will not be displayed on the page.

This may sound useless, but it's a great way to work with modem-speed connections. Once you've preloaded an image, you can replace any of the images on the page with that image—and because it's already cached, the change happens instantly.

You can cache an image by creating a new image object, using the new keyword. Here's an example:

```
Image2 = new Image();
Image2.src = "arrow1.gif";
```

> You learned about the new keyword and its other uses for object-oriented programming in Hour 15, "Creating Custom Objects."

Creating Rollovers

The most common use of JavaScript's dynamic image feature is to create *rollovers*, which are images that change when you move the mouse pointer over them.

Rollovers are usually used for images that are links. Using this feature, you can highlight the current link with a different color or a border, or even by changing the image entirely.

You can turn an image into a rollover by adding an onMouseOver event handler that replaces the image with a highlighted version and an onMouseOut handler that returns the original image. Listing 13.2 shows an example that uses four images as rollovers.

LISTING 13.2   An example of rollovers

```html
<html>
<head>
<title>Roll Over, Spot. Good Dog.</title>
</head>
<body>
<h1>An Example of Rollovers</h1>
<hr>
The images below will change when you move the mouse over them.
<p>
<a href="home.html"
onMouseOver="document.images[0].src='home1.gif';"
onMouseOut="document.images[0].src='home.gif';">
<img src="home.gif" width=192 height=47 alt="" border="0">
</a>
<br>
<a href="links.html"
onMouseOver="document.images[1].src='links1.gif';"
onMouseOut="document.images[1].src='links.gif';">
<img src="links.gif" width=93 height=42 alt="" border="0">
</a>
<br>
<a href="guest.html"
onMouseOver="document.images[2].src='guest1.gif';"
onMouseOut="document.images[2].src='guest.gif';">
<img src="guest.gif" width=195 height=42 alt="" border="0">
</a>
<br>
<a href="email.html"
onMouseOver="document.images[3].src='email1.gif';"
onMouseOut="document.images[3].src='email.gif';">
<img src="email.gif" width=185 height=42 alt="" border="0">
</a>
</body>
</html>
```

In this example, two versions of each image are used. For example, `guest.gif` is the guest book graphic, and `guest1.gif` is the same graphic with a border around it. Each link includes `onMouseOver` and `onMouseOut` handlers that change the image. Figure 13.2 shows Internet Explorer's display of this script.

13

 You can highlight your images in other ways—for example, change their color. Another method is to place a smaller image to the side of each image that starts out as blank and changes to an arrow or other symbol when the mouse cursor is over the link image.

FIGURE **13.2.**

Using JavaScript for image rollovers.

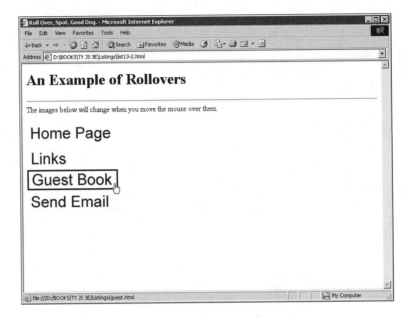

Workshop: Creating a Simple Animation

Although rollovers are undoubtedly the most practical use for JavaScript's dynamic images, you can also use the feature for simple animations. JavaScript isn't always the best way to do animations, but it's very useful in cases where you want to control the animation from a script.

> If you just want an animated image that repeats over and over, an animated GIF image is often a better choice. Many graphic software packages are available that automate the process of creating animated GIF images.

As a simple example of JavaScript animation, you will now create a script that moves an animated character across the browser display.

Creating the Images

The first step in creating a JavaScript animation is to create the images themselves. For this example, you will make an animated mouse move across the page. (You could use anything, of course, but this mouse is the only thing I can draw.)

The mouse animation uses a series of eight images, shown in Figure 13.3. To create these images, draw the mouse in a 100×100 square and then shift it to the left and right to create the various steps in the animation.

Figure 13.3.

The eight images for the mouse animation.

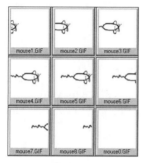

Call these images `mouse1.gif` through `mouse8.gif`. You will also need a blank image for those times when the mouse isn't there; call that `mouse0.gif`. All of these files are available on this book's Web site (www.jsworkshop.com), so you can try the example yourself.

Creating the HTML Document

Next, you'll need to create the HTML document for the animation. You will animate the mouse through five adjacent images on the page so it appears to move from one end to the other. Here is the basic HTML to lay out the graphics:

```
<h1>Animation in JavaScript</h1>
<hr>
<center>
<img src="mouse0.gif" width=100 height=100 alt="" border="0">
<img src="mouse0.gif" width=100 height=100 alt="" border="0">
<img src="mouse0.gif" width=100 height=100 alt="" border="0">
<img src="mouse0.gif" width=100 height=100 alt="" border="0">
<img src="mouse0.gif" width=100 height=100 alt="" border="0">
</center>
```

At this point, all five of the images on the page are displaying the `mouse0.gif` image and are therefore invisible. Because these are the first five images on the page, the script will be able to access them as `images[0]` through `images[4]`.

Defining the Variables

To begin the actual script, define some global variables. Here is the beginning of the script:

```
var cbox=0;
var nbox=1;
var cimage=0;
var nimage=0;
```

13

The cbox variable will store a value from 0 to 4, indicating which of the five images the mouse is currently running through. Part of the mouse may protrude into the next image, so use the nbox variable to store the position of the right half of the mouse, if required.

The cimage variable will store the value of the image (from 1 to 8) to be stored in the current box. Similarly, nimage will store the value of the image for the part of the mouse that protrudes into the next box, if needed.

Stepping through the Animation

Next, create the actual animation. You'll use a function called next to move the mouse to its next position, and use the setTimeout method to call this function regularly.

The first step in the next function is to increment the image in the current box. Here is the function definition and the increment statement:

```
function next() {
cimage += 1;
```

After incrementing the value of cimage, the script needs to make sure it hasn't gone past 8 because there are eight images. The next part of the script checks for values greater than 8:

```
if (cimage > 8) {
        cimage = 4;
        document.images[cbox].src = "mouse0.gif";
        cbox = (cbox + 1) % 5;
        nbox = (cbox + 1) % 5;
}
```

If the current image has a value greater than 8, this code increments the value of cbox and assigns nbox to the next value. Both of these statements use the modulo (%) operator, which prevents the position from reaching a value greater than 4. Instead, the mouse will start over at the left side of the page.

The preceding script also resets cimage to 4. (Because the current box was previously the next box, it's already moved through images 1, 2, and 3.)

Next, the script needs to calculate the image for the next box, if any:

```
nimage = cimage - 5;
if (nimage <= 0) nimage = 0;
```

The first statement here assigns nimage to five less than cimage. If you look at the images in Figure 13.3, you'll notice that images 6, 7, and 8 match up with images 1, 2, and 3, respectively, to form a complete mouse. If the subtraction results in a negative value, there shouldn't be a next image, so assign 0 to nimage.

Finally, the end of the next function assigns the images indicated by cimage and nimage to the locations indicated by cbox and nbox:

```
document.images[cbox].src = "mouse" + cimage + ".gif";
document.images[nbox].src = "mouse" + nimage + ".gif";
window.setTimeout("next();",100);
}
```

The final statement here sets a timeout so that the next function will be called again in a tenth of a second. (You can increase or decrease this value to change the mouse's speed.)

Putting It All Together

You now have all of the components of a working animation script. Listing 13.3 shows the complete HTML document and script. The <BODY> tag includes an onLoad event handler that calls the preload function to preload the mouse images. This function then calls the next function after a timeout to get the animation started.

LISTING 13.3   The complete animation example

```
<html>
<head>
<title>Primitive Animation in JavaScript</title>
<script LANGUAGE="JavaScript" type="text/javascript">
var cbox=0;
var nbox=1;
var cimage=0;
var nimage=0;
function preload() {
    a1 = new Image();
    a1.src = "mouse1.gif";
    a2 = new Image();
    a2.src = "mouse2.gif";
    a3 = new Image();
    a3.src = "mouse3.gif";
    a4 = new Image();
    a4.src = "mouse4.gif";
    a5 = new Image();
    a5.src = "mouse5.gif";
    a6 = new Image();
    a6.src = "mouse6.gif";
    a7 = new Image();
    a7.src = "mouse7.gif";
```

13

LISTING 13.3   Continued

```
        a8 = new Image();
        a8.src = "mouse8.gif";
        window.setTimeout("next();",500) ;
    }
    function next() {
        cimage += 1;
        if (cimage > 8) {
            cimage = 4;
            document.images[cbox].src = "mouse0.gif";
            cbox = (cbox + 1) % 5;
            nbox = (cbox + 1) % 5;
        }
        nimage = cimage - 5;
        if (nimage <= 0) nimage = 0;
        document.images[cbox].src = "mouse" + cimage + ".gif";
        document.images[nbox].src = "mouse" + nimage + ".gif";
        window.setTimeout("next();",100);
    }
    </script>
    </head>
    <body onLoad="preload();">
    <H1>Animation in JavaScript</H1>
    <HR>
    <center>
    <img src="mouse0.gif" width=100 height=100 alt="" border="0">
    <img src="mouse0.gif" width=100 height=100 alt="" border="0">
    <img src="mouse0.gif" width=100 height=100 alt="" border="0">
    <img src="mouse0.gif" width=100 height=100 alt="" border="0">
    <img src="mouse0.gif" width=100 height=100 alt="" border="0">
    </center>
    <HR>
    </body>
    </html>
```

To test the script, load it into a browser. Be sure the HTML document is in the same directory as the mouse0 through mouse8 image files. If everything works, you should see a little mouse scurrying across the screen, as shown in Figure 13.4.

You may notice a slight gap between the five images as the mouse moves across the screen. To remedy this, remove the spaces and carriage returns between the <img> tags in the body of the page, making them into one long line.

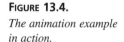

FIGURE 13.4.

The animation example in action.

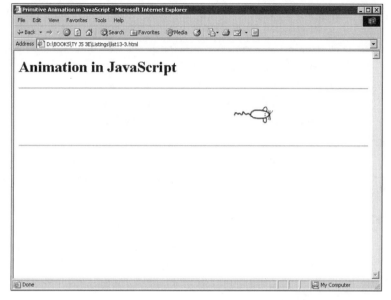

Summary

In this hour, you learned how to use JavaScript to work with graphics. JavaScript can work with image maps, and can be used to create image rollovers and simple animations.

You've reached the end of Part III! In Part IV, you'll learn more techniques that are helpful in creating scripts for the Web. In the next hour, you'll learn how to detect browser versions and create scripts that work on multiple browsers.

Q&A

Q I created an onMouseOver event handler for rollovers, and it works in Internet Explorer but not Netscape. What's wrong?

A This is probably because you used the onMouseOver handler in the <img> tag. This is supported only by Internet Explorer. For Netscape, you need to make the image a link and use event handlers in the <a> tag. (This will also work in Internet Explorer.)

Q Can I use rollovers in an image map?

A No, you'll need to replace the entire map image to do this. Usually, it's easier and faster to divide the map image into a number of sections and use those as the rollovers.

13

Q JavaScript animation seems a bit basic. Is there a way to do more complex or interactive animation?

A Not in JavaScript. For these purposes, you may want to look into using Java or Macromedia's Flash. See this URL for more information about Flash: `http://www.macromedia.com/software/flash/`.

Q I created a JavaScript program on a page with images, and my event handlers don't seem to be working. What's wrong?

A JavaScript requires you to use `HEIGHT` and `WIDTH` attributes on all `<img>` tags. Adding them will most likely make the event handlers work properly. See Hour 17, "Debugging JavaScript Applications," for other debugging techniques.

Quiz

Test your knowledge of JavaScript graphics and animation by answering the following questions.

Questions

1. Which two event handlers are used for a rollover?

    a. `onMouseOver` and `onClick`

    b. `onMouseOver` and `onMouseUnder`

    c. `onMouseOver` and `onMouseOut`

2. Which types of image maps can be used with JavaScript?

    a. Server-side image maps

    b. Client-side image maps

    c. Both types

3. What is the JavaScript object for the second image on a page?

    a. `image[2]`

    b. `images[2]`

    c. `images[1]`

Answers

1. c. You create rollovers with the `onMouseOver` and `onMouseOut` event handlers.

2. b. Client-side image maps can be used with JavaScript.

3. c. The second image on a page is represented by `images[1]`.

Exercises

If you want to study JavaScript graphics further, perform these exercises:

- Change the image map example in Listing 13.1 to link to HTML documents rather than displaying alert messages.
- In the rollover example in Listing 13.2, try adding a third image that is displayed while the mouse is clicked. You can use the onMouseDown event handler.

13

PART IV

Moving on to Advanced JavaScript Features

Hour

HOUR 14

Creating Cross-Browser Scripts

Welcome to Part IV. Up until now, most of the scripts you've written will work in the latest versions of either of today's most popular browsers: Netscape Navigator and Internet Explorer. Between these two, your scripts will work for a vast majority of the Web audience.

As you move on, however, you'll start working with topics that aren't so compatible. The latest features, such as dynamic HTML, tend to work differently on different browsers, and some features are specific to one or another.

The new DOM (Document Object Model) standard has eliminated many of the most troubling browser differences, but you'll still run into situations where you need to create different code for different browsers. You can use JavaScript to differentiate between browsers, supporting all of them either within one page or on separate pages.

Hour 14 covers the following topics:

- Using JavaScript to get browser information
- Displaying browser details with JavaScript
- Making a page browser-specific
- Dealing with browsers without JavaScript support
- Creating a script for multiple browser support

Reading Browser Information

In Hour 9, "Working with the Document Object Model," you learned about the various objects (such as window and document) that represent portions of the browser window and the current Web document. JavaScript also includes an object called navigator that you can use to read information about the user's browser.

The navigator object isn't part of the DOM, so you can refer to it directly. It includes a number of properties, each of which tells you something about the browser. These include the following:

- navigator.appCodeName is the browser's internal code name, usually Mozilla.
- navigator.appName is the browser's name, usually Netscape or Microsoft Internet Explorer.
- navigator.appVersion is the version of the browser being used—for example, 4.0(Win95;I).
- navigator.userAgent is the user-agent header, a string that the browser sends to the Web server when requesting a Web page. It includes the entire version information, for example Mozilla/4.0(Win95;I).
- navigator.language is the language (such as English or Spanish) of the browser. This is stored as a two-letter code, such as "en" for English. This property is supported only by Netscape.
- navigator.platform is the computer platform of the current browser. This is a short string, such as Win16, Win32, or MacPPC. You can use this to enable any platform-specific features (for example, ActiveX components).

You will usually use these properties in an if statement. For example, the following statement sends the user to a different URL if the navigator object specifies Netscape 4.x:

```
if (navigator.userAgent.indexOf("Mozilla/4") == -1)
    window.location="non_netscape.html";
```

As you might have guessed, the navigator object is named after Netscape Navigator, the browser that originally supported JavaScript. Fortunately, this object is also supported by Internet Explorer.

Displaying Browser Information

As an example of how to read the navigator object's properties, Listing 14.1 shows a script that displays a list of the properties and their values for the current browser.

LISTING 14.1　A script to display information about the browser

```
<html>
<head>
<title>Browser Information</title>
</head>
<body>
<h1>Browser Information</h1>
<hr>
<p>
The <b>navigator</b> object contains the following information
about the browser you are using.
</p>
<ul>
<script LANGUAGE="JavaScript" type="text/javascript">
document.write("<li><b>Code Name:</b> " + navigator.appCodeName);
document.write("<li><b>App Name:</b> " + navigator.appName);
document.write("<li><b>App Version:</b> " + navigator.appVersion);
document.write("<li><b>User Agent:</b> " + navigator.userAgent);
document.write("<li><b>Language:</b> " + navigator.language);
document.write("<li><b>Platform:</b> " + navigator.platform);
</script>
</ul>
<hr>
</body>
</html>
```

You can download this and the other listings for this hour from this book's Web site: http://www.jsworkshop.com/.

14

This script includes a basic HTML document. A script is used within the body of the document to display each of the properties of the navigator object using the docu-ment.write statement.

To try this script, load it into the browser of your choice. If you have more than one browser or browser version handy, try it in each one. Netscape 6's display of the script is shown in Figure 14.1.

FIGURE 14.1.

Netscape displays the browser information script.

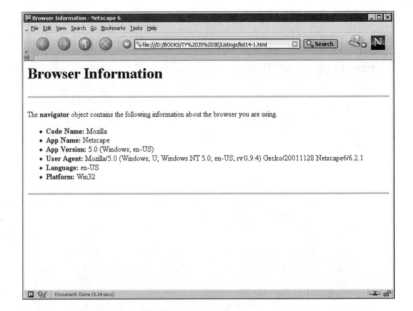

Dealing with Dishonest Browsers

If you tried the browser information script in Listing 14.1 using one of the latest versions of Internet Explorer, you probably got a surprise. Figure 14.2 shows how Internet Explorer 6.0 displays the script.

There are several unexpected things about this display. First of all, the navigator.lan-guage property is listed as undefined. This isn't much of a surprise because this property isn't yet supported by Internet Explorer.

More importantly, you'll notice that the word Mozilla appears in the code name and user agent fields. The full user agent string reads as follows:

```
Mozilla/4.0 (compatible; MSIE 6.0; Windows 98)
```

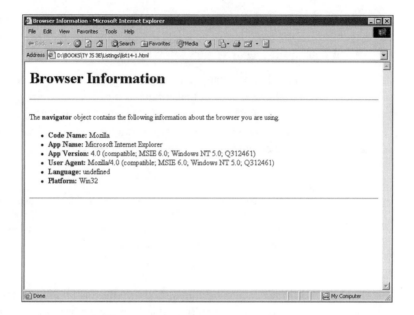

FIGURE 14.2.

Internet Explorer displays the browser information script.

Believe it or not, Microsoft did have a good reason for this. At the height of the browser wars, about the time Netscape 3.0 and IE 3.0 came out, it was becoming common to see "Netscape only" pages. Some Webmasters who used features such as frames and JavaScript set their servers to turn away browsers without `Mozilla` in their user agent string. The problem with this was that most of these features were also supported by Internet Explorer.

Microsoft solved this problem in IE 4.0 by making IE's user agent read `Mozilla`, with the word `compatible` in parentheses. This allows IE users to view those pages, but still includes enough details to tell Web servers which browser was in use.

Many Web servers keep statistics about which browsers people use to access them. When Microsoft changed IE's user agent string, many of the statistics programs were not aware of the change. As a result, they counted a visit by IE as a visit by Netscape. Ironically, Microsoft's move to make their browser more compatible caused Netscape's market share statistics to improve, at least for a while.

14

You've probably already noticed the other problem with Internet Explorer 6.0's User agent string: the portion reading `Mozilla/4.0`. Not only is IE claiming to be Netscape—it's also masquerading as version 4.0. Why?

As it turns out, this was another effort by Microsoft to stay one step ahead of the browser wars, although this one doesn't make quite as much sense. Since poorly-written scripts were checking specifically for "Mozilla/4" for dynamic HTML pages, Microsoft was concerned that its 5.0 version would fail to run these pages. Since changing it now would only create more confusion, this tradition continues with IE 6.0.

Microsoft isn't alone in confusing browser IDs. Netscape version 6 displays a user agent string beginning with `Mozilla/5`, and an app version of 5.0. (Netscape 5.0 is Netscape's open-source browser, code named Mozilla, that formed the foundation of what is now Netscape 6.)

Although these are two interesting episodes in the annals of the browser wars, what does all this mean to you? Well, you'll need to be careful when your scripts are trying to differentiate between IE and Netscape, and between different versions. For example, the following statement was presented earlier in this hour as an example of the `navigator` properties:

```
if (navigator.userAgent.indexOf("Mozilla/4") == -1)
   window.location="non_netscape.html";
```

As it turns out, this statement checks for the string `Mozilla/4`—which will actually allow either Netscape 4.x or Internet Explorer 4.x, or even IE 5.x. This isn't necessarily a bad thing, but what if you want to look specifically for Netscape 4.0? In that case, you can be more specific:

```
if (navigator.appName.indexOf("Netscape") == -1
|| navigator.appVersion.indexOf("4.0") == -1)
    window.location="non_netscape.html";
```

This longer `if` statement first checks the `navigator.appName` property, which will contain the appropriate value of `Netscape` or `Microsoft`. Next, it checks the `navigator.appVersion` property. If the name isn't `Netscape` or the version isn't `4.0`, it sends the user to another page.

This example uses the `indexOf` string method, which searches for a string within another string. To refresh your memory about this and other string functions, see Hour 5, "Using Strings and Arrays."

In conclusion, don't trust the code name or app version properties, and always test your cross-browser scripts with several browsers before you put them online. In the Workshop section of this hour, you'll learn a practical way to check specifically for 5.0 and later browsers.

Supporting Browsers with JavaScript

If you're using features that are on the cutting edge and require a particular browser or version, there are several ways of using JavaScript to steer users in the right direction. The following sections explain three different methods.

Creating a Browser-Specific Page

The easiest solution—and the least polite—is to pick a browser version to support and kick everyone out who isn't using it. This is easy to do with a script in the header or body of the page. Here's a simple example:

```
<script language="JavaScript" type="text/javascript">
if (navigator.appName.indexOf("Netscape") == -1
|| navigator.appVersion.indexOf("5.0") == -1)
window.alert("Download Netscape now, or else.");
window.location = "http://www.netscape.com/";
</script>
```

If you're using a non-Netscape browser or a version of Netscape other than 5.0/6.0, this script displays a rude message and sends you to Netscape's Web page. Needless to say, there are more polite ways of saying this.

If you must make a page browser-specific, be sure you have a good reason to do so. If other browsers can display the page's content—even if your cute buttons or animations don't work—you should support them. Few users are willing to download a new browser just for your page, so you'll be losing a good part of your audience.

Branching to Separate Pages

In most cases, it's not hard to support more than one browser. If you want to fine-tune your pages to display perfectly on both Netscape and IE, one convenient way is to create a separate version of the page for each browser. You can then use JavaScript to send the user to the appropriate page.

14

For example, here is a script that could be placed on the introductory page of a site. After detecting the browser version, it sends the user to the appropriate page.

```
<script language="Javascript" type="text/javascript">
if (navigator.appName.indexOf("Netscape") > -1
 && navigator.appVersion.indexOf("5") > -1)
    window.location = "netscape.html";
if (navigator.appName.indexOf("Microsoft") > -1
 && navigator.appVersion.indexOf("4") > -1)
    window.location = "ie.html";
window.location = "default.html";
</SCRIPT>
```

This script sends the user to one of three pages: `netscape.html` for Netscape 5.x or 6.x, `ie.html` for Internet Explorer 4.x or later, or `default.html` for any other browser.

> You might have noticed that there is no third `if` statement in this script. The statement to send the user to `default.html` is unconditional. This works because if either of the `if` statements was true, the browser would have been sent to a different page, immediately aborting the current script. The only browsers that make it to the last line are those that aren't detected specifically.

Making a Multiple-Browser Page

The third alternative is to make a single page that supports more than one type of browser. You can use a script in the page to detect the browser, and then use script commands to include different HTML codes in the document depending on the browser.

This method uses only one document, but you might find that it transforms a long, complicated page into a long, *impossibly* complicated page. A short example of a page that does this is included in this hour's Workshop section.

Using Feature Sensing

The examples so far in this hour have used *browser sensing* to differentiate between browsers: They look at the `navigator` object's properties to determine which browser is in use. While this is sometimes the only way to support all browsers, *feature sensing* is often a better way.

Feature sensing detects whether a feature is supported, rather than being concerned with the exact browser in use. For example, if your script uses dynamic images, you could use this statement to determine whether they are supported:

```
if (document.images) alert("dynamic images are supported.");
```

This statement checks for the existence of the images array. If it exists, the browser most likely supports dynamic images—if it doesn't exist, this statement won't cause an error and you'll know dynamic images aren't supported.

Feature sensing has some advantages: First, it doesn't rely on specific browser versions, so a new browser release is less likely to break your script. Second, it's often easier than dealing with all of the possible navigator properties used in different browsers.

> Feature sensing is especially useful when dealing with Dynamic HTML. You'll learn more about it and create some examples in Hour 19, "Using Dynamic HTML (DHTML)."

Supporting Non-JavaScript Browsers

What about browsers that don't support JavaScript at all? You can't detect them with a script because they won't even *run* the script. However, there are ways of dealing with these browsers.

With 99% of Web users using a recent copy of Netscape or IE, where are the non-JavaScript browsers? First, there are still some older browsers out there, and text browsers such as Lynx don't support scripting. Second, and more importantly, many Netscape and IE users have JavaScript support turned off, either due to security concerns or just to avoid watching scrolling messages in the status line.

In the last few years, a wide variety of new browsers have also emerged. Palmtop computers, such as 3Com's PalmPilot and the Windows CE platform, support Web browsing, as do some cellular phones and other appliances. Since none of these support JavaScript, it's even more important to provide an alternative when possible.

One way to be friendly to non-JavaScript browsers is to use the <noscript> tag. Supported in Netscape 3.0 and later, this tag displays a message to non-JavaScript browsers. Browsers that support JavaScript ignore the text between the <noscript> tags, while others display it. Here is a simple example:

```
<noscript>
This page requires JavaScript. You can either download a copy
of netscape from <a href="http://www.netscape.com/"> their page,
or switch to the <a href="nojs.html">Non-JavaScript</a> version of
this page.
</noscript>
```

14

The main problem with using <noscript> is that Netscape 2.0 will display the text between the tags, even though it does support some JavaScript. While Netscape 2.0 isn't too common these days, there is a way to solve this problem. The following script detects non-JavaScript browsers and displays a message:

```
<script LANGUAGE="JavaScript" type="text/javascript">
    <!-- //hide from old browsers
    ...script commands go here...
    /* (start JavaScript comment, end HTML comment)
    -->
    You're using a non-JavaScript browser! Shame on you.
    <!-- */ // -->
</script>
```

This uses the HTML comment tags (<!-- and -->) to hide the script commands from old browsers. It then uses JavaScript comment tags (/* and */) to enclose the message for non-JavaScript browsers, so it will be disregarded by browsers that support JavaScript.

An easier alternative is to send users with JavaScript support to another page. This can be accomplished with a single JavaScript statement:

```
<script LANGUAGE="JavaScript" type="text/javascript">
window.location="JavaScript.html";
</script>
```

This simply sends the user to a different page. If the browser doesn't support JavaScript, of course, the script won't be executed.

The final alternative is to simply make your scripts unobtrusive. Use comments to hide them from other browsers, as described in Hour 3, "How JavaScript Programs Work," and be sure they're not essential to navigate or read the page.

Workshop: Scripting for Multiple Browsers

As an example of the techniques you learned in this hour, you can create a script that uses reliable methods to determine which of the following categories the current browser falls into:

- Either Internet Explorer or Netscape, 5.0 or later
- Netscape 4.x
- Internet Explorer 4.x
- All others

This is useful because the 5.0 and later browsers support the new DOM for dynamic HTML. You may also want to support the 4.x browsers, which support dynamic features but in incompatible ways. Last but not least, older browsers can be supported with a minimal script.

As a simple example, this script will determine the browser in use and set a variable, browser, to the appropriate code. Listing 14.2 shows the browser detection example.

LISTING 14.2 The browser detection example

```html
<html>
<head>
<title>Browser Detection</title>
<script language="Javascript" type="text/javascript">
// check for 5.0 or later browsers
if (parseInt(navigator.appVersion) >= 5
   || navigator.appVersion.indexOf("MSIE 5") != -1) {
   browser="DOM";
} else if (navigator.userAgent.indexOf("Mozilla/4") != -1)
   {
   if (navigator.appName.indexOf("Netscape") != -1)
      browser="NS4";
   if (navigator.appVersion.indexOf("MSIE 4") != -1)
      browser="IE4";
   } else browser="Other";
</script>
</head>
<body>
<h1>Browser Detection Example</h1>
<script language="Javascript" type="text/javascript">
document.write("browser detected: " + browser + "<br>");
</script>
</body>
</html>
```

The script in the header of this document assigns the variable browser the value of DOM for 5.0 browsers, NS4 for Netscape 4.x, and IE4 for Internet Explorer 4.x. The body of this document simply displays the variable, but your script could use it to change the output according to the browser.

Summary

In this hour, you've learned various ways to use JavaScript to read information about the user's browser and to accommodate multiple browsers.

In the next hour, you'll learn more about JavaScript's object model and how to simplify your scripts with custom objects.

14

Q&A

Q **What if my page requires a particular plug-in? Is there a way to detect that with JavaScript?**

A Yes, the `navigator` object includes properties for detecting plug-ins. These are described in Hour 16, "Working with Sounds and Plug-Ins." However, this method doesn't work in Internet Explorer.

Q **Can I detect the user's email address using the `navigator` object or another technique?**

A No, there is no reliable way to detect users' email addresses using JavaScript. (If there was, you would get hundreds of advertisements in your mailbox every day from companies that detected your address as you browsed their pages.) You can use a signed script to obtain the user's email address, but this requires the user's permission and only works in some versions of Netscape.

Q **Do I need to worry about browsers besides Netscape and Internet Explorer, since they don't support JavaScript anyway?**

A Actually, there is a Windows browser called Opera that supports JavaScript, and you never know when a new browser may come out. It's always best to support all of them if you can. To learn more about Opera, visit its Web page at www.operasoftware.com.

Quiz

Test your knowledge of cross-browser scripting in JavaScript by answering the following questions.

Questions

1. Which of the following `navigator` object properties is the same in both Netscape and IE?

    a. `navigator.appCodeName`

    b. `navigator.appName`

    c. `navigator.appVersion`

2. Which of the following is something you *can't* do with JavaScript?

    a. Send users of Netscape to a different page.

    b. Send users of IE to a different page.

    c. Send users of non-JavaScript browsers to a different page.

3. What does the <noscript> tag do?

   a. Encloses text to be displayed by non-JavaScript browsers.

   b. Prevents scripts on the page from executing.

   c. Describes certain low-budget movies.

Answers

1. a. The navigator.appCodeName property is the same ("Mozilla") in the latest Netscape and Microsoft browsers.

2. c. You can't use JavaScript to send users of non-JavaScript browsers to a different page because the script won't be executed at all.

3. a. The <noscript> tag encloses text to be displayed by non-JavaScript browsers.

Exercises

If you want to gain more experience detecting browsers in JavaScript, perform these exercises:

- Create a script, based on this hour's examples, that sends users of IE 5.0 or Netscape 6.0 to one page and users of earlier versions to a different page.

- Modify the example in Listing 14.2 to assign a separate specific code to the browser variable for 3.x versions of IE or Netscape.

14

HOUR 15

Creating Custom Objects

Earlier in this book, you learned to use JavaScript's built-in objects, such as Date. You've also learned about the objects in the DOM (Document Object Model), which allow you to manipulate Web documents. These are the most commonly used JavaScript objects, but you can also create custom objects.

In this hour, you'll learn how to create your own custom objects with JavaScript, and in the process learn a bit more about how JavaScript handles all kinds of objects. Hour 15 covers the following topics:

- How objects can simplify scripts
- Defining an object
- Adding methods to an object
- Creating instances of an object
- Using objects to store and manage data

Using Objects to Simplify Scripting

Although JavaScript's variables and arrays are versatile ways to store data, sometimes you need a more complicated structure. For example, suppose you are creating a script to work with a business card database that contains names, addresses, and phone numbers for a variety of people.

If you were using regular variables, you would need several separate variables for each person in the database: a name variable, an address variable, and so on. This would be very confusing.

Arrays would improve things slightly. You could have a names array, an addresses array, and a phone number array. Each person in the database would have an entry in each array. This would be more convenient, but still not perfect.

With objects, you can make the variables that store the database as logical as business cards. Each person is represented by a Card object, which has properties for name, address, and phone number. You can even add methods to the object to display or work with the information.

In the following sections, you'll use JavaScript to actually create the Card object and its properties and methods. Later in this hour, you'll use the Card object in a script to display information for several members of the database.

Defining an Object

The first step in creating an object is to name it and its properties. We've already decided to call the object a Card object. Each object will have the following properties:

- name
- address
- workphone
- homephone

The first step in using this object in a JavaScript program is to create a function to create new Card objects. This function is called the *constructor* for an object. Here is the constructor function for the Card object:

```
function Card(name,address,work,home) {
   this.name = name;
   this.address = address;
   this.workphone = work;
   this.homephone = home;
}
```

The constructor is a simple function that accepts parameters to initialize a new object and assigns them to the corresponding properties. This function accepts several parameters from the statement that calls the function, and then assigns them as properties of an object. Because the function is called Card, the object is the Card object.

Notice the `this` keyword. You'll use it anytime you create an object definition. Use `this` to refer to the current object—the one that is being created by the function.

Defining an Object Method

Next, you will create a method to work with the `Card` object. Because all `Card` objects will have the same properties, it might be handy to have a function that prints out the properties in a neat format. Let's call this function `PrintCard`.

Your `PrintCard` function will be used as a method for `Card` objects, so you don't need to ask for parameters. Instead, you can use the `this` keyword again to refer to the current object's properties. Here is a function definition for the `PrintCard()` function:

```
function PrintCard() {
   line1 = "Name: " + this.name + "<br>\n";
   line2 = "Address: " + this.address + "<br>\n";
   line3 = "Work Phone: " + this.workphone + "<br>\n";
   line4 = "Home Phone: " + this.homephone + "<hr>\n";
   document.write(line1, line2, line3, line4);
}
```

This function simply reads the properties from the current object (`this`), prints each one with a caption, and skips to a new line.

You now have a function that prints a card, but it isn't officially a method of the `Card` object. The last thing you need to do is make `PrintCard` part of the function definition for `Card` objects. Here is the modified function definition:

```
function Card(name,address,work,home) {
   this.name = name;
   this.address = address;
   this.workphone = work;
   this.homephone = home;
   this.PrintCard = PrintCard;
}
```

The added statement looks just like another property definition, but it refers to the `PrintCard` function. This will work so long as the PrintCard function is defined with its own function definition.

Creating an Object Instance

Now let's use the object definition and method you created above. To use an object definition, you create a new object. This is done with the `new` keyword. This is the same keyword you've already used to create `Date` and `Array` objects.

The following statement creates a new `Card` object called `tom`:

```
tom = new Card("Tom Jones", "123 Elm Street", "555-1234", "555-9876");
```

As you can see, creating an object is easy. All you do is call the `Card()` function (the object definition) and give it the required attributes, in the same order as the definition.

Once this statement executes, a new object is created to hold Tom's information. This is called an *instance* of the `Card` object. Just as there can be several string variables in a program, there can be several instances of an object you define.

Rather than specify all the information for a card with the `new` keyword, you can assign them after the fact. For example, the following script creates an empty `Card` object called `holmes`, and then assigns its properties:

```
holmes = new Card();
holmes.name = "Sherlock Holmes";
holmes.address = "221B Baker Street";
holmes.workphone = "555-2345";
holmes.homephone = "555-3456";
```

Once you've created an instance of the `Card` object using either of these methods, you can use the `PrintCard()` method to display its information. For example, this statement displays the properties of the `tom` card:

```
tom.PrintCard();
```

Customizing Built-In Objects

JavaScript includes a feature that enables you to extend the definitions of built-in objects. For example, if you think the `String` object doesn't quite fit your needs, you can extend it, adding a new property or method. This might be very useful if you were creating a large script that used many strings.

You can add both properties and methods to an existing object by using the `prototype` keyword. (A *prototype* is another name for an object's definition, or constructor function.) The `prototype` keyword allows you to change the definition of an object outside its constructor function.

As an example, let's add a method to the `String` object definition. You will create a method called `heading`, which converts a string into an HTML heading. The following statement defines a string called `title`:

```
title = "Fred's Home Page";
```

This statement would output the contents of the `title` string as an HTML Level 1 header:

```
document.write(title.heading(1));
```

Listing 15.1 adds a `heading` method to the `String` object definition that will display the string as a heading, and then displays a simple example.

LISTING 15.1 Adding a method to the `String` object

```
<html>
<head><title>Test of heading method</title>
</head>
<body>
<script LANGUAGE="JavaScript1.1" type="text/javascript1.1">
function addhead (level) {
   html = "H" + level;
   text = this.toString();
   start = "<" + html + ">";
   stop = "</" + html + ">";
   return start + text + stop;
}
String.prototype.heading = addhead;
document.write ("This is a test".heading(1));
</script>
</body>
</html>
```

Don't forget that you can download this listing from this book's Web site (`http://www.jsworkshop.com/`) rather than typing it in.

First, you define the `addhead()` function, which will serve as the new string method. It accepts a number to specify the heading level. The `start` and `stop` variables are used to store the HTML "begin header" and "end header" tags, such as `<h1>` and `</h1>`.

After the function is defined, use the `prototype` keyword to add it as a method of the `String` object. You can then use this method on any `String` object, or in fact any JavaScript string. This is demonstrated by the last statement, which displays a quoted text string as a Level 1 header.

Workshop: Storing Data in Objects

Now you've created a new object to store business cards and a method to print them out. As a final demonstration of objects, properties, functions, and methods, you will now use this object in a Web page to display data for several cards.

The HTML document will need to include the function definition for PrintCard, along with the function definition for the Card object. You will then create three cards and print them out in the body of the document. Listing 15.2 shows the complete HTML document.

LISTING 15.2   An HTML document that uses the Card object

```
<html>
<head>
<title>JavaScript Business Cards</title>
<script LANGUAGE="JavaScript" type="text/javascript">
function PrintCard() {
line1 = "<b>Name: </b>" + this.name + "<br>\n";
line2 = "<b>Address: </b>" + this.address + "<br>\n";
line3 = "<b>Work Phone: </b>" + this.workphone + "<br>\n";
line4 = "<b>Home Phone: </b>" + this.homephone + "<hr>\n";
document.write(line1, line2, line3, line4);
}
function Card(name,address,work,home) {
    this.name = name;
    this.address = address;
    this.workphone = work;
    this.homephone = home;
    this.PrintCard = PrintCard;
}
</script>
</head>
<body>
<h1>JavaScript Business Card Test</h1>
<p>Script begins here.</p><hr>
<script LANGUAGE="JavaScript" type="text/javascript">
// Create the objects
sue = new Card("Sue Suthers", "123 Elm Street", "555-1234", "555-9876");
phred = new Card("Phred Madsen", "233 Oak Lane", "555-2222", "555-4444");
henry = new Card("Henry Tillman", "233 Walnut Circle", "555-1299", "555-1344");
// And print them
sue.PrintCard();
phred.PrintCard();
henry.PrintCard();
</script>
End of script.
</body>
</html>
```

Notice that the PrintCard() function has been modified slightly to make things look good with the captions in boldface. The browser's display of this example is shown in Figure 15.1.

This example isn't a very sophisticated database because you have to include the data for each person in the HTML document. However, an object like this could be used to store a database record retrieved from a database server with thousands of records.

15

FIGURE 15.1.
Internet Explorer displays the output of the business card example.

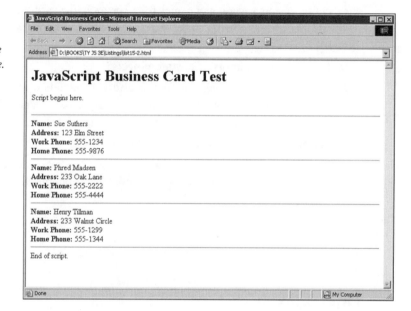

Summary

In this hour, you've learned how to create your own objects in JavaScript. You created an object definition, added object properties and methods, created object instances, and learned to use all of them together in a complete script. You also learned how to modify JavaScript's built-in objects, such as the String object.

In the next hour, you'll learn another advanced JavaScript topic: how to make your scripts work with sounds and plug-in objects.

Q&A

Q **The objects described in Hour 9 included parent and child objects. Can I include child objects in my custom object definitions?**

A Yes. Just create a constructor function for the child object, and then add a property to the parent object that corresponds to it. For example, if you created a `Nicknames` object to store several nicknames for a person in the card file example, you could add it as a child object in the `Card` object's constructor: `this.nick = new Nicknames();`

Q **Can I create an array of custom objects?**

A Yes. First, create the object definition as usual and define an array with the required number of elements. Then use a loop to assign a new object to each array element (for example, `cardarray[1] = new Card();`).

Q **Which browsers support custom objects?**

A The features described in this hour are included in JavaScript 1.1 and later, and should be supported by Netscape 3.0 or later and Internet Explorer 4.0 and later.

Quiz

Test your knowledge of JavaScript's object-oriented features by answering the following questions.

Questions

1. What JavaScript keyword is used to create an instance of an object?

    a. `object`

    b. `new`

    c. `instance`

2. What is the meaning of the `this` keyword in JavaScript?

    a. The current object.

    b. The current script.

    c. It has no meaning.

3. What does the `prototype` keyword allow you to do in a script?

    a. Change the syntax of JavaScript commands.

    b. Modify the definitions of built-in objects.

    c. Modify the user's browser so only your scripts will work.

15

Answers

1. b. The `new` keyword creates an object instance.
2. a. The `this` keyword refers to the current object.
3. b. The `prototype` keyword allows you to modify the definitions of built-in objects.

Exercises

If you'd like to gain more experience in using custom objects, perform the following exercises:

- Modify the definition of the `Card` object to include a property called `email` for the person's email address. Modify the `PrintCard` function to include this property.

- Make a script that adds a `first5` method, which returns the first five characters, to the `String` object. You'll need to use the `substring` method, described in Hour 5, "Using Strings and Arrays."

HOUR 16

Working with Sounds and Plug-Ins

In the last two hours, you learned some of JavaScript's advanced features. In this hour, you'll learn another advanced feature: using JavaScript with plug-ins.

Plug-ins are browser add-ons that allow you to use additional types of information in the browser: sounds, videos, and so forth. You can use JavaScript to control the behavior of these plug-ins, allowing your scripts to do just about anything.

Hour 16 covers the following topics:

- How JavaScript works with plug-ins
- Detecting plug-ins with JavaScript
- Checking available MIME types
- Scripting objects in plug-ins
- Creating an application using sounds

Introducing Plug-Ins

Plug-ins were introduced by Netscape in Navigator 3.0. Rather than adding support directly to the browser for media types such as formatted text, video, and audio, Netscape created a modular architecture that allows programmers to write their own browser add-ons for these features.

There are now hundreds of plug-ins available for both Netscape and Internet Explorer. Here are a few of the most popular:

- Macromedia's ShockWave and Flash plug-ins support animation and video.
- Adobe's Acrobat plug-in supports precisely formatted, cross-platform text.
- RealPlayer supports streaming audio and video.
- Headspace's Beatnik plug-in supports music in Web pages.

Netscape and Internet Explorer use different plug-in formats and usually require different versions of a plug-in. Additionally, some plug-ins are available only for one platform, such as Windows or Macintosh.

Because Netscape's LiveAudio plug-in and Microsoft's Windows Media Player are included with Netscape 4.x and Internet Explorer, you can assume that much of your Web page's audience will have a plug-in for playing sounds. The workshop section of this hour will use these plug-ins to play sounds.

All of the examples in this hour use plug-ins that are available for both Microsoft and Netscape, but the plug-in detection examples require Netscape 3.0 or later. Netscape 6 does not currently include a plug-in for playing sounds.

Using the `<embed>` Tag

You can include a file that uses a plug-in in a Web document with the `<embed>` tag. This tag specifies the filename for the content and any parameters required by the plug-in. Here is a simple example:

```
<embed SRC="sound.wav" HIDDEN=true AUTOSTART=false LOOP=false>
```

This example embeds the file sound.wav. The <embed> tag for sounds uses the following attributes:

- The SRC attribute specifies the filename of the sound file.

- The HIDDEN attribute makes the embedded object invisible on the page; without this attribute, a control panel is displayed to play or stop the sound.

- The AUTOSTART attribute controls whether the sound should play immediately when the page loads.

- The LOOP attribute specifies whether the sound will repeat—this is more useful for MIDI music files than simple sounds.

- The CONTROLS attribute specifies the type of control panel that is used if HIDDEN is not specified. Values include "console" for a large panel, "smallconsole" for a smaller panel, or "playbutton" for a simple Play button.

- The WIDTH and HEIGHT attributes control the size of the control panel, if it is not hidden.

16

These attributes are valid for Internet Explorer with Windows Media Player or Netscape 4.x with LiveAudio. Other browsers or plug-ins could have different attributes.

Using the <object> Tag

The <embed> tag has been deprecated in the HTML 4.0 standard in favor of a new tag, <object>. This tag allows you to specify the same parameters and many others to embed a sound or other plug-in object. Here is an example <object> tag to include a sound within a Web page:

```
<object type="audio/x-wav" data="sound.wav" width="100" height="50">
  <param name="src" value="sound.wav">
  <param name="autostart" value="false">
  <param name="hidden" value="true">
</object>
```

This tag embeds a hidden sound object, similar to the <embed> tag example in the previous section.

While `<object>` is now the standard tag for embedding sound, it is currently supported only by Internet Explorer 4.0 and later. The `<embed>` tag is still supported by the latest browsers and is currently a better choice for compatibility.

Understanding MIME Types

Multipurpose Internet Mail Extensions (MIME) is a standard for classifying different types of files and transmitting them over the Internet. The different types of files are known as *MIME types*.

You've already worked with a few MIME types: HTML (MIME type `text/html`), text (MIME type `text/plain`), and GIF images (MIME type `image/gif`). Although Web browsers don't normally support many more than these types, external applications and plug-ins can provide support for additional types.

When a Web server sends a document to a browser, it includes that document's MIME type in the heading. If the browser supports that MIME type, it displays the file. If not, you're asked what to do with the file (such as when you click on a `.zip` or `.exe` file to download it).

Working with Plug-In Objects

The JavaScript `navigator` object, which you learned about in Hour 9, "Working with the Document Object Model," includes a child object called `plugins`. This object is an array, with one entry for each plug-in installed on the browser.

Unfortunately, the `navigator.plugins` object is supported only by Netscape 3.0 and later. There is no easy way to detect installed plug-ins in Internet Explorer.

Each plug-in has an entry in the array. Each entry has the following properties:

- `name` is the name of the plug-in.
- `filename` is the executable file that was loaded to install the plug-in.
- `description` is a description of the plug-in, supplied by the developer.
- `mimeTypes` is an array with one entry for each `MIME` type supported by the plug-in.

You can use these properties in a script to find out about the installed plug-ins, as you'll see in the next section.

> Netscape's `navigator` object also has a child object called `mimeTypes`, which includes an array element for each MIME type supported by the browser or one of its plug-ins.

Checking for Plug-Ins

What if you want to use a hot new plug-in on your pages, but you know that not everyone has the plug-in installed? One of the handiest uses for JavaScript is to detect a plug-in before loading the page that contains that plug-in's content.

For example, the following simple script checks for the QuickTime plug-in (or any other plug-in that handles QuickTime movies). If a plug-in is found, the script writes the `<embed>` tag to include a movie in the document. If not, it displays a still image.

```
test=navigator.mimeTypes["video/quicktime"];
if (test)
    document.writeln("<embed SRC='quick.mov' HEIGHT=100 WIDTH=100>");
else
    document.writeln("<img SRC='quick.gif' HEIGHT=100 WIDTH=100>");
```

If your script does not detect the appropriate plug-in, you can provide a link to the download location for the plug-in or to a non-plug-in version of the page.

Listing Plug-Ins

As an example of the `plugins` array, you can use JavaScript to list the plug-ins supported by your browser. Listing 16.1 shows a script that lists the plug-ins in a table, with filenames and descriptions.

LISTING 16.1   Listing plug-ins with JavaScript

```
<html>
<head>
<title>List of Plug-Ins</title>
</head>
<body>
<h1>List of Plug-Ins</h1>
<hr>
<p>The following is a list of the plug-ins installed in this
copy of Netscape, generated using the JavaScript
```

LISTING 16.1   Continued

```
navigator.plugins object:</p>
<hr>
<table BORDER>
<tr><th>Plug-in Name</th>
<th>Filename</th>
<th>Description</th>
</tr>
<script LANGUAGE="JavaScript" type="text/javascript">
for (i=0; i<navigator.plugins.length; i++) {
    document.write("<tr><td>");
    document.write(navigator.plugins[i].name);
    document.write("</td><td>");
    document.write(navigator.plugins[i].filename);
    document.write("</td><td>");
    document.write(navigator.plugins[i].description);
    document.write("</td></tr>");
}
</script>
</table>
</body>
</html>
```

The action of the script is performed by the `<script>` section in the body. This begins with a `for` loop that loops from 0 to the number of plug-ins (the `length` property of the `plugins` array).

The `document.write` statements within the loop display the properties for a single `plugin` object, along with some HTML tags to make the table. This script's output in Netscape 6 is shown in Figure 16.1.

Using Objects in Plug-Ins

You now know how to use the `navigator` object's properties to detect plug-ins. You can also use objects to manipulate plug-ins themselves.

Each embedded object in a document is represented by an element in the `embeds` array, which is a child of the `document` array. For example, if a document contains a single embedded object, it is represented by `document.embeds[0]`.

While the earlier plug-in detection examples work only with Netscape, the `embeds` array and the sound-playing example in the next section will also work with Internet Explorer 4.0 or later.

FIGURE 16.1.

The list of plug-ins as displayed by Netscape.

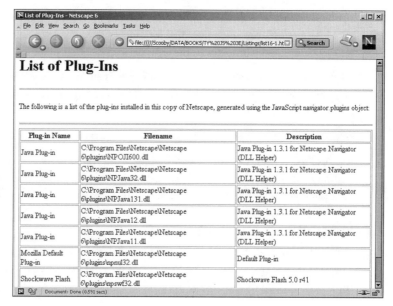

16

The properties and methods of the embed object depend on the plug-in in use. For example, the LiveAudio plug-in includes play and stop methods for controlling audio output. Some plug-ins may not be scriptable at all.

Workshop: Playing Music with the Mouse

As an example of controlling a plug-in with JavaScript, you will now create a script to play sounds. I've created some graphics that vaguely resemble a piano keyboard and audio files for each note. Your script can detect mouse clicks on the keys and play the appropriate notes.

> You can download the audio files and graphics used in this example from this book's Web site at http://www.jsworkshop.com/.

Embedding the Sounds

For this example, I've created sound files in WAV format for each of the 13 notes in a single octave of a piano keyboard. Each file is named after the note it contains. Your HTML document will need to include these sounds using the <embed> tag.

Normally, when you embed a sound, it plays as soon as the page loads. You don't want all 13 notes to play at once (and that wouldn't work anyway), so use the AUTOSTART=false parameter to prevent the sounds from playing.

Also include the HIDDEN=true parameter to prevent the browser from displaying cute little control panels for each of the sounds. The <embed> tag for a single note (the bottom C) would look like this:

```
<embed SRC="C0.wav" HIDDEN=true AUTOSTART=false>
```

Because the HTML document will include a tag like this for each sound, the 13 sounds will be loaded (but not played) immediately. This will prevent the browser from having to communicate with the server to load a file each time you click on a piano key.

Displaying the Keyboard

For the keyboard display, I've created two GIF graphics: a white key and a black key. The HTML document simply needs to include whitekey.gif and blackkey.gif in the right combination to display the 13 keys.

For a better-looking keyboard, you could use an image map. The script in this hour's workshop sticks to linked graphics for simplicity; see this book's Web site for a fancier version. Here's the HTML link tag for a single piano key:

```
<a href="#" onClick="playnote(0);">
    <img border=0 SRC="whitekey.gif" ALIGN=TOP></a>
```

This displays the white key graphic. It is linked with "#" as a target (which will prevent the browser from loading a different page), and the onClick event handler runs a JavaScript function to play the note.

Playing the Sounds

The playnote function handles the playing of the appropriate sound. It accepts a parameter, note (a number from 0 to 12 representing one of the embedded sounds) and uses the play method to play the sound. Here's the function:

```
function playnote(note) {
document.embeds[note].play();
}
```

While it isn't used by this example, you can also use the stop() method of sound objects to stop a sound that is currently playing.

A Word About Audio Plug-ins

When you're dealing with plug-ins, you need to make sure you (and the users of your Web site) have the correct plug-ins. While most browsers include a plug-in for WAV files, installing other software can often remove or interfere with the included plug-ins. Here are some tips for getting sounds to play in the latest browsers:

- For Netscape 4.x, make sure the LiveAudio component is installed.

- For Internet Explorer 4.0 and later for Windows, install the latest version of the Windows Media Player component. If other audio software has been installed, you may need to re-install Windows Media Player to get sounds working.

- At the time of this writing, Netscape 6 does not include a plug-in for playing sounds. While you can install plug-ins to play sounds in Netscape 6, such as Apple's QuickTime and Microsoft's Windows Media Player, they are not currently scriptable using the techniques presented here. A future release of LiveAudio from Netscape may solve this problem.

16

Putting It All Together

Listing 16.2 shows the complete HTML document for the piano. This listing may look long, but most of the lines are just repeated forms of the ones in the previous sections: 13 <embed> tags, and 13 links and images for the keyboard display. Each link sends a different parameter to the play function to play the appropriate note.

LISTING 16.2 The complete HTML and script for the piano example

```
<html>
<head>
<title>JavaScript Piano</title>
<script LANGUAGE="JavaScript" type="text/javascript">
function playnote(note) {
  document.embeds[note].play();
}
</script>
</head>
<body>
<embed SRC="C0.wav" HIDDEN=true AUTOSTART=false>
<embed SRC="Cs0.wav" HIDDEN=true AUTOSTART=false>
<embed SRC="D0.wav" HIDDEN=true AUTOSTART=false>
<embed SRC="Ds0.wav" HIDDEN=true AUTOSTART=false>
<embed SRC="E0.wav" HIDDEN=true AUTOSTART=false>
<embed SRC="F0.wav" HIDDEN=true AUTOSTART=false>
<embed SRC="Fs0.wav" HIDDEN=true AUTOSTART=false>
<embed SRC="G0.wav" HIDDEN=true AUTOSTART=false>
<embed SRC="Gs0.wav" HIDDEN=true AUTOSTART=false>
```

LISTING **16.2**   Continued

```
<embed SRC="A0.wav" HIDDEN=true AUTOSTART=false>
<embed SRC="As0.wav" HIDDEN=true AUTOSTART=false>
<embed SRC="B0.wav" HIDDEN=true AUTOSTART=false>
<embed SRC="C1.wav" HIDDEN=true AUTOSTART=false>
<h1>The JavaScript Piano</h1>
<hr>
<p>Click on the funny-looking piano keys below to play a melody.</p>
<hr>
<a HREF="#" onClick="playnote(0);">
   <img border=0 SRC="whitekey.gif" ALIGN=TOP></a>
<a HREF="#" onClick="playnote(1);">
   <img border=0 SRC="blackkey.gif" ALIGN=TOP></a>
<a HREF="#" onClick="playnote(2);">
   <img border=0 SRC="whitekey.gif" ALIGN=TOP></a>
<a HREF="#" onClick="playnote(3);">
   <img border=0 SRC="blackkey.gif" ALIGN=TOP></a>
<a HREF="#" onClick="playnote(4);">
   <img border=0 SRC="whitekey.gif" ALIGN=TOP></a>
<a HREF="#" onClick="playnote(5);">
   <img border=0 SRC="whitekey.gif" ALIGN=TOP></a>
<a HREF="#" onClick="playnote(6);">
   <img border=0 SRC="blackkey.gif" ALIGN=TOP></a>
<a HREF="#" onClick="playnote(7);">
   <img border=0 SRC="whitekey.gif" ALIGN=TOP></a>
<a HREF="#" onClick="playnote(8);">
   <img border=0 SRC="blackkey.gif" ALIGN=TOP></a>
<a HREF="#" onClick="playnote(9);">
   <img border=0 SRC="whitekey.gif" ALIGN=TOP></a>
<a HREF="#" onClick="playnote(10);">
   <img border=0 SRC="blackkey.gif" ALIGN=TOP></a>
<a HREF="#" onClick="playnote(11);">
   <img border=0 SRC="whitekey.gif" ALIGN=TOP></a>
<a HREF="#" onClick="playnote(12);">
   <img border=0 SRC="whitekey.gif" ALIGN=TOP></a>
<hr>
</body>
</html>
```

To try out the piano, put the HTML document in the same directory as the required graphic and sound files, either on your local computer or a Web server. You can then load the document and begin playing the piano. (You can't play chords, but they're only used by the most advanced musicians anyway.)

This example won't work unless you have an audio player plug-in configured. For Netscape 3.0 and 4.x, the included LiveAudio plug-in will work; for Internet Explorer 4.0 and later, make sure the Windows Media Player component is installed. Netscape 6 does not currently include a plug-in for playing sounds.

16

Figure 16.2 shows Internet Explorer's display of the piano keyboard. Books aren't nearly as multimedia-ready as the Web, so you'll have to try the script yourself to hear the sounds.

FIGURE 16.2.

Internet Explorer displays the piano keyboard script.

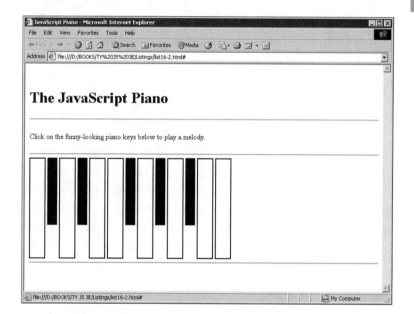

Summary

In this hour, you learned about the JavaScript features that work with plug-ins. You learned how to detect or list plug-ins with JavaScript, and how to use JavaScript objects to control plug-ins. Finally, you created a script that uses a plug-in to play sounds.

You've nearly reached the end of Part IV. In the final hour of this part, you'll learn how to debug JavaScript applications and avoid common scripting errors.

Q&A

Q **Can I force the browser to download a plug-in automatically to support my document?**

A No, although a future version of Netscape may support this feature, and Internet Explorer provides an option to allow the download of plug-ins on demand. If the user does download and install the plug-in, you can use the `navigator.plugins.reload` method to refresh the list of plug-ins.

Q **Where can I find a list of the exact properties and methods supported by a plug-in?**

A Check the plug-in vendor's Web site. For the plug-ins that are bundled with Netscape, you can find information on Netscape's site.

Q **Just how supported are plug-ins? Will I be abandoning part of my audience by using them?**

A In the case of basic plug-ins such as Quicktime and audio players, you're pretty safe to use them but you will run into problems with some users. More complicated plug-ins are far less common. I suggest that you only use these when they're required (for example, a game that requires Macromedia Flash) or when you've provided a plug-in-free alternative to access your content.

Q **I get an error message saying "Object does not support this property or method" when attempting to play sounds with JavaScript.**

A This usually happens when the browser doesn't have a plug-in installed for the type of sound file you are using. For Internet Explorer, installing the latest Windows Media Player component from Microsoft will fix the problem.

Quiz

Test your knowledge of JavaScript's plug-in and multimedia features by answering the following questions.

Questions

1. Which HTML tag is often used to include a plug-in object within a Web page?

    a. `<sound>`

    b. `<embed>`

    c. `<plugin>`

2. The `plugins` object is a child of which browser object?

    a. `document`

    b. `window`

    c. `navigator`

3. Which plug-in for playing sounds is included with Netscape 4.x?

    a. LiveConnect

    b. LiveAudio

    c. No plug-in is included; you must make the sounds with your mouth

16

Answers

1. b. The `<embed>` tag embeds a plug-in object.

2. c. The `plugins` object is a child of the `navigator` object.

3. b. The LiveAudio plug-in is included with Netscape 4.x.

Exercises

If you want to gain more experience using JavaScript with plug-ins, try these exercises:

- Modify Listing 16.1 to detect a plug-in and display a message with a link to the plug-in vendor's site if it is not supported.

- Expand the piano keyboard in Listing 16.2 to include more notes. (Audio files for all 88 keys of a piano are available at this book's Web site (`http://www.jsworkshop.com`) if you want to go all out. An imagemap version of the keyboard with more keys is also available.)

Hour 17

Debugging JavaScript Applications

You've reached the end of Part IV. As you move on to more advanced JavaScript applications in the remaining hours, it's important to know how to deal with problems in your scripts.

In this hour, you'll learn a few pointers on keeping your scripts bug-free, and you'll look at the tools and techniques you can use to find and eliminate bugs when they occur. Hour 17 covers the following topics:

- Using good programming practices to avoid bugs
- Tips for debugging with the JavaScript console
- Using alert messages and status messages to debug scripts
- Creating custom error handlers
- Debugging an actual script

Avoiding Bugs

A bug is an error in a program that prevents it from doing what it should do. If you've tried writing any scripts on your own, you've probably run into one or more bugs. If not, you will—no matter how careful you are.

Although you'll undoubtedly run into a few bugs if you write a complex script, you can avoid many others by carefully writing and double-checking your script.

Using Good Programming Practices

There's not a single programmer out there whose programs always work the first time, without any bugs. However, good programmers share a few habits that help them avoid some of the more common bugs. Here are a few good habits you can develop to improve your scripts:

- Format your scripts neatly and try to keep them readable. Use consistent spacing and variable names that mean something. It's hard to determine what's wrong with a script when you can't even remember what a particular line does.

- Similarly, use JavaScript comments liberally to document your script. This will help if you need to work on the script after you've forgotten the details of how it works—or if someone else inherits the job.

- End all JavaScript statements with semicolons. Although this is optional, it makes the script more readable. Additionally, it may help the browser to produce meaningful error messages.

- Declare all variables with the var keyword. This is optional in most cases, but it will help make sure you really mean to create a new variable and will avoid problems with variable scope.

- Divide complicated scripts into functions. This will make the script easier to read, and it will also make it easy to pinpoint the cause of a problem.

- Write a large script in several phases and test the script at each phase before adding more features. This way, you can avoid having several new errors appear at once.

Avoiding Common Mistakes

Along with following scripting practices, you should also watch for common mistakes in your scripts. Different people make different mistakes in JavaScript programming, but the following sections explore some of the most common ones.

Syntax Errors

A syntax error is an incorrect keyword, operator, punctuation mark, or other item in a script. Most often, it's caused by a typing error.

Syntax errors are usually obvious—both to you when you look at the script and to the browser's JavaScript interpreter when you load the script. These errors usually result in an error message and can easily be corrected.

Assignment and Equality

One of the most common syntax errors made by beginning JavaScript programmers is confusing the assignment operator (=) with the equality operator (==). This can be a hard error to spot because it may not result in an error message.

If you're confused about which operator to use, follow this simple rule: use = to change the value of a variable and == to compare two values. Here's an example of a statement that confuses the two:

```
If (a = 5) alert("found a five.");
```

The statement looks logical enough, but a = 5 will actually assign the value 5 to the a variable rather than comparing the two. Netscape usually detects this type of error and displays an error message in the JavaScript console, but the opposite type of error (using == when you mean =) may not be detected.

Local and Global Variables

Another common mistake is confusing local and global variables, such as trying to use the value of a variable that was declared in a function outside the function. If you actually need to do this, you should either use a global variable or return a value from the function.

Hour 4, "Using Functions and Variables," describes the differences between local and global variables in detail.

Using Objects Correctly

Another common error is referring to JavaScript objects incorrectly. It's important to use the correct object names and to remember when to explicitly name the parent of an object.

For example, you can usually refer to the window.alert method as simply alert. However, there are some cases when you must use window.alert, such as in some event handlers. If you find that alert or another method or property is not recognized by the browser, try specifying the window object.

Another common mistake is to assume that you can omit the document object's name, such as using write instead of document.write. This won't work because most scripts have a window object as their scope.

HTML Errors

Last but not least, don't forget that JavaScript isn't the only language that can have errors. It's easy to accidentally create an error in an HTML document—for example, forgetting to include a closing </table> tag, or even a closing </script> tag.

While writing proper HTML is beyond the scope of this book, you should be aware that sometimes improper HTML can cause errors in your JavaScript. When you experience bugs, be sure to double-check the HTML, especially the objects (such as forms or images) that your script manipulates.

Basic Debugging Tools

If checking your script for common mistakes and obvious problems doesn't fix things, it's time to start debugging. This is the process of finding errors in a program and eliminating them. Some basic tools for debugging scripts are described in the following sections.

Netscape's JavaScript Console

The first thing you should do if your script doesn't work is check for error messages. In Netscape 4.5 and later, the messages are not displayed by default, but are logged to the JavaScript console.

To access the console, type **javascript:** in Netscape's Location field or select Tasks, Tools, JavaScript Console from the menu. The console displays the last few error messages that have occurred, as shown in Figure 17.1.

Along with reading the error messages, you can use the console to type a JavaScript command or expression and see its results. This is useful if you need to make sure a line of your script uses the correct syntax.

FIGURE 17.1.

The JavaScript console displays recent error messages.

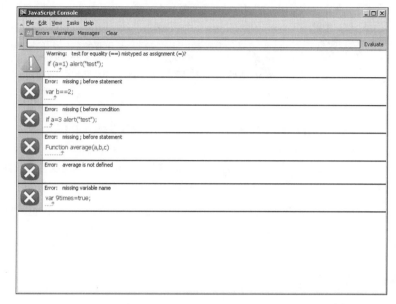

Some versions of Netscape 6 don't accept the `javascript:` command. You should still be able to access the console by selecting Tasks, Tools, JavaScript Console from the menu.

Displaying Error Messages in Internet Explorer

Microsoft Internet Explorer 4.0 and later do not display JavaScript error messages by default. While this can make browsing poorly-written pages a more pleasant experience, it can be frustrating to JavaScript programmers.

To enable the display of error messages in Internet Explorer, select Internet Options from the Tools menu. Select the Advanced tab. In the list under browsing, deselect the "Disable script debugging" option and enable the "Display a notification about every script error" option.

If you haven't enabled the display of error messages, Internet Explorer still displays an error icon on the status line when an error occurs. You can double-click this icon to display the error message.

17

Netscape's JavaScript console is a better debugging tool than Internet Explorer's error messages, so you may want to test your scripts in Netscape even if IE is your default browser. More importantly, you should test all scripts in both browsers to ensure compatibility.

Alert Messages and the Status Line

If you're lucky, the error messages in the console will tell you how to fix your script. However, your script may not generate any error messages at all—but still fail to work correctly. In this case, the real debugging process begins.

One useful debugging technique is to add temporary statements to your script to let you know what's going on. For example, you can use an alert message to display the value of a variable. Once you understand what's happening to the variable, you can figure out what's wrong with the script.

You can also display messages on the status line using the `window.status` property. This technique is especially useful when you are displaying lots of messages and don't want to acknowledge a dialog box for each one.

You can also display debugging information in a separate browser window or frame. You can use `document.write` in some cases, but this only works when the document hasn't finished loading yet and thus isn't a reliable debugging tool.

Using Comments

When all else fails, you can use JavaScript comments to eliminate portions of your script until the error goes away. If you do this carefully, you can pinpoint the place where the error occurred.

You can use `//` to begin a single-line comment, or `/*` and `*/` around a section of any length. Using comments to temporarily turn off statements in a program or script is called *commenting out* and is a common technique among programmers.

JavaScript comments were introduced and described in more detail in Hour 3, "How JavaScript Programs Work."

Other Debugging Tools

Although you can use alert messages and a little common sense to quickly find a bug in a simple script, larger scripts can be difficult to debug. Here are a few tools you may find useful as you develop and debug larger JavaScript applications:

- HTML validators can check your HTML documents to see if they meet the HTML standard. The validation process can also help you find errors in your HTML. The W3C has a validator online at `http://validator.w3.org/`.

- Netscape's JavaScript debugger allows you to set breakpoints, display variable values, and perform other debugging tasks. You can download the debugger at this URL: `http://developer.netscape.com/software/jsdebug.html`. The debugger does not yet support Netscape 6, but a version is in development: `http://www.mozilla.org/projects/venkman/`.

- Microsoft Script Debugger is similar, but works with Internet Explorer. It is available from this URL: `http://msdn.microsoft.com/library/en-us/sdbug/Html/sdbug_1.asp`.

- While text and HTML editors are good basic editing tools, they can also help with debugging by displaying line numbers and using color codes to indicate valid commands.

Appendix B, "Tools for JavaScript Developers," includes links to HTML validators, editors, and other debugging tools.

Creating Error Handlers

In some cases, there may be times when an error message is unavoidable, and in a large JavaScript application errors are bound to happen. Your scripts can respond to errors in a friendlier way using error handlers.

Using the onerror Property

You can set up an error handler by assigning a function to the `onerror` property of the `window` object. When an error occurs in a script in the document, the browser calls the function you specify instead of the normal error dialog. For example, these statements set up a function that displays a simple message when an error occurs:

```
function errmsg(message,url,line) {
    alert("There wasn't an error. Nothing to see here.");
    return true;
}
window.onerror=errmsg;
```

These statements define a function, errmsg, that handles errors by displaying a simple dialog. The last statement assigns the errmsg function to the window.onerror property.

The return true; statement tells the browser that this function has handled the error, and prevents the standard error dialog from being displayed. If you use return false; instead, the standard error dialog will be displayed after your function exits.

> You can't define an onError event handler in HTML. You must define it using the window.onerror property as shown here.

Displaying Information About the Error

When the browser calls your error-handling function, it passes three parameters: the error message, the URL of the document where the error happened, and the line number. The simple error handler in the previous example didn't use these values. You can create a more sophisticated handler that displays the information.

> As usual, you can download this hour's examples from this book's Web site: http://www.jsworkshop.com/.

Listing 17.1 shows a complete example including an enhanced errmsg function. This version displays the error message, URL, and line number in a dialog box.

LISTING 17.1   Handling errors with a JavaScript function

```
<html><head>
<title>Error handling test</title>
<script language="JavaScript1.1" type="text/javascript1.1">
function errmsg(message,url,line) {
    amsg = "A JavaScript error has occurred. Please let us know about it.\n";
    amsg += "Error Message: " + message + "\n";
    amsg += "URL: " + url + "\n";
    amsg += "Line #: " + line;
    alert(amsg);
    return true;
}
window.onerror=errmsg;
</script>
</head>
<body>
```

LISTING 17.1 Continued

```html
<h1> Error handling test</h1>
<p>This page includes a JavaScript function to handle errors.
Test it by clicking the button below.</p>
<form>
  <input type="button" value="ERROR" onClick="garble">
</form>
</body>
</html>
```

This example includes a button with a nonsensical event handler. To test the error handler, click the button to generate an error. Figure 17.2 shows the example in action in Internet Explorer with the alert message displayed.

FIGURE 17.2

The error handler example in action.

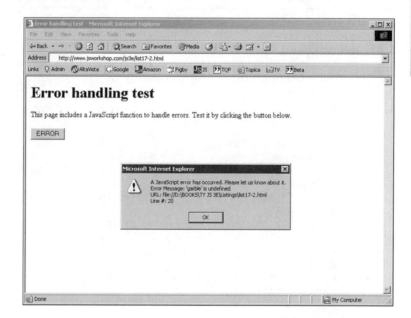

 If you try to use an error handler and still get error messages, make sure there isn't a syntax error in your error handler itself.

Workshop: Debugging a Script

You should now have a good understanding of what can go wrong with JavaScript programs and the tools you have available to diagnose these problems. You can now try your hand at debugging a script.

Listing 17.2 shows a script I wrote to play the classic "Guess a Number" game. The script picks a number between 1 and 100 and then allows the user 10 guesses. If a guess is incorrect, it provides a hint as to whether the target number is higher or lower.

This is a relatively simple script with a twist: It includes at least one bug and doesn't work at all in its present form.

LISTING 17.2   The number guesser script, complete with bugs

```
<html>
<head>
<title>Guess a Number</title>
<script LANGUAGE="JavaScript" type="text/javascript">
var num = Math.random() * 100 + 1;
var tries = 0;
function Guess() {
var g = document.form1.guess1.value;
tries++;
status = "Tries: " + tries;
if (g < num)
    document.form1.hint.value = "No, guess higher.";
if (g > num)
    document.form1.hint.value = "No, guess lower.";
if (g == num) {
    window.alert("Correct! You guessed it in " + tries + " tries.");
    location.reload();
    }
if (tries == 10) {
    window.alert("Sorry, time's up. The number was: " + num);
    location.reload();
    }
}
</script>
</head>
<body>
<h1>Guess a Number</h1>
<hr>
<p>I'm thinking of a number between 1 and 100. Try to guess
it in less than 10 tries.</p>
<form NAME="form1">
<input TYPE="text" SIZE=25 NAME="hint" VALUE="Enter your Guess.">
<br>
```

LISTING 17.2 Continued

```
<b>Guess:</b>
<input TYPE="text" NAME="guess1" SIZE="5">
<input TYPE="BUTTON" VALUE="Guess"  onClick="guess();">
</form>
</body>
</html>
```

Here's a summary of how this script should work:

- The first line within the <script> section picks a random number and stores it in the num variable.
- The Guess function is defined in the header of the document. This function is called each time the user enters a guess.
- Within the Guess function, several if statements test the user's guess. If it is incorrect, a hint is displayed in the text box. If the guess is correct, the script displays an alert message to congratulate the user.

Testing the Program

To test this program, load the HTML document into your browser. It appears to load correctly and does not immediately cause any errors. However, when you enter a guess and press the Guess button, a JavaScript error occurs.

According to Netscape's JavaScript Console, the error message is this:

```
Line 36: guess is undefined
```

Internet Explorer's error message refers to the same line number:

```
Line 36, character 1: Object expected
```

Fixing the Error

As the error message indicates, there must be something wrong with the function call to the Guess function, in the event handler on line 36. The line in question looks like this:

```
<input TYPE="BUTTON" VALUE="Guess"  onClick="guess();">
```

Upon further examination, you'll notice that the first two lines of the function are as follows:

```
function Guess() {
var guess = document.form1.guess1.value;
```

Although this may look correct at first glance, there's a problem here: guess() is lower-case in the event handler, while the function definition uses a capitalized Guess(). This is easy to fix. Simply change the function call in the event handler from guess to Guess. The corrected line will look like this:

```
<input TYPE="BUTTON" VALUE="Guess"  onClick="Guess();">
```

Testing the Script Again

Now that you've fixed the error, try the script again. This time it loads without an error, and you can enter a guess without an error. The hints about guessing higher or lower are even displayed correctly.

However, to truly test the script, you'll need to play the game all the way through. When you do, you'll discover that there's still another problem in the script: You can't win, no matter how hard you try.

After your 10 guesses are up, an alert message informs you that you've lost the game. Coincidentally, this alert message also tells you what's wrong with the script. Figure 17.3 shows how the browser window looks after a complete game, complete with this dialog box.

FIGURE 17.3.

The number guesser script's display after a game is finished.

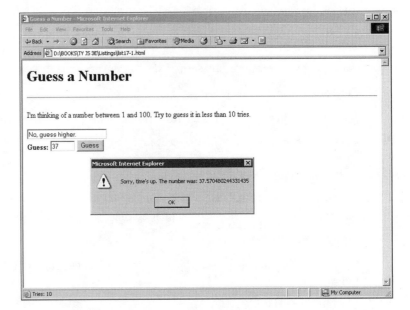

As you can see from the alert message, it's no wonder you didn't win: The random number the computer picked includes more than 10 decimal places, and you've been guessing integers. You could guess decimal numbers, but you'd need a whole lot more than 10 guesses, and the game would start to lose its simplicity and charm.

To fix this problem, look at the statement at the beginning of the script that generates the random number:

```
var num = Math.random() * 100 + 1;
```

This uses the `Math.random` method, which results in a random number between 0 and 1. The number is then multiplied and incremented to result in a number between 1 and 100.

This statement does indeed produce a number between 1 and 100, but not an integer. To fix the problem, you can add the `Math.floor` method to chop off the decimal portion of the number. Here's a corrected statement:

```
var num = Math.floor(Math.random() * 100) + 1;
```

To fix the script, make this change and then test it again. If you play a game or two, you'll find that it works just fine. Listing 17.3 shows the complete, debugged script.

17

LISTING 17.3   The complete, debugged number guesser script

```html
<html>
<head>
<title>Guess a Number</title>
<script LANGUAGE="JavaScript" type="text/javascript">
var num = Math.floor(Math.random() * 100) + 1;
var tries = 0;
function Guess() {
var g = document.form1.guess1.value;
tries++;
status = "Tries: " + tries;
if (g < num)
    document.form1.hint.value = "No, guess higher.";
if (g > num)
    document.form1.hint.value = "No, guess lower.";
if (g == num) {
    window.alert("Correct! You guessed it in " + tries + " tries.") ;
    location.reload();
    }
if (tries == 10) {
    window.alert("Sorry, time's up. The number was: " + num);
    location.reload();
    }
}
</script>
```

LISTING 17.3   Continued

```
</head>
<body>
<h1>Guess a Number</h1>
<hr>
<p>I'm thinking of a number between 1 and 100. Try to guess
it in less than 10 tries.</p>
<form NAME="form1">
<input TYPE="text" SIZE=25 NAME="hint" VALUE="Enter your Guess.">
<br>
<b>Guess:</b>
<input TYPE="text" NAME="guess1" SIZE="5">
<input TYPE="BUTTON" VALUE="Guess"  onClick="Guess();">
</form>
</body>
</html>
```

Figure 17.4 shows the debugged example in action in Netscape 6, after a successful game.

FIGURE 17.4

The number guesser example after a successful game.

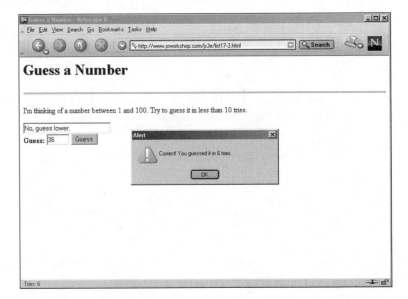

Summary

In this hour, you've learned how to debug JavaScript programs. You examined some techniques for producing scripts with a minimum of bugs and learned about some tools that will help you find bugs in scripts. Finally, you tried your hand at debugging a script.

Congratulations—you're nearing the final hours of your JavaScript education. In the next three hours, you will learn how you can use Dynamic HTML (DHTML) to add sophisticated effects to your scripts.

Q&A

Q **Why are some errors displayed after the script runs for a time, while others are displayed when the script loads?**

A The JavaScript interpreter looks at scripts in the body or heading of the document, such as function definitions, when the page loads. Event handlers aren't checked until the event happens. Additionally, a statement might look fine when the page loads, but will cause an error because of the value of a variable it uses later.

Q **What is the purpose of the `location.reload` statements in the number guesser script?**

A This is an easy way to start a new game because reloading the page reinitializes the variables. This results in a new number being picked, and the default "Guess a Number" message is displayed in the hint field.

Q **The JavaScript console in Netscape is useful for testing JavaScript commands when I'm not sure of the syntax. Is there an equivalent in Internet Explorer?**

A Not a built-in one, but I've created a JavaScript-based console that works in Netscape or Internet Explorer. It can't display errors like Netscape's console, but it is useful for testing commands interactively. You can find it at this book's Web site: `http://www.jsworkshop.com/`.

Quiz

Test your knowledge of avoiding and debugging JavaScript errors by answering the following questions.

Questions

1. If you mistype a JavaScript keyword, which type of error is the result?

   a. Syntax error

   b. Function error

   c. Pilot error

17

2. The process of dealing with errors in a script or program is known as:

   a. Error detection

   b Frustration

   c. Debugging

3. Which of the following is a useful technique when a script is not working but does not generate an error message?

   a. Rewriting from scratch

   b. Removing `<script>` tags

   c. Adding `alert` statements

Answers

1. a. A syntax error can result from a mistyped JavaScript keyword.

2. c. Debugging is the process of finding and fixing errors in a program.

3. c. You can add `alert` statements to a script to display variables or the current status of the script and aid in debugging.

Exercises

If you want to gain more experience debugging JavaScript programs, try these exercises:

- Although the number guesser script in Listing 17.3 avoids JavaScript errors, it is still vulnerable to user errors. Add a statement to verify that the user's guess is between 1 and 100. If it isn't, display an alert message and make sure that the guess doesn't count toward the total of 10 guesses.

- Load Listing 17.2, the number guesser script with bugs, into Netscape's JavaScript Debugger or Microsoft's Script Debugger. Try using the watch and breakpoint features and see if you find this an easier way to diagnose the problem.

PART V

Working with Dynamic HTML (DHTML)

Hour

HOUR 18

Working with Style Sheets

Welcome to Part V! In the next three hours, you'll learn how to use some of the more recent additions to the Web developer's arsenal, and how to use JavaScript to control these features.

This hour begins with an introduction to style sheets, which you can use to take more control over how the browser displays your document. You can also use JavaScript with style sheets to change the display dynamically.

Hour 18 covers the following topics:

- Why style sheets are needed
- How to define Cascading Style Sheets (CSS)
- How to use a style sheet in a document
- Using an external style sheet file
- Using JavaScript to change styles dynamically

Style and Substance

If you've ever tried to make a really good-looking Web page, you've probably encountered some problems. First of all, HTML doesn't give you very much control over a page's appearance. For example, you can't change the amount of space between words—in fact, you can't even use two spaces between words because they'll be converted to a single space.

Second, even when you do your best to make a perfect-looking document using HTML, you will find that it doesn't necessarily display the same way on all browsers—or even on different computers running the same browser.

The reason for these problems is simple: HTML was never meant to handle such things as layout, justification, and spacing. HTML deals with a document's *structure*—in other words, how the document is divided into paragraphs, headings, lists, and other elements.

This isn't a bad thing. In fact, it's one of the most powerful features of HTML. You only define the structure of the document, so it can be displayed in all sorts of different ways without changing its meaning. For example, a well-written HTML document can be displayed in Netscape or Internet Explorer, which generally treat elements the same way—there is a space between paragraphs, headings are in big, bold text, and so on.

Because HTML only defines the structure, the same document can be displayed in a text-based browser, such as Lynx. In this case, the different elements will be displayed differently, but you can still tell which text is a heading, which is a list, and so on.

 Text-based browsers aren't the only alternate way of displaying HTML. Browsers designed for the blind can read a Web page using a speech synthesizer, with different voices or sounds that indicate the different elements.

As you should now understand, HTML is very good at its job—defining a document's structure. Not surprisingly, using this language to try to control the document's *presentation* will only drive you crazy.

Fortunately, the World Wide Web Consortium (W3C) realized that Web authors need to control the layout and presentation of documents. This resulted in the *Cascading Style Sheets (CSS)* standard.

CSS adds a number of features to standard HTML to control style and appearance. More importantly, it does this without affecting HTML's ability to describe document structures. While style sheets still won't make your document look 100% identical on all browsers and all platforms, it is certainly a step in the right direction.

Let's look at a real-world example. If you're browsing the Web with a CSS-supported browser and come across a page that uses CSS, you'll see the document exactly as it was intended. You can also turn off your browser's support for style sheets if you'd rather view all the pages in the same consistent way.

Defining and Using CSS Styles

You can define a CSS style sheet using the `<style>` tag. The opening `<style>` tag specifies the type of style sheet—CSS is currently the only valid type—and begins a list of styles to apply to the document. The `</style>` tag ends the style sheet. Here's a simple example:

```
<style TYPE="text/css">
H1 {color: blue;}
</style>
```

Since the style sheet definition itself doesn't create any output on the page, you should place the `<style>` tags in the `<head>` section of the HTML document.

18

 You can only use style sheet rules within the `<style>` tags. No other HTML tags are valid within a style sheet.

Creating Rules

Each element within the `<style>` tags is called a *rule*. To create a rule, you specify the HTML elements that it will affect, as well as a list of properties and values that control the appearance of those elements. We'll look at the properties in the next section.

As a simple example, the following style sheet contains a single rule—All Level 1 headings are blue:

```
<style TYPE="text/css">
H1 {color: blue;}
</style>
```

Each rule includes three components:

- A *selector* (H1 in the example) describing which HTML tags will be affected
- One or more *property names* (color in the example)
- A *value* for each property name (blue in the example)

Each rule uses braces to surround the list of properties and values, and a semicolon after each value. The semicolon is optional if you are only specifying one property and value.

You can specify multiple HTML tags for the selector, as well as multiple properties and values. For example, the following style sheet specifies that all headers are blue, italic, and centered:

```
<style TYPE="text/css">
H1,H2,H3,H4,H5,H6 {color: blue;
                   font-style: italic;
                   text-align: center; }
</style>
```

 If you make a rule that sets the style of the <body> tag, it will affect the entire document. This becomes the default rule for the document and you can override it with the styles of elements within the body of the page.

Setting Styles for Specific Elements

Rather than setting the style for all elements of a certain type, you can specify a style for an individual element only. For example, the following HTML tag represents a Level 1 header colored red:

```
<H1 STYLE="color: red; text-align: center;">This is a blue header.</H1>
```

This is called an *inline style* since it's specified in the HTML tag itself. You don't need to use <style> tags with this type of style. If you have used both, an inline style overrides a style sheet—for example, if the above tag appeared in a document that sets H1 headings to be blue in a style sheet, the heading would still be red.

Using ID Attributes

You can also create a rule within a style sheet that will only apply to a certain element. The ID attribute of an HTML tag allows you to assign a unique identifier to that element. For example, this tag defines a paragraph with the ID attribute intro:

```
<p ID="intro">This is a paragraph</p>
```

Once you've assigned this attribute to the tag, you can include a rule for it as part of a style sheet. CSS uses the pound sign (#) to indicate that a rule applies to a specific ID. For example, the following style sheet sets the intro paragraph to be red in color:

```
<style type="text/css">
   #intro {color: red;}
</style>
```

Using Classes

While the ID attribute is useful, you can only use each unique ID with a single HTML tag. If you need to apply the same style to several tags, you can use the CLASS attribute instead. For example, this HTML tag defines a paragraph in a class called smallprint:

```
<p class="smallprint">This is the small print</p>
```

To refer to a class within a style sheet, you use a period followed by the class name. Here is a style sheet that defines styles for the smallprint class:

```
<style type="text/css">
   .smallprint {color: black;
                font-size: 10px; }
</style>
```

Using CSS Properties

CSS supports a wide variety of properties, such as color and text-align in the previous example. The following sections list some of the most useful CSS properties for aligning text, changing colors, working with fonts, and setting margins and borders.

This is only an introduction to CSS, and there are many properties beyond those listed here. For more details about CSS, consult one of the Web resources or books listed in Appendix A, "Other JavaScript Resources."

18

Aligning Text

One of the most useful features of style sheets is the capability to change the spacing and alignment of text. Most of these features aren't available using standard HTML. You can use the following properties to change the alignment and spacing of text:

- letter-spacing—Specifies the spacing between letters.

- text-decoration— Allows you to create lines over, under, or through the text, or to choose blinking text. The value can be none (default), underline, overline, line-through, or blink. Blinking text is supported by Netscape 4 only.

- vertical-align— Allows you to move the element up or down to align with other elements on the same line. The value can be baseline, sub, super, top, text-top, middle, text-bottom, and bottom.

- text-align— Specifies the justification of text. This can be left, right, center, or justify. The justify option is supported by Netscape 6 and Internet Explorer 5.0 and later only.

- text-transform— Changes the capitalization of text. capitalize makes the first letter of each word uppercase; uppercase makes *all* letters uppercase; and lower-case makes all letters lowercase.

- text-indent— Allows you to specify the amount of indentation for paragraphs and other elements.

- line-height— This allows you to specify the distance between the top of one line of text and the top of the next.

Changing Colors and Background Images

You can also use style sheets to gain more control over the colors and background images used on your Web page. CSS includes the following properties for this purpose:

- color— Specifies the text color of an element. This is useful for emphasizing text or for using a specific color scheme for the document. You can specify a named color (for example, red) or red, green, and blue values (for example, #0522A5).

- background-color— Specifies the background color of an element. By setting this value, you can make paragraphs, table cells, and other elements with unique background colors. As with color, you can specify a color name or numeric color.

- background-image— Specifies a GIF format image to be used as the background for the element.

- background-repeat— Specifies whether the background image is repeated (tiled). The image can be repeated horizontally, vertically, or both.

- background-attachment— Controls whether the background image scrolls when you scroll through the document. fixed means that the background image stays still while the document scrolls; scroll means the image scrolls with the document (like background images on normal Web documents).

- background-position— Allows you to offset the position of the background image.

- background—This provides a quick way to set all of the background elements in this list. You can specify all of the attributes in a single background rule.

Working with Fonts

Style sheets also allow you to control the fonts used on the Web document and how they are displayed. You can use the following properties to control fonts:

- `font-family`— Specifies the name of a font, such as `arial` or `helvetica`, to use with the element. Because not all users have the same fonts installed, you can list several fonts. The CSS specification also supports several generic font families that are guaranteed to be available: `serif`, `sans-serif`, `cursive`, `fantasy`, and `mono-space`.

- `font-style`— Specifies the style of a font, such as `normal`, `italic`, or `oblique`.

- `font-variant`— This value is `normal` for normal text, and `small-caps` to display lowercase letters as small capitals.

- `font-weight`— Allows you to specify the weight of text: `normal` or `bold`. You can also specify a numeric font weight for a specific amount of boldness.

- `font-size`— The point size of the font.

- `font`— This is a quick way to set all the font properties in this list. You can list all the values in a single `font` rule.

Margins and Borders

Last but not least, you can use style sheets to control the general layout of the page. The following properties affect margins, borders, and the width and height of elements on the Web page:

- `margin-top`, `margin-bottom`, `margin-left`, `margin-right`—These properties specify the margins of the element. You can specify the margins as an exact number or as a percentage of the page's width.

- `margin`— Allows you to specify a single value for all four of the margins.

- `width`— Specifies the width of an element, such as an image.

- `height`— Specifies the height of an element.

- `float`— Allows the text to flow around an element. This is particularly useful with images or tables.

- `clear`— Specifies that the text should stop flowing around a floating image.

Along with these features, CSS style sheets allow you to create sections of the document that can be positioned independently. This feature is described in Hour 19, "Using Dynamic HTML (DHTML)."

18

Units for Style Sheets

Style sheet properties support a wide variety of *units*, or types of values you can specify. Most properties that accept a numeric value support the following types of units:

- px: Pixels (for example, 15px). Pixels are the smallest addressable units on a computer screen or other device. In some devices with non-typical resolutions (for example, handheld computers) the browser may rescale this value to fit the device.

- pt: Points (for example, 10pt). Points are a standard unit for font size. The size of text of a specified point size varies depending on the monitor resolution. Points are equal to 1/72 of an inch.

- ex: Approximate height of the letter x in the current font (for example, 1.2ex).

- em: Approximate width of the letter m in the current font (for example, 1.5em). This is usually equal to the font-size property for the current element.

- %: Percentage of the containing object's value (for example, 150%).

Which unit you choose to use is generally a matter of convenience. Point sizes are commonly used for fonts, pixel units for the size and position of layers or other objects, and so on.

Creating a Simple Style Sheet

As an example of CSS, you can now create a Web page that uses a wide variety of styles:

- For the entire body, the text is blue.
- Paragraphs are centered and have a wide margin on either side.
- Level 1, 2, and 3 headings are red.
- Bullet lists are boldface and green by default.

The following is the CSS style sheet to define these properties, using the <style> tags:

```
<style type="text/css">
BODY {color: blue}
P {text-align: center;
   margin-left:20%;
   margin-right:20%}
H1, H2, H3 {color: red}
UL {color: green;
    font-weight: bold}
</style>
```

Here's a rundown of how this style sheet works:

- The <style> tags enclose the style sheet.
- The BODY section sets body's default text color to blue.
- The P section defines the style for paragraphs.
- The H1, H2, H3 section defines the style for header tags.
- The UL section defines a style for bullet lists.

To show how this style sheet works, Listing 18.1 shows a document that includes this style sheet and a few examples of overriding styles for particular elements. Figure 18.1 shows Internet Explorer's display of this example.

LISTING 18.1   An example of a document using CSS style sheets

```
<html>
<head><title>Style Sheet Example</title>
<style type="text/css">
BODY {color: blue}
P {text-align: center;
   margin-left:20%;
   margin-right:20%}
H1, H2, H3 {color: red}
UL {color: green;
   font-weight: bold}
</style>
</head>
<body>
<h1>Welcome to this page</h1>
<p>The above heading is red, since we specified that H1-H3 headers
are red. This paragraph is blue, which is the default color for
the entire body. It's also centered and has 20% margins, which we
specified as the default for paragraphs.
</p>
<p STYLE="color:black">This paragraph has black text, because it overrides
the default color in the paragraph tag. We didn't override the centering,
so this paragraph is also centered.</p>
<ul>
<li>This is a bullet list.
<li>It's green and bold, because we specified those defaults for bullet lists.
<li STYLE="color:red">This item is red, overriding the default.
<li>This item is back to normal.
</ul>
<p>This is another paragraph with the default paragraph style.</p>
</body>
</html>
```

18

Remember that you can download the code for this listing from this book's Web site: http://www.jsworkshop.com/.

FIGURE 18.1.

The style sheet example as displayed by Internet Explorer.

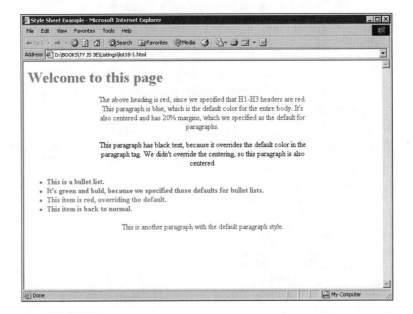

Using External Style Sheets

The preceding example only changes a few aspects of the HTML document's appearance, but it adds about 10 lines to its length. If you were trying to make a very stylish page and had defined new styles for all of the attributes, you would end up with a very long and complicated document.

For this reason, you can use a CSS style sheet from a separate file in your document. This makes your document short and to the point. More importantly, it allows you to define a single style sheet and use it to control the appearance of all of the pages on your site.

To define an external style sheet, place the commands you would normally use between the <style> tags in a separate file. You can then refer to that file using the <link> tag in the header of one or more documents:

```
<link REL=STYLESHEET TYPE="text/css" HREF="style.css">
```

This tag refers to an external CSS style sheet stored in the style.css file.

Creating External `.css` Files

Once you've linked to an external `.css` file, you need to create the file itself. The external style sheet is a simple text file that you can create with the same editor you use for HTML documents.

The `.css` file should contain a list of CSS rules, in the same format you would use between `<style>` tags. However, the file should not include `<style>` tags or any other HTML tags. Here is what the styles from the previous example would look like as an external style sheet:

```
BODY {color: blue}
P {text-align: center;
   margin-left:20%;
   margin-right:20%}
H1, H2, H3 {color: red}
UL {color: green;
   font-weight: bold}
```

Controlling Styles with JavaScript

The new W3C DOM (Document Object Model) makes it easy for JavaScript applications to control the styles on a page. Whether you use style sheets or not, you can use JavaScript to modify the style of any element on a page.

As you learned in Hour 9, "Working with the Document Object Model," the DOM allows you to access the entire HTML document and all of its elements as scriptable objects. You can change any object's style by modifying its `style` object values.

The names and values of objects under the `style` object are the same as you've learned in this Hour. For example, you can change an element's color by modifying its `style.color` attribute:

```
element.style.color="blue";
```

Here, `element` represents the object for an element. There are many ways of finding an element's corresponding object, which you will learn about in detail in Hour 19, "Using Dynamic HTML (DHTML)."

In the meantime, an easy way to find an element's object is to assign an identifier to it with the `ID` attribute. The following statement creates an `<h1>` element with the identifier `"head1"`:

```
<h1 ID = "head1">This is a heading</h1>
```

18

Now that you've assigned an identifier, you can use the `getElementById` method to find the DOM object for the element:

```
element = document.getElementById("head1");
```

You can also use a shortcut to set styles and avoid the use of a variable by directly working with the `getElementbyId` method:

```
document.getElementById("head1").style.color="blue";
```

This statement combines the examples above by directly assigning the blue color style to the `head1` element of the page. You'll use this technique to create a dynamic page in the Workshop section.

Workshop: Creating Dynamic Styles

Using the DOM style objects, you can create a page that allows you to directly control the colors used in the page's text. To begin with, you will need a form with which to select colors. The following is a basic form using `<select>` tags to define options for head and body colors:

```
<FORM NAME="form1">
<B>Heading color: </B>
<select name="heading" onChange="changehead();">
    <option value="black">Black</option>
    <option value="red">Red</option>
    <option value="blue">Blue</option>
    <option value="green">Green</option>
    <option value="yellow">Yellow</option>
</select>
<br>
<B>Body text color: </B>
<select name="body" onChange="changebody();">
    <option value="black">Black</option>
    <option value="red">Red</option>
    <option value="blue">Blue</option>
    <option value="green">Green</option>
    <option value="yellow">Yellow</option>
</select>
</FORM>
```

If you are unsure of the syntax used in forms, you might want to review Hour 12, "Getting Data with Forms."

Notice that this form uses onChange attributes in the <select> tags to call two functions, changehead and changebody, when their respective selection changes. Next, you will need to create these functions. The following script defines the style changing functions:

```
<script language="Javascript" type="text/javascript">
function changehead() {
  i = document.form1.heading.selectedIndex;
  headcolor = document.form1.heading.options[i].value;
  document.getElementById("head1").style.color = headcolor;
}
function changebody() {
  i = document.form1.body.selectedIndex;
  doccolor = document.form1.body.options[i].value;
  document.getElementById("p1").style.color = doccolor;
}
</script>
```

This script first defines the changehead function. This reads the index for the currently selected heading color, then reads the color value for the index. This function uses the getElementById method described in the previous section to change the color. The changebody function uses the same syntax to change the body color.

Last but not least, you will need some basic HTML, including a heading and some body text to be changed by the functions. Listing 18.2 shows the complete HTML document, including the script and form you created earlier.

LISTING 18.2   The complete dynamic styles example

```
<HTML>
<HEAD>
<TITLE>Controlling Styles with JavaScript</TITLE>
<script language="Javascript" type="text/javascript">
function changehead() {
  i = document.form1.heading.selectedIndex;
  headcolor = document.form1.heading.options[i].value;
  document.getElementById("head1").style.color = headcolor;
}
function changebody() {
  i = document.form1.body.selectedIndex;
  doccolor = document.form1.body.options[i].value;
  document.getElementById("p1").style.color = doccolor;
}
</script>
</HEAD>
```

18

LISTING 18.2   Continued

```
<BODY>
<h1 ID="head1">
Controlling Styles with JavaScript</h1>
<hr>
<p ID="p1">
Select the color for paragraphs and headings using the form below.
The colors you specified will be dynamically changed in this document.
The change occurs as soon as you change the value of either of the
drop-down lists in the form.
</p>
<FORM NAME="form1">
<B>Heading color: </B>
<select name="heading" onChange="changehead();">
   <option value="black">Black</option>
   <option value="red">Red</option>
   <option value="blue">Blue</option>
   <option value="green">Green</option>
   <option value="yellow">Yellow</option>
</select>
<br>
<B>Body text color: </B>
<select name="body" onChange="changebody();">
   <option value="black">Black</option>
   <option value="red">Red</option>
   <option value="blue">Blue</option>
   <option value="green">Green</option>
   <option value="yellow">Yellow</option>
</select>
</FORM>
</BODY>
</HTML>
```

Notice that the <h1> tag has an ID attribute of "head1", and the <p> tag has an ID of
"p1". These are the values the script uses in the getElementById function.

To test the dynamic styles script, load Listing 18.2 into the browser. Select the colors,
and notice the immediate change in the heading or body of the page. Figure 18.2 shows a
typical display of this document after the colors have been changed.

FIGURE 18.2.

*The dynamic styles
example in action.*

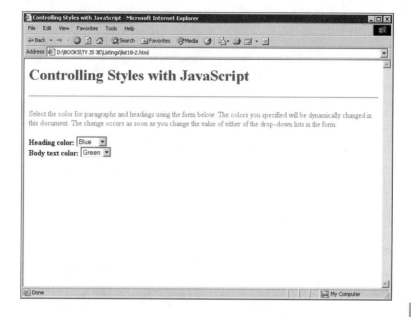

Summary

In this hour, you've used style sheets to control the appearance of Web documents. You've learned the CSS syntax for creating style sheets, and used JavaScript to control the styles of a document.

In the next hour, you will move on to Dynamic HTML (DHTML) using layers and other features of the new W3C DOM.

Q&A

Q What's the difference between changing the appearance of text with traditional tags, such as <b> and <i>, and using a style sheet?

A Functionally, there is no difference. If you're only using simple boldface, italics, and such, it's probably best to avoid style sheets. On the other hand, if you need to use more specific formatting, style sheets are ideal.

Q What happens if two style sheets affect the same text?

A The CSS specification is designed to allow style sheets to overlap, or cascade. Thus, you can specify a style for the body of the document and override it for specific elements, such as headings and paragraphs. You can even go one step further and override the style for one particular instance of an element.

Q What if users don't like the styles I use in my pages?

A This is another distinct advantage style sheets have over browser-specific tags. With the latest browsers, users will be able to choose a default style sheet of their own and override any properties they want.

Quiz

Test your knowledge of style sheets and JavaScript by answering the following questions.

Questions

1. Which of the following tags is the correct way to begin a CSS style sheet?

   a. `<style>`

   b. `<style TYPE="text/css">`

2. Why isn't the normal HTML language very good at defining layout and presentation?

   a. Because it was designed by programmers.

   b. Because magazines feared the competition.

   c. Because its main purpose is to describe document structure.

3. Which feature of new browsers allows you to use JavaScript statements to change styles?

   a. HTML 4.0

   b. The DOM

   c. CSS 2.0

Answers

1. b. You begin a CSS style sheet with the tag `<style TYPE="text/css">`.

2. c. HTML is primarily intended to describe the structure of documents.

3. b. The DOM (Document Object Model) allows you to change styles using JavaScript.

Exercises

If you want to gain more experience using style sheets, try the following exercise:

- Modify Listing 18.2 to include an <h2> tag with a subheading. Add a form element to select this tag's color, and a corresponding changeh2 function in the script.
- Now that Listing 18.2 has three different changeable elements, there is quite a bit of repetition in the script. Create a single ChangeColor function that takes a parameter for the element to change, and modify the onChange event handlers to send the appropriate element ID as a parameter to this function.

18

HOUR 19

Using Dynamic HTML (DHTML)

Throughout this book you've learned about the DOM (Document Object Model), JavaScript's way of referencing objects within Web documents. In the last hour you learned to modify style sheet properties on the fly using JavaScript.

During this hour, you'll learn more about how the DOM represents the objects that make up a Web document, and how to use DOM objects to move objects within a page. Hour 19 covers the following topics:

- How the DOM's objects are structured
- Understanding nodes, parents, children, and siblings
- Creating positionable layers
- Controlling positioning with JavaScript
- Differences between newer and older browsers
- Creating an animation using DOM objects

Understanding DOM Structure

In Hour 9, "Working with the Document Object Model," you learned about how some of the most important DOM objects are organized: The `window` object contains the `document` object, and so on. While these objects were the only ones available in older browsers, the new DOM adds objects under the `document` object for every element of a page.

To better understand this concept, let's look at the simple HTML document in Listing 19.1. This document has the usual `<head>` and `<body>` sections, a heading, and a single paragraph of text.

LISTING 19.1   A simple HTML document

```
<html>
<head>
<title>A simple HTML Document</title>
</head>
<body>
<h1>This is a Heading</h1>
<p>This is a paragraph</p>
</body>
</html>
```

Like all HTML documents, this one is composed of various *containers* and their contents. The `<html>` tags form a container that includes the entire document, the `<body>` tags contain the body of the page, and so on.

In the DOM, each container within the page and its contents are represented by an object. The objects are organized into a tree-like structure, with the `document` object itself at the root of the tree, and individual elements such as the heading and paragraph of text at the leaves of the tree. Figure 19.1 shows a diagram of these relationships.

In the following sections, you will examine the structure of the DOM more closely.

FIGURE 19.1.
How the DOM represents an HTML document.

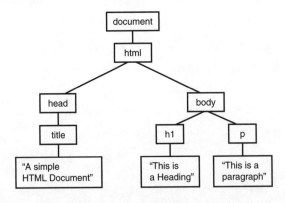

Don't worry if this tree structure confuses you; you can do almost anything by simply assigning IDs to elements and referring to them. This is the method used in the previous hour, as well as in the Workshop section of this hour. In Hour 20, "Using Advanced DOM Features," you will look at more complicated examples that require you to understand the way objects are organized in the DOM.

Nodes

Each container or element in the document is called a *node* in the DOM. In the example in Figure 19.1, each of the objects in boxes is a node, and the lines represent the relationships between the nodes.

You will often need to refer to individual nodes in scripts. You can do this by assigning an ID, or by navigating the tree using the relationships between the nodes.

Parents and Children

As you learned earlier in this book, each JavaScript object can have a *parent*—an object that contains it—and can also have *children*—objects that it contains. The DOM uses the same terminology.

In Figure 19.1, the document object is the parent object for the remaining objects, and does not have a parent itself. The html object is the parent of the head and body objects, and the h1 and p objects are children of the body object.

Text nodes work a bit differently. The actual text in the paragraph is a node in itself, and is a child of the p object. Similarly, the text within the <h1> tags is a child of the h1 object.

19

In Hour 20, you will learn methods of referring to objects by their parent and child relationships, as well as ways of adding and removing nodes from the document.

Siblings

The DOM also uses another term for organization of objects: *siblings*. As you might expect, this refers to objects that have the same parent—in other words, objects at the same level in the DOM object tree.

In Figure 19.1, the h1 and p objects are siblings: both are children of the body object. Similarly, the head and body objects are siblings under the html object.

Creating Positionable Elements

Netscape 4.0 included a <layer> tag, which defined a portion of the Web page that could be moved, shown, or hidden separately from the rest of the page. While this was proprietary, the CSS (Cascading Style Sheets) specification also includes methods of positioning elements.

Under the new DOM, you can control any element in the page. You can effectively create a layer, or a group of HTML objects that can be controlled as a group, using the <div> or <span> tags.

> The <div> and <span> tags are part of the HTML 3.0 standard. <span> defines an arbitrary section of the HTML document, and does not specify any formatting for the text it contains. <div> is similar, but includes a line break before and after its contents.

To create a layer with <div>, enclose the content of the layer between the two division tags and specify the layer's properties in the style attribute of the <div> tag. Here's a simple example:

```
<DIV ID="layer1" STYLE="position:absolute; left:100; top:100">
<p>This is the content of the layer.</p>
</DIV>
```

This code defines a layer with the name layer1. This is a moveable layer positioned 100 pixels down and 100 pixels to the right of the upper-left corner of the browser window. You'll learn more details about the layer properties in the next section.

> As with all CSS properties, you can specify the position property and other layer properties in a <style> block, in an external style sheet, or in the style attribute of an HTML tag.

Setting Object Position and Size

You can use various properties in the `style` attribute of the `<div>` tag when you define a layer to set its position, visibility, and other features. The following properties control the object's position and size:

- `position` is the main positioning attribute and can affect the properties below. The `position` property can have one of three values:
  - `static` defines items that are laid out in normal HTML fashion, and cannot be moved. This is the default.
  - `absolute` specifies that an item will be positioned using coordinates you specify.
  - `relative` defines an item that is offset a certain amount from the `static` position, where the element would normally have been laid out within the HTML page.
- `left` and `top` specify offsets for the position of the item. For absolute positioning, this is relative to the main browser window or a containing item. For relative positioning, it's relative to the usual static position.
- `right` and `bottom` are an alternate way to specify the position of the item. You can use these when you need to align the object's right or bottom edge.
- `width` and `height` are similar to the standard HTML `width` and `height` attributes and specify a width and height for the item.
- `z-index` specifies how items overlap. Normally indexes start with 1 and go up with each layer added "on top" of the page. By changing this value, you can specify which item is on top.

19

Properties such as `left` and `top` work in pixels by default. You can also use any of the units described in the previous hour: px, pt, ex, em, or percentages.

Setting Overflow Properties

Sometimes the content inside a layer is larger than the size of the layer can display. Two properties affect how the layer is displayed in this case:

- `clip` specifies the clipping rectangle for an item. Only the portion of the item inside this rectangle is displayed.

- `overflow` indicates whether the clipping rectangle cuts off the item or a scroll bar allows viewing the rest of the item. Values include `visible`, `hidden`, `scroll` to display scroll bars, `auto` to let the browser decide whether to display scroll bars, or `inherit` to use a parent object's setting.

Using Visibility Properties

Along with positioning objects, you can use CSS positioning to control whether the objects are visible at all, and how the document is formatted around them. These properties control how objects are displayed:

- `display` specifies whether an item is displayed in the browser. A value of "none" hides the object. Other values include `block` to display the object preceded and followed by line breaks, `inline` to display it without line breaks, and `list-item` to display it as part of a list.
- `visibility` specifies whether an item is visible. Values include `visible` (default), `hidden`, and `inherit`. A value of `inherit` means the item inherits the visibility of any item it appears within (such as a table or paragraph).

Setting Background and Border Properties

You can use the following properties to set the color and background image for a layer or other object and control whether borders are displayed:

- `background-color` specifies the color for the background of any text in the layer.
- `background-image` specifies a background image for any text in the layer.
- `border-width` sets the width of the border for all four sides. This can be a numeric value or the keywords `thin`, `medium`, or `thick`.
- `border-style` sets the style of border. Values include `none` (default), `dotted`, `dashed`, `solid`, `double`, `groove`, `ridge`, `inset`, or `outset`.
- `border-color` sets the color of the border. As with other color properties, this can be a named color such as `blue` or an RGB color such as `#FF03A5`.

Controlling Positioning with JavaScript

As you learned in the previous hour, you can control the style attributes for an object with the attributes of the object's `style` property. You can control the positioning attributes listed in the previous section the same way.

Suppose you have created a layer with the following <div> tags:

```
<div ID="layer1" STYLE="position:absolute; left:100; top:100">
<p>This is the content of the layer.</p>
</div>
```

To move this layer up or down within the page using JavaScript, you can change its `style.top` attribute. For example, the following statements move the layer 100 pixels down from its original position:

```
var obj = document.getElementById("layer1");
obj.style.top=200;
```

The `document.getElementById` method returns the object corresponding to the layer's <div> tag, and the second statement sets the object's `top` positioning property to 200. As you learned in the previous hour, you can also combine these two statements:

```
document.getElementById("layer1").style.top = 200;
```

This simply sets the `style.top` property for the layer without assigning a variable to the layer's object. You will use this technique to create an animation in this hour's Workshop section.

Some CSS properties, such as `text-indent` and `border-color`, have hyphens in their names. Since this would cause JavaScript errors, you combine the hyphenated sections and use a capital letter when working with them in JavaScript: `textIndent` and `borderColor`.

Dealing with Older Browsers

While the new DOM makes it easy to manipulate styles, positions, and even portions of a document themselves, you should be aware that these features are only standardized and supported in Internet Explorer 5.0 and later, and Netscape 6.0 and later.

Furthermore, since the DOM features are new, you may run into differences in the ways the browsers implement these features. You should test any DOM-dependent scripts on both the latest Netscape and Internet Explorer browsers before publishing it.

Equally importantly, you should be aware that many users are using older browsers and will be for some time. Since Netscape 4.0 and Internet Explorer 4.0 support many of these features, although in non-standard ways, you can use browser detection to support these browsers as well as newer DOM-compliant browsers.

19

You learned the techniques used in browser detection in Hour 14, "Creating Cross-Browser Scripts."

In particular, the layer positioning techniques you learned in this hour can be accomplished equally well in Netscape 4.0 or Internet Explorer 4.0. To begin with, both of these browsers support the CSS method of defining a layer with the `<div>` tag. These statements create the same layer in both 4.0 and DOM-compliant browsers:

```
<div ID="layer1" STYLE="position:absolute; left:100; top:100">
<p>This is the content of the layer.</p>
</div>
```

The difference is in the way you use JavaScript to control layer positioning. Here is the DOM method of changing the layer's top position to 200, as you learned above:

```
var obj = document.getElementById("layer1");
obj.style.top=200;
```

Internet Explorer 4.0 uses a similar syntax, but stores all objects under the `document.all` object rather than in a tree structure. Here is IE4's method of performing the same position change:

```
var obj=document.all.layer1;
obj.style.top=200;
```

Last but not least, Netscape 4.0 uses the `layers` array to store information about layer positions. Here is the Netscape 4.0 method of changing the layer's position:

```
var obj=document.layers["layer1"];
obj.top=200;
```

As you can see, the new DOM will make multiple-browser compatibility much easier when the latest browsers complete replace older ones. In the meantime, be sure to support older browsers if it's possible and practical for your pages.

Using Feature Sensing

In Hour 14, you learned how to detect the browser in use using the `navigator` object. While you could use this technique to support the 4.0 browsers for DHTML, using *feature sensing* makes your script easier to write and more compatible with future browsers.

In feature sensing, you detect whether an object or method exists rather than detecting the browser version. For example, this statement detects whether Netscape's `document.layers` object exists:

```
if (document.layers) alert ("layers!");
```

Using this technique, you can create a function that finds the correct object to manipulate regardless of the browser in use:

```
function GetStyleObject(id) {
    if (document.getElementById)
        return document.getElementById(id).style;
    else if (document.layers)
        return document.layers[id];
    else if (document.all)
        return document.all[id].style;
    else {
        alert("DHTML support not found.");
        return false;
    }
}
```

The GetStyleObject function determines whether to use getElementById for version 5-6 browsers, document.layers for Netscape 4.x, and document.all for Internet Explorer 4.x. It returns the correct parent object to use with style objects. If you add this function to a document and use it in place of the document.getElementById method, you can often make the script work in 4.x browsers.

Workshop: Creating Dynamic HTML Animation

One of the most common uses for positioning is to create animation. In Hour 13, "Using Graphics and Animation," you used JavaScript to create a simple animation. Using the DOM's positioning properties, you can animate the mouse from Hour 13 using a simpler approach.

Just to make things more fun (and because mice are still the only thing I can draw), you will animate three mice at a time using dynamic HTML. Using this technique for the animation provides smoother animation and is easier to program. Listing 19.2 shows the dynamic HTML animation script.

19

LISTING 19.2   The dynamic HTML animation script

```
<html>
<head>
<title>Animation with Dynamic HTML</title>
<script LANGUAGE="JavaScript" type="text/javascript">
var pos1=-95;
var pos2=-95;
var pos3=-95;
```

LISTING 19.2 Continued

```
var speed1 = Math.floor(Math.random()*10)+2;
var speed2 = Math.floor(Math.random()*10)+2;
var speed3 = Math.floor(Math.random()*10)+2;
function next() {
    pos1 += speed1;
    pos2 += speed2;
    pos3 += speed3;
    if (pos1 > 795) pos1 = -95;
    if (pos2 > 795) pos2 = -95;
    if (pos3 > 795) pos3 = -95;
    document.getElementById("mouse1").style.left = pos1;
    document.getElementById("mouse2").style.left = pos2;
    document.getElementById("mouse3").style.left = pos3;
    window.setTimeout("next();",10);
}
</script>
</head>
<body onLoad="next();">
<h1>Animation with Dynamic HTML</h1>
<hr>
<div ID="mouse1" STYLE="position:absolute; left:0; top:100;
width:100; height:100; visibility:show">
<img src="mouse5.gif" width=100 height=100 alt="" border="0">
</div>
<div ID="mouse2" STYLE="position:absolute; left:0; top:200;
width:100; height:100; visibility:show">
<img src="mouse5.gif" width=100 height=100 alt="" border="0">
</div>
<div ID="mouse3" STYLE="position:absolute; left:0; top:300;
width:100; height:100; visibility:show">
<img src="mouse5.gif" width=100 height=100 alt="" border="0">
</div>
</body>
</html>
```

As usual, to test this script, load the HTML document into a browser. Remember, since this example uses the new DOM features, it requires Internet Explorer 5.0 or later or Netscape 6.0 or later. Netscape 6's display of the example is shown in Figure 19.2.

 Don't forget that the mouse graphics used in this example, along with the example code itself, are available on this book's Web site: http://www.jsworkshop.com/.

FIGURE 19.2

*Netscape 6 displays
the animation
example.*

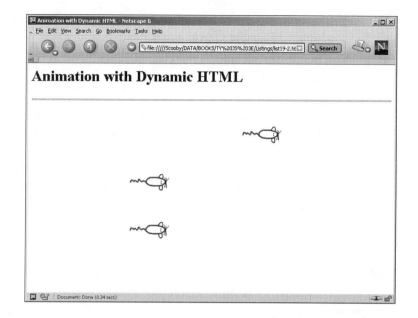

Summary

In this hour, you learned how the W3C DOM (Document Object Model) represents objects within a Web page, and how to use these objects to control the position of elements within a page.

In the next hour, you will move on to advanced features of the DOM, including the properties and methods you can use to navigate the DOM object tree, add elements, and modify text within a page.

19

Q&A

Q What happens when my Web page includes multiple HTML documents, such as when frames are used?

A In this case, each window or frame has its own document object that stores the elements of the HTML document it contains.

Q I created a page that uses browser detection to use DOM features on 5.0 or 6.0 browsers only, but it does not work in Internet Explorer 5.0. What could cause this?

A Remember, Internet Explorer 5.0's version number is listed as "4.0," for reasons only Microsoft understands. See Hour 14 for a consistent way of detecting 5.0 and 6.0 browsers, or use feature sensing as described in this hour.

Q **If the new DOM allows any object to be dynamically changed, why does the animation example need to use the `<div>` tags around the image?**

A Actually, you can animate the `<img>` tag directly rather than using the `<div>` tag. In the example, I used `<div>` to make it easier to support older browsers (see the Exercises section).

Q **The new DOM makes cross-browser scripting easy, but what's to stop version 7.0 of Netscape or Internet Explorer from changing everything again and breaking my scripts?**

A There's no guarantee that things won't change, of course—but the W3C DOM is designed to accommodate future versions of HTML and XML, and both Netscape and Microsoft have committed to supporting it. With any luck, cross-browser scripting will continue to get easier.

Quiz

Test your knowledge of the W3C Document Object Model (DOM) by answering the following questions.

Questions

1. Which of the following tags is used to create a cross-browser layer?

   a. `<layer>`

   b. `<div>`

   c. `<style>`

2. Which attribute controls an element's left-to-right position?

   a. `left`

   b. `width`

   c. `lrpos`

3. Which object is supported by Internet Explorer 4.0 and later but is not part of the W3C DOM?

   a. `document`

   b. `layer`

   c. `document.all`

Answers

1. b. The `<div>` tag can be used to create cross-browser layers.

2. a. The `left` attribute controls an element's left-to-right position.

3. c. The `document.all` object is supported by Internet Explorer 4.0 and later, but not by the W3C DOM.

Exercises

If you want to gain more experience using positionable elements with JavaScript, try these exercises:

- Modify Listing 19.2 to make one of the mice run the race from right to left instead of left to right. (For the full effect, use a reversed version of the graphic.)

- Modify Listing 19.2 to make the animation work in Netscape 4.x and Internet Explorer 4.x as well as newer browsers. You can use the `GetStyleObject` function introduced in this hour.

19

Hour **20**

Using Advanced DOM Features

In the last hour, you learned about the tree-like structure of the DOM (Document Object Model) and how its nodes represent the HTML that makes up a Web document. You also learned how to use DOM positioning attributes to animate an object.

During this hour, you will take a closer look at the objects in the DOM, and the properties and methods you can use to control them. You will also explore several examples of dynamic HTML pages using these DOM features. Hour 20 covers the following topics:

- Using the properties of DOM nodes
- Understanding DOM node methods
- Hiding and showing objects within a page
- Modifying text within a page
- Adding text to a page
- Creating a DOM-based scrolling message

Working with DOM Nodes

As you learned in Hour 19, "Using Dynamic HTML (DHTML)," the DOM organizes objects within a Web page into a tree-like structure. Each node (object) in this tree can be accessed in JavaScript. In the next sections you will learn how you can use the properties and methods of nodes to manage them.

 The sections below only describe the most important properties and methods of nodes, and those that are supported by current browsers. For a complete list of available properties, see the W3C's DOM specification at http://www.w3.org/TR/DOM-Level-2/.

Basic Node Properties

You have already used the style property of nodes to change their stylesheet values. Each node also has a number of basic properties that you can examine or set. These include the following:

- nodeName is the name of the node (not the ID). For nodes based on HTML tags, such as <p> or <body>, the name is the tag name: P or BODY. For the document node, the name is a special code: #document. Similarly, text nodes have the name #text.

- nodeType is an integer describing the node's type: 1 for normal HTML tags, 3 for text nodes, and 9 for the document node.

- nodeValue is the actual text contained within a text node.

- innerHTML is the HTML content of any node. You can assign a value including HTML tags to this property and change the DOM child objects for a node dynamically.

Node Relationship Properties

In addition to the basic properties described above, each node has a number of properties that describe its relation to other nodes. These include the following:

- firstChild is the first child object for a node. For nodes that contain text, such as h1 or p, the text node containing the actual text is the first child.

- lastChild is the node's last child object.

- childNodes is an array that includes all of a node's child nodes. You can use a loop with this array to work with all the nodes under a given node.

- previousSibling is the sibling (node at the same level) previous to the current node.

- nextSibling is the sibling after the current node.

 Remember that, like all JavaScript objects and properties, the node properties and functions described here are case-sensitive. Be sure you type them exactly as shown.

Document Methods

The document node itself has several methods you may find useful. You have already used one of these, getElementById, to refer to DOM objects by their ID properties. The document node's methods include the following:

- getElementById(*ID*) returns the element with the specified ID attribute.

- getElementsByTagName(*tag*) returns an array of all of the elements with a specified tag name. You can use the wildcard "*" to return an array containing all the nodes in the document.

- createTextNode(*text*) creates a new text node containing the specified text, which you can then add to the document.

- createElement(*tag*) creates a new HTML element for the specified tag. As with createTextNode, you need to add the element to the document after creating it. You can assign content within the element by changing its child objects or the innerHTML property.

Node Methods

Each node within a page has a number of methods available. Which of these are valid depends on the node's position in the page, and whether it has parent or child nodes. These include the following:

- appendChild(*new*) appends the specified new node after all of the object's existing nodes.

- insertBefore(*new,old*) inserts the specified new child node before the specified old child node, which must already exist.

- replaceChild(*new,old*) replaces the specified old child node with a new node.

- removeChild(*old*) removes a child node from the object's set of children.

20

- `hasChildNodes()` returns a boolean value of `true` if the object has one or more child nodes, or `false` if it has none.
- `cloneNode()` creates a copy of an existing node. If a parameter of `true` is supplied, the copy will also include any child nodes of the original node.

Hiding and Showing Objects

We will now move on to a number of real-world examples using the DOM objects to manipulate Web pages. As a simple example, you can create a script that hides or shows objects within a page.

As you learned in Hour 18, "Working with Style Sheets," objects have a `visibility` style property that specifies whether they are currently visible within the page:

```
Object.style.visibility="hidden"; // hides an object
Object.style.visibility="visible"; // shows an object
```

Using this property, you can create a script that hides or shows objects in either browser. Listing 20.1 shows the HTML document for a script that allows two headings to be shown or hidden.

LISTING 20.1   Hiding and Showing Objects

```html
<html>
<head>
<title>Hiding and Showing Objects</title>
<script language="Javascript" type="text/javascript">
function ShowHide() {
    var head1 = document.getElementById("head1");
    var head2 = document.getElementById("head2");
    var showhead1 = document.form1.head1.checked;
    var showhead2 = document.form1.head2.checked;
    head1.style.visibility=(showhead1) ? "visible" : "hidden";
    head2.style.visibility=(showhead2) ? "visible" : "hidden";
}
</script>
</head>
<body>
<h1 ID="head1">This is the first heading</h1>
<h1 ID="head2">This is the second heading</h1>
<p>Using the W3C DOM, you can choose
whether to show or hide the headings on
this page using the checkboxes below.</p>
<form name="form1">
```

LISTING 20.1 Continued

```
<input type="checkbox" name="head1"
   checked onClick="ShowHide();">
<b>Show first heading</b><br>
<input type="checkbox" name="head2"
   checked onClick="ShowHide();">
<b>Show second heading</b><br>
</form>
</body>
</html>
```

Remember, the examples in this hour use the new DOM, and thus require Netscape 6.0 or later, or Internet Explorer 5.0 or later. All of this hour's examples will work with either of these browsers. Online versions are available on this book's Web site: http://www.jsworkshop.com/.

The <h1> tags in this document define headings with the identifiers head1 and head2. The <form> section defines a form with two check boxes, one for each of the headings. When a check box is modified, the onClick method is used to call the ShowHide function.

This function is defined within the <script> statements in the header. The function assigns the head1 and head2 variables to the objects for the headings, using the getElementById method. Next, it assigns the showhead1 and showhead2 variables to the contents of the check boxes. Finally, the function uses the style.visibility attributes to set the visibility of the headings.

The lines that set the visibility property may look a bit strange. The ? and : characters create *conditional expressions*, a shorthand way of handling if statements. To review conditional expressions, see Hour 6, "Testing and Comparing Values."

20

Figure 20.1 shows this example in action in Internet Explorer 6. In the figure, the second heading's check box has been unchecked, so only the first heading is visible.

FIGURE 20.1

*The text hiding/show-
ing example in Internet
Explorer.*

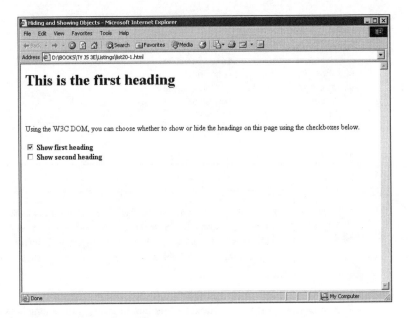

Modifying Text within a Page

Next, you can create a simple script to modify the contents of a heading within a Web page. As you learned earlier this hour, the nodeValue property of a text node contains its actual text, and the text node for a heading is a child of that heading. Thus, the syntax to change the text of a heading with the identifier head1 would be:

```
Var head1=document.getElementById("head1");
Head1.firstChild.nodeValue="New Text Here";
```

This assigns the variable head1 to the heading's object. The firstChild property returns the text node that is the only child of the heading, and its nodeValue property contains the heading text.

Using this technique, it's easy to create a page that allows the heading to be changed dynamically. Listing 20.2 shows the complete HTML document for this script.

LISTING 20.2   The Complete Text-Modifying Example

```
<html>
<head>
<title>Dynamic Text in JavaScript</title>
<script language="Javascript" type="text/javascript">
function ChangeTitle() {
    var newtitle = document.form1.newtitle.value;
    var head1 = document.getElementById("head1");
```

LISTING 20.2 Continued

```
      head1.firstChild.nodeValue=newtitle;
}
</script>
</head>
<body>
<h1 ID="head1">Dynamic Text in JavaScript</h1>
<p>Using the W3C DOM, you can dynamically
change the heading at the top of this
page. Enter a new title and click the
Change button.</p>
<form name="form1">
<input type="text" name="newtitle" size="25">
<input type="button" value="Change!"
  onClick="ChangeTitle();">
</form>
</body>
</html>
```

This example defines a form that allows the user to enter a new heading for the page. Pressing the button calls the ChangeTitle function, defined in the header. This function gets the value the user entered in the form, and changes the heading's value to the new text.

Figure 20.2 shows this page in action in Internet Explorer 6, after a new title has been entered and the Change button has been clicked.

FIGURE 20.2

The heading-changing example in action.

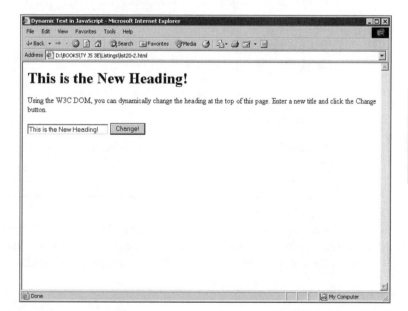

20

Adding Text to a Page

Next, you can create a script that actually adds text to a page. To do this, you must first create a new text node. This statement creates a new text node with the text "this is a test":

```
var node=document.createTextNode("this is a test");
```

Next, you can add this node to the document. To do this, you use the appendChild method. The text can be added to any element that can contain text, but we will use a paragraph. The following statement adds the text node defined above to the paragraph with the identifier p1:

```
document.getElementById("p1").appendChild(node);
```

Listing 20.3 shows the HTML document for a complete example that uses this technique, using a form to allow the user to specify text to add to the page.

LISTING 20.3   Adding Text to a Page

```
<html>
<head>
<title>Adding to a page</title>
<script language="Javascript" type="text/javascript">
function AddText() {
   var sentence=document.form1.sentence.value;
   var node=document.createTextNode(" " + sentence);
   document.getElementById("p1").appendChild(node);
}
</script>
</head>
<body>
<h1>Create Your Own Content</h1>
<p ID="p1">Using the W3C DOM, you can dynamically
add sentences to this paragraph. Type a sentence
and click the Add button.</p>
<form name="form1">
<input type="text" name="sentence" size="65">
<input type="button" value="Add" onClick="AddText();">
</form>
</body>
</html>
```

In this example, the <p> section defines the paragraph that will hold the added text. The <form> section defines a form with a text field called sentence and an add button, which calls the AddText function. This function is defined in the header.

The AddText function first assigns the sentence variable to the text typed in the text field. Next, it creates a new text node containing the sentence, and appends the new text node to the paragraph.

Load this document into a browser to test it, and try adding several sentences by typing them and clicking the Add button. Figure 20.3 shows Netscape 6's display of this document after several sentences have been added to the paragraph.

FIGURE 20.3

Netscape 6 shows the text-adding example.

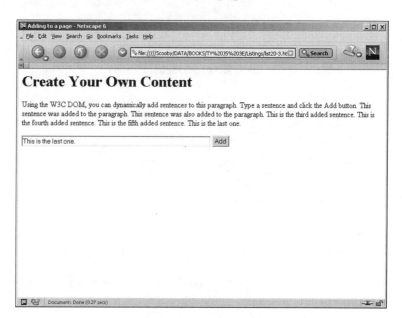

Workshop: A Better Scrolling Message

In Hour 5, "Using Strings and Arrays," you created a script that scrolls a message across the browser's status line. Using the DOM objects, you can create a better scrolling message—one that scrolls within the Web page itself.

To do this, you can start with the scrolling message example from Hour 5. Instead of assigning the message to the window.status variable, you can display it in a text node within the page. Listing 20.4 shows the complete HTML document for this example.

LISTING 20.4 The New Scrolling Message Example

```
<html>
<head>
<title>Scrolling Message Example</title>
```

20

LISTING 20.4　Continued

```
<script language="JavaScript" type="text/javascript">
msg = "This is an example of a scrolling message ";
msg += "that appears in the body of the page. ";
msg = "......." + msg;
pos = 0;
function ScrollMessage() {
    var newtext = msg.substring(pos, msg.length) + msg.substring(0, pos);
    var td = document.getElementById("scroll");
    td.firstChild.nodeValue = newtext;
    pos++;
    if (pos > msg.length) pos = 0;
    window.setTimeout("ScrollMessage()",150);
}
</script>
</head>
<body onLoad="ScrollMessage();">
<h1>A Better Scrolling Message</h1>
<p>Rather than using the status line, this page uses
the DOM to scroll a message within the small table below.</p>
<table width="90%" border>
<tr>
<td ID="scroll" width="90%"> The scrolling message goes here.</td>
</tr>
</table>
</body>
```

In this example, the <table> section defines a simple table to contain the scrolling message. The <td> tag has an identifier of scroll, and will be the actual container for the scrolling text.

The <script> section in the header initializes the variables for this script, and the ScrollMessage function performs the actual scrolling. This function is first called by the document's onLoad method.

The first two lines of the ScrollMessage function scroll the message within the newtext string. Next, the function assigns the td variable to the table cell where the scrolling will happen using getElementById, and sets the cell's text node value to the new version of the message.

Finally, the pos counter is updated for the current scroll position, and the setTimeout method is used to call the ScrollMessage function again after a short delay. Figure 20.4 shows this example in action in Netscape 6.

This example uses a table to form a frame around the scrolling message. You could actually scroll the message in any text element, such as a heading or a paragraph.

FIGURE 20.4

The new scrolling message, as displayed by Netscape 6.

Summary

In this hour, you learned some of the advanced features of the new W3C DOM (Document Object Model). You learned the functions and properties you can use to manage DOM objects, and used example scripts to hide and show elements within a page, modify text, and add text. Finally, you created a scrolling message using DOM features.

Congratulations—you've reached the end of Part V! Now that you've learned all about JavaScript and DHTML, the final hours will allow you to use this knowledge to create some complete examples. You'll begin in Hour 21 with a JavaScript-enhanced Web page.

20

Q&A

Q **Can I avoid assigning an ID attribute to every DOM object I want to handle with a script?**

A Yes. While the scripts in this hour typically use the ID attribute for convenience, you can actually locate any object in the page by using combinations of node properties such as firstChild and nextSibling.

Q **Can I include HTML tags, such as <b>, in the new text I assign to a text node?**

A Text nodes are limited to text if you use the nodeValue attribute. However, the innerHTML property does not have this limitation and can be used to insert any HTML.

Q **Is there a reference that specifies which DOM properties and methods work in which browser versions?**

A Yes, several Web sites are available that keep up-to-date lists of browser features. Some of these are listed in Appendix A, "Other JavaScript Resources."

Quiz

Test your knowledge of JavaScript's advanced DOM features by answering the following questions.

Questions

1. If para1 is the DOM object for a paragraph, what is the correct syntax to change the text within the paragraph to "New Text"?

   a. `para1.value="New Text";`

   b. `para1.firstChild.nodeValue="New Text";`

   c. `para1.nodeValue="New Text";`

2. Which of the following DOM objects never has a parent node?

   a. `body`

   b. `div`

   c. `document`

3. Which of the following is the correct syntax to get the DOM object for a heading with the identifier head1?

   a. `document.getElementById("head1")`

   b. `document.GetElementByID("head1")`

   c. `document.getElementsById("head1")`

Answers

1. b. The actual text is the nodeValue attribute of the text node, which is a child of the paragraph node.

2. c. The document object is the root of the DOM object tree, and has no parent object.

3. a. getElementById has a lowercase "g" at the beginning, and a lowercase "d" at the end, contrary to what you might know about normal English grammar.

Exercises

If you want to gain more experience using the DOM in JavaScript, try these exercises:

- Add a third check box to Listing 20.1 to allow the paragraph of text to be shown or hidden. You will need to add an ID attribute to the <p> tag, add a check box to the form, and add the appropriate lines to the script.

- Modify Listing 20.3 to add the entered text at the beginning of the paragraph instead of the end. You will need to replace the appendChild method with the insertBefore method.

- Modify Listing 20.4 to scroll a short message in the heading of the page instead of in the table.

20

PART VI

Putting It All Together

Hour

Hour **21**

Improving a Web Page with JavaScript

You should now know quite a bit about JavaScript's features and how to write and debug JavaScript programs. In the next three hours of this book, you will apply this knowledge by creating some complete applications.

This hour, you will start with a simple application: an ordinary Web page with a few JavaScript features to make it friendlier and easier to navigate. Hour 21 covers the following topics:

- Creating a basic HTML document
- Adding a drop-down navigation bar
- Adding status-line descriptions for links
- Adding graphic links and rollovers
- Combining these features into a complete Web page

Creating the HTML Document

For this example, you'll start with the Web page of a small (and hopeless) software company known as Fictional Software Company (FSC). Their Web page is rather unimpressive, but you've got to start somewhere.

The main FSC Web page is shown in Figure 21.1. It includes a logo at the top, three paragraphs of information, and a simple bulleted list of links to the various subpages. This page is defined using the HTML in Listing 21.1.

FIGURE 21.1

A simple Web page using only HTML.

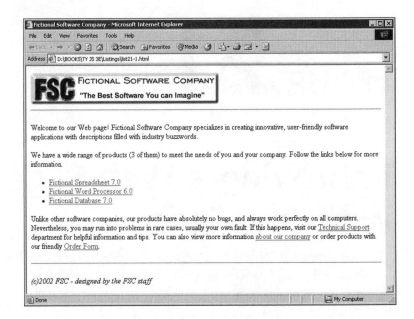

LISTING 21.1   The HTML Document for the Initial FSC Web Page

```
<html>
<head><title>Fictional Software Company</title></head>
<body>
<img SRC="fsclogo.gif" alt="Fictional Software Company">
<hr>
<p>Welcome to our Web page! Fictional Software Company
specializes in creating innovative, user-friendly software
applications with descriptions filled with industry
buzzwords.</p>
<p>We have a wide range of products (3 of them) to meet
the needs of you and your company. Follow the links
below for more information.
</p>
```

LISTING 21.1 Continued

```
<ul>
<li><a HREF="spread.html">Fictional Spreadsheet 7.0</a>
<li><a HREF="word.html">Fictional Word Processor 6.0</a>
<li><a HREF="data.html">Fictional Database 7.0</a>
</ul>
<p>
Unlike other software companies, our products have
absolutely no bugs, and always work perfectly on all
computers. Nevertheless, you may run into problems in
rare cases, usually your own fault. If this happens,
visit our <a HREF="support.html">Technical Support</a>
department for helpful information and tips. You can
also view more information <a HREF="company.html">about
our company</a> or order products with our friendly
<a href="order.html">Order Form</a>.</p>
<hr>
<p><i>(c)2002 FSC - designed by the FSC staff</i></p>
</body>
</html>
```

The various links on the page send you to the company's other pages. One describes all of the company's products, another contains information about the company, and another gives technical support information. There's also a link to an order form.

Using Drop-Down Lists for Navigation

More recently, FSC decided to add more detailed information to its pages. The main page remains the same, but each product's page is now a menu of links to subpages with various categories of information.

As it is, the pages can be difficult to navigate. For example, if you want to view the system requirements for the Fictional Word Processor product, you must select the product name from the main page, wait for the page to load, and then select the System Requirements link.

With JavaScript, you can create a friendly interface to all the pages on the main page without taking up much space. Let's use one drop-down list to choose a product and another drop-down list to choose the type of information to view about the product.

Naming the Pages

In writing a program, the programming isn't always the hardest part. You should define the task the program will perform and the data it will use in advance, simplifying the actual task of writing the program.

21

To make programming the navigation bar easier, choose simple, meaningful names for the subpages. Construct their names based on the value of the selection lists. Assign a one-letter code to each product: w for the word processor, s for the spreadsheet, and d for the database. Then follow that with an underscore and a word indicating the type of information.

Here are the categories of information and their corresponding codes:

- tech—Technical support for the product
- sales—Sales and availability information
- feat—A list of features
- price—Pricing information for the product
- tips—Tips for getting the most out of the product

For example, s_feat.html is the features list for the spreadsheet program. Meaningful names like this make it easier to maintain HTML pages. When you're automating with JavaScript, they can make a big difference.

To try this example yourself, you'll need all the individual HTML files. You can download them from this book's Web site at http://www.jsworkshop.com/.

Creating the Data Structures and HTML

Before you write the function to navigate the pages, you need to store the needed data. In this case, you need to store the three codes for the software products and the five codes for the types of pages. You could create an array for each list, but that isn't necessary in this case.

Rather than creating an array, you can simply place the information in the HTML page itself and it will be stored in the properties of the form object by the JavaScript interpreter. You will use the codes as the VALUE attribute of each option.

You will need to define an HTML selection list for each of the lists of information. In addition, the user needs a way to visit the page after selecting it. You can do this with a Go button next to the drop-down lists.

The following shows the HTML to add to the main page. You'll include it toward the end of the page, but it's generally self-contained and could be placed anywhere:

```
<form name="navform">
<select name="program">
<option VALUE="x" SELECTED>Select a Product
<option VALUE="w">Fictional Word Processor
<option VALUE="s">Fictional Spreadsheet
<option VALUE="d">Fictional Database
</select>
<select name="category">
<option VALUE="x" SELECTED>Select a Category
<option VALUE="tech">Technical Support
<option VALUE="sales">Sales and Availability
<option VALUE="feat">List of Features
<option VALUE="price">Pricing Information
<option VALUE="tips">Tips and Techniques
</select>
<input TYPE="button" NAME="go" VALUE="Go to Page"
onClick="Navigate();">
</form>
```

In addition to the categories discussed, there's an additional option with the value x in each selection list. These are the default options and display instructions until another selection is made. Selecting the Go button while one of these options is selected does nothing.

Creating the Function for the Navigation Bar

You defined an onClick event handler for the Go button, which calls the Navigate() function. Next, you need to create this function. It will read the current value of both selection lists, construct a filename, and then load that file into the browser.

The following is the definition for the Navigate function. Next you will look at the features of this function in detail.

```
function Navigate() {
    prod = document.navform.program.selectedIndex;
    cat = document.navform.category.selectedIndex;
    prodval = document.navform.program.options[prod].value;
    catval = document.navform.category.options[cat].value;
    if (prodval == "x" || catval == "x")
        alert("Select a product and category.");
    else window.location = prodval + "_" + catval + ".html";
}
```

To begin, this function sets two variables—prod and cat —to hold the currently selected index for each selection list. Next, prodval and catval are assigned to the corresponding value properties.

21

The if statement checks both lists for the x value, meaning that the user hasn't yet selected an item. If no value has been selected in either list, it displays an alert message reminding the user to select both.

Finally, the new document filename is constructed by concatenating the two codes, the underscore (_), and the html suffix. This value is assigned to the window.location property, which causes the new page to be loaded.

> Because changing the location property loads the new document, you can't do anything more in the current JavaScript program. In fact, the Navigate function never returns. However, you could include JavaScript functions on the next page.

Adding Link Descriptions

Some users will undoubtedly prefer traditional hyperlinks to the navigation bar. To make these links more friendly, you can display descriptions of them on the status line when the user moves the mouse pointer over them.

You can accomplish this easily with onMouseOver event handlers. When the user moves the mouse over a link, this event will call a function to display the appropriate message on the status line. For example, the following HTML defines a link with a friendly status line:

```
<a HREF="order.html"
onMouseOver="window.status='Allows you to order products';return true;"
onMouseOut="window.status='';">
Order form</a>
```

This sets the value of window.status to display the message. In addition, the true value is returned; this is necessary to override the normal action (displaying the URL) for the status line. The onMouseOut event handler clears the status line when the mouse pointer moves off the link.

> You learned the basics of window objects, including the window.status object, in Hour 9, "Working with the Document Object Model." Event handlers are described in Hour 10, "Responding to Events."

The following shows the result of adding onMouseOver functions to the links in the original version of the FSC Software page. The page is shown in action in Figure 21.2, with the mouse pointer currently over the Spreadsheet link.

```
<ul>
<li><a HREF="spread.html"
onMouseOver="window.status='Spreadsheet Information';return true;"
onMouseOut="window.status='';">
Fictional Spreadsheet 7.0</a>
<li><a HREF="word.html"
onMouseOver="window.status='Word Processor Info';return true;"
 onMouseOut="window.status='';">
Fictional Word Processor 6.0</a>
 <li><a HREF="data.html"
 onMouseOver="window.status='Database Information';return true;"
  onMouseOut="window.status='';">
Fictional Database 7.0</a>
</ul>
```

FIGURE 21.2

The HTML document with link descriptions.

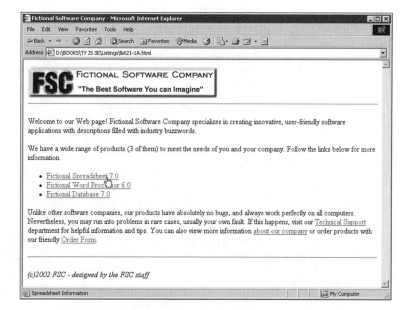

Adding Graphic Links

As an alternative to the drop-down navigation bar, you can use graphics in a navigation bar at the top of the page. You'll use rollovers to change the graphics when the mouse moves over them, as described in Hour 13, "Using Graphics and Animation."

21

Creating the Graphics

To begin creating the rollovers, you will need to create graphics for the links. For each one, you'll need a highlighted and unhighlighted version. The highlighting can be a different color, an added line or circle, or anything you want.

For this example, I've created graphics for the major links: Spreadsheet, Word Processor, Database, and Order Form. The highlighted versions are negatives of the normal graphics. For simplicity, call the standard graphics spread.gif, word.gif, data.gif, and order.gif. The highlighted versions will have an added numeral 2, as in order2.gif.

 When you're creating graphics for rollovers, remember that the highlighted and unhighlighted versions of an image must be the same size. Otherwise, the images may be distorted or may not be replaced correctly.

Creating Event Handlers

Once you've created the graphics, you simply need to add the graphic links with onMouseOver and onMouseOut event handlers. The following is the HTML for the graphics, including the event handlers:

```
<a HREF="spread.html"
    onMouseOver="document.images[1].src='spread2.gif';"
    onMouseOut ="document.images[1].src='spread.gif';">
<img BORDER=0 SRC="spread.gif" height=28 width=173></a>
<a HREF="word.html"
    onMouseOver="document.images[2].src='word2.gif';"
    onMouseOut ="document.images[2].src='word.gif';">
<img BORDER=0 SRC="word.gif" height=28 width=225></a>
<a HREF="data.html"
    onMouseOver="document.images[3].src='data2.gif';"
    onMouseOut ="document.images[3].src='data.gif';">
<img BORDER=0 SRC="data.gif" height=28 width=121></a>
<a HREF="order.html"
    onMouseOver="document.images[4].src='order2.gif';"
    onMouseOut ="document.images[4].src='order.gif';">
<img BORDER=0 SRC="order.gif" height=28 width=152></a>
```

In this case, all the code for the rollover is included in the HTML event handler, rather than in a separate function. Each link's event handlers change the source of the appropriate image when the mouse enters or exits the area.

To ensure that image rollovers work quickly and reliably, you should preload any images that are not initially displayed on the page, as described in Hour 13. The full script in the next section includes this feature.

Workshop: Finishing up the Page

Over the course of this hour, you've added three different navigational tools to the FSC Web page: ordinary links with status-line descriptions, a drop-down navigation bar, and graphic links that change when the mouse moves over them.

Each of these methods has its advantages and disadvantages. For the best of all three worlds, you can add all these features to the same Web page. Listing 21.2 is the original Web document combined with the functions for the navigation bar, rollovers, and status-line messages.

LISTING 21.2 The Complete HTML Document

```html
<html>
<head>
<title>Fictional Software Company</title>
<script LANGUAGE="JavaScript1.1" type="text/javascript1.1">
o2 = new Image();
o2.src = "order2.gif";
d2 = new Image();
d2.src = "data2.gif";
w2 = new Image();
w2.src = "word2.gif";
s2 = new Image();
s2.src = "spread2.gif";
function Navigate() {
    var prod = document.navform.program.selectedIndex;
    var cat = document.navform.category.selectedIndex;
    var prodval = document.navform.program.options[prod].value;
    var catval = document.navform.category.options[cat].value;
    if (prodval == "x" || catval == "x")
        alert("Select a product and category.");
    else window.location = prodval + "_" + catval + ".html";
}
</script>
</head>
<body>
```

21

LISTING 21.2 Continued

```
<img SRC="fsclogo.gif" alt="Fictional Software Company"
width=405 height=65>
<hr>
<a HREF="spread.html"
   onMouseOver="document.images[1].src='spread2.gif';"
   onMouseOut ="document.images[1].src='spread.gif';">
<img BORDER=0 SRC="spread.gif" height=28 width=173></a>
<a HREF="word.html"
   onMouseOver="document.images[2].src='word2.gif';"
   onMouseOut ="document.images[2].src='word.gif';">
<img BORDER=0 SRC="word.gif" height=28 width=225></a>
<a HREF="data.html"
   onMouseOver="document.images[3].src='data2.gif';"
   onMouseOut ="document.images[3].src='data.gif';">
<img BORDER=0 SRC="data.gif" height=28 width=121></a>
<a HREF="order.html"
   onMouseOver="document.images[4].src='order2.gif';"
   onMouseOut ="document.images[4].src='order.gif';">
<IMG BORDER=0 SRC="order.gif" height=28 width=152></a>
<p>Welcome to our web page! Fictional Software Company
specializes in creating innovative, user-friendly software
applications with descriptions filled with industry
buzzwords.
We have a wide range of products:
</p>
<ul>
<li><a HREF="spread.html"
onMouseOver="window.status='Spreadsheet Information';return true;"
  onMouseOut="window.status='';">
Fictional Spreadsheet 7.0</a>
<li><a HREF="word.html"
onMouseOver="window.status=' Word Processor Info';return true;"
  onMouseOut="window.status='';">
Fictional Word Processor 6.0</a>
<li><a HREF="data.html"
onMouseOver="window.status='Database Information';return true;"
  onMouseOut="window.status='';">
Fictional Database 7.0</a>
</ul>
<p>
Unlike other software companies, our products have
absolutely no bugs, and always work perfectly on all
computers. Nevertheless, you may run into problems in
rare cases, usually your own fault. If this happens,
```

LISTING 21.2 Continued

```
visit our <a HREF="support.html"
onMouseOver="window.status='Technical Support';return true;"
  onMouseOut="window.status='';">
Technical Support</a>
department for helpful information and tips. You can
also view more information <a HREF="company.html"
onMouseOver="window.status=' FSC Software Co.';return true;"
  onMouseOut="window.status='';">
about our company</a> or order products with our friendly
<a href="order.html"
onMouseOver="window.status='Order products';return true;"
  onMouseOut="window.status='';">
Order Form</a>.</p>
<form name="navform">
<select name="program">
<option VALUE="x" SELECTED>Select a Product
<option VALUE="w">Fictional Word Processor
<option VALUE="s">Fictional Spreadsheet
<option VALUE="d">Fictional Database
</select>
<select name="category">
<option VALUE="x" SELECTED>Select a Category
<option VALUE="tech">Technical Support
<option VALUE="sales">Sales and Availability
<option VALUE="feat">List of Features
<option VALUE="price">Pricing Information
<option VALUE="tips">Tips and Techniques
</select>
<input TYPE="button" NAME="go" VALUE="Go to Page"
onClick="Navigate();">
</form>
<hr>
<p><i>(c)1998 FSC - designed by the FSC staff</i></p>
</body>
</html>
```

Figure 21.3 shows this page as it appears in Netscape. Of course, on a page with this little actual content, all of these navigation features can make it look cluttered. This shouldn't be a problem if your page has more to say than this one.

21

FIGURE 21.3

The complete HTML document displayed by Netscape.

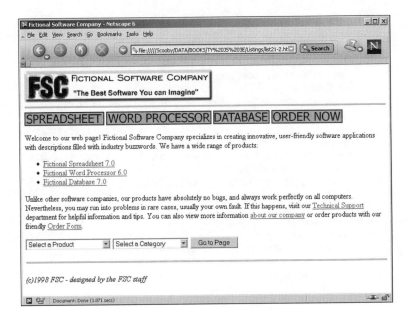

Summary

In this hour, you've used various JavaScript techniques you learned throughout this book to improve a Web page's appearance and user-friendliness.

In the next hour, you'll move on to a more complex JavaScript application: a complete game with graphics and user interaction.

Q&A

Q Is there any way to use some kind of "floating hints" or "balloon help" with links instead of using the status bar?

A Yes, you can use dynamic HTML to achieve this effect. See Hour 19, "Using Dynamic HTML (DHTML)," for information.

Q Can the navigation bar in this hour be used with browsers that don't support JavaScript?

A Yes. You could easily modify it to send the selections to a CGI script, which could send the user to the correct page. This would be slower, but would still work.

Q Can I add status-line descriptions to the graphic links along with rollovers?

A Yes. Because this would lengthen the event handlers considerably, a function would simplify things in this case.

Quiz

To test your knowledge of JavaScript's uses in improving Web pages, answer the following questions.

Questions

1. In the navigation script, what does `document.navform.category.selectedIndex` refer to?

   a. The number of the currently selected option

   b. The text of the currently selected option

   c. An index to another document

2. When creating rollovers, which HTML tag should include the `onMouseOver` event handler?

   a. `<a>`

   b. `<img>`

   c. `<moose>`

3. What's wrong with using the `onMouseOver="window.status='test';"` event handler for a link?

   a. It should include a better description of the link

   b. It doesn't return a value of `true`

   c. It should read `onMouseOut`

Answers

1. a. This refers to the number of the currently selected index.

2. a. The event handler should be included with the link tag, `<a>`. Internet Explorer and Netscape 6 support event handlers in the `<img>` tag, but earlier versions of Netscape do not.

3. b. The event handler should return a value of `true` to prevent the status line from being erased.

21

Exercises

If you want to gain more experience in improving Web pages with JavaScript, try adding one of the following to the page in Listing 21.2 and making sure it works along with the other features:

- A scrolling message (Hour 5)
- Back and Forward buttons (Hour 9)

Hour **22**

Creating a JavaScript Game

Only three more hours to go until you're done with your 24-hour tour of JavaScript. In this hour, you'll create a JavaScript-based game. This is the longest and most complex script you've dealt with so far.

Hour 22 covers the following topics:

- Creating graphics for the game
- Choosing variables to store data
- Designing the HTML document
- Creating the game program

Planning the Program

In this hour you'll create a JavaScript program that plays a game. It will be a casino-style draw poker game, although it won't cost you a penny to play. In the process you'll learn what it's like to create a complex JavaScript program, complete with graphics, user interaction, and complex calculations.

Creating Graphics

Because this is a card game, you will need graphics for each of the 52 cards in the deck. In case you're not an artist, I've made a set of cards available on this book's Web site at `http://www.jsworkshop.com/`. (When you look at them, you'll see that I'm not an artist either.)

Five cards will be displayed on the screen at the same time, so I used graphics files with a width of 106 and height of 136. This will allow the game to be played on a 640×480 monitor, and should also look good at other resolutions.

One of the main considerations in a program like this is the naming of the graphics files. Although names like `Ten of Spades.gif` are friendly to users, they would be difficult for the JavaScript interpreter to work with.

To make it easy for the script, I've named the files with the numbers 1–13 (Ace is 1; Jack, Queen, and King are 11, 12, and 13). The file names are simply this number plus a letter representing the suit (c, h, s, or d). As an example, the Jack of Clubs would be `11c.gif`.

I've also created a title graphic, a Hold button to be displayed under each dealt card, and Deal and Draw buttons to control the gameplay.

Choosing Variables

The next step in planning the script is to choose the variables that will be used. You can add variables later, but choosing them beforehand helps you plan the way the script will store data.

The variables you'll need for this game include the following:

- `score`—An integer representing the player's current score. This starts at 100. One point will be bet each time the cards are dealt, and the score will increase based on the poker hand's score.
- `dealt`—A flag that you'll use to indicate that the cards have been dealt, and the player can now hold or draw cards.

- hand—An array that stores the values of the five cards in the current hand.
- held—An array of flags that indicate whether each card should be held or discarded.
- deck—An array that stores the deck of 52 cards that will be shuffled and dealt from.

The following JavaScript code declares these global variables—it will be included in the header of the HTML document:

```
var score = 100;
var dealt = false;
var hand = new Array(6);
var held = new Array(6);
var deck = new Array(53);
```

To simplify data storage, you will next create an object that represents a card. This object will store the card's number, its suit, and a function to calculate the graphics filename to display the card. Here is the definition for the Card object:

```
// Make a filename for an image, given Card object
function fname() {
    return this.num + this.suit + ".gif";
}
// Constructor for Card objects
function Card(num,suit) {
    this.num = num;
    this.suit = suit;
    this.fname = fname;
}
```

This defines the fname function, which calculates the filename for a card, and the constructor function for the Card object. The deck and hand arrays will store a Card object for each card.

Creating the HTML Document

You should perform one more task before you do any actual scripting: design the HTML layout for the game. Listing 22.1 shows a basic layout, using an HTML table to align the cards and buttons.

LISTING 22.1 The HTML Document for the Game

```
<html>
<head>
<title>Draw Poker</title>
</head>
<body>
```

LISTING 22.1 Continued

```html
<img src="title.gif" width=381 height=81>
<hr>
<form NAME="form1">
<table>
<tr>
  <td> <img border=0 src="blank.gif" height=136 width=106>
  <td> <img border=0 src="blank.gif" height=136 width=106>
  <td> <img border=0 src="blank.gif" height=136 width=106>
  <td> <img border=0 src="blank.gif" height=136 width=106>
  <td> <img border=0 src="blank.gif" height=136 width=106>
  <td> </td>
</tr>
<tr>
  <td> <a href="#" onClick="Hold(1);">
       <img border=0 src="hold.gif" height=50 width=106></a>
  <td> <a href="#" onClick="Hold(2);">
       <img border=0 src="hold.gif" height=50 width=106></a>
  <td> <a href="#" onClick="Hold(3);">
       <img border=0 src="hold.gif" height=50 width=106></a>
  <td> <a href="#" onClick="Hold(4);">
       <img border=0 src="hold.gif" height=50 width=106></a>
  <td> <a href="#" onClick="Hold(5);">
       <img border=0 src="hold.gif" height=50 width=106></a>
</tr>
<tr>
  <td> <B>Total<BR>Score:</B>
       <input TYPE="TEXT" SIZE=6 NAME="total" VALUE="100"></td>
  <td colspan=2> <B>Current <BR>Hand:</B>
       <input TYPE="TEXT" SIZE=20 NAME="message"
        VALUE="Press DEAL to begin.">
  <td>
  <td> <a href="#" onClick="DealDraw();">
       <img border=0 src="deal.gif" height=50 width=106></a>
</tr>
</table>
</form>
</body>
</html>
```

Here's a breakdown of the HTML components used in this document:

- The <table> tag starts an HTML table, which will line up the elements on the page.
- The first <tr> section defines a row of the table that displays the five cards. A blank picture (blank.gif) is used as the source because no cards have been dealt yet.

- The second `<tr>` section defines the second row of the table. This row contains Hold buttons for each card.
- The third `<tr>` section defines the third row. This row includes text fields for the total score and the status of the current hand, as well as the Deal button (which will change into a Draw button after the cards are dealt).

Figure 22.1 shows the HTML document as displayed by Internet Explorer, before a game has started.

FIGURE 22.1

The completed HTML layout for the game.

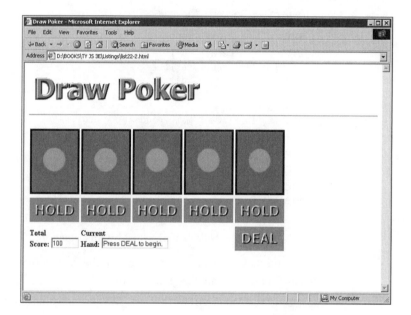

Writing the Program

You're now ready to write the actual script to play the game. Because this is a game, the script will be entirely controlled by the user. Each of the functions is called by an event handler in the HTML document.

Handling the Deal/Draw Button

Because the Deal and Draw buttons are the same button, you will need a function that determines which action should be performed. The `DealDraw` function will be called by the button's event handler:

```
function DealDraw() {
   if (dealt == true) Draw();
   else Deal();
}
```

This function checks whether the cards have been dealt. If they have, it calls the Draw function; otherwise, it calls the Deal function.

Shuffling the Deck

The Deal function deals five cards into the five spaces in your HTML document. To begin, you first need a shuffled deck of cards. The first half of the Deal function fills the deck array with cards and then shuffles them:

```
function Deal() {
// fill the deck (in order, for now)
   for (i=1; i<14; i++) {
      deck[i] = new Card(i,"c");
      deck[i+13] = new Card(i,"h");
      deck[i+26] = new Card(i,"s");
      deck[i+39] = new Card(i,"d");
   }
// shuffle the deck
   var n = Math.floor(400 * Math.random() + 500);
   for (i=1; i<n; i++) {
      card1 = Math.floor(52*Math.random() + 1);
      card2 = Math.floor(52*Math.random() + 1);
      temp = deck[card2];
      deck[card2] = deck[card1];
      deck[card1] = temp;
   }
```

Here's a breakdown of the actions performed by this function:

- The statements within the first for loop fill the deck with cards. To begin with, the cards are in order by number and then by suit.

- The second for loop shuffles the deck. This is accomplished by picking a random number and starting a loop based on that number. In each loop iteration, two random cards are chosen and swapped.

Dealing the Cards

The second half of the Deal function will actually deal the cards:

```
// Deal and Display cards
   for (i=1; i<6; i++) {
      hand[i] = deck[i];
      document.images[i].src = hand[i].fname();
      document.images[i+5].src = "hold.gif";
      held[i] = false;
   }
   dealt = true;
   score = score - 1; //deduct one for bet amount
```

```
    document.form1.total.value = score;
    document.images[11].src="draw.gif";
    Addscore();
}
```

This half includes the following actions:

- The for keyword begins a loop that will range from 1 to 5, using the variable i.
- The next card in the shuffled deck is assigned to the next position in the hand array.
- The document.images array is used to display the dealt card and to change the button below the card to the standard hold.gif. (An alternate version will be loaded when the user presses the button.)
- The held flag is set to false for the current card.
- After the loop is completed, the function sets the dealt flag and subtracts the bet from the total score.
- The current score is displayed in the text field.
- Now that the cards have been dealt, the function uses document.images to change the Deal button to the Draw button.
- Finally, the function calls the Addscore function to calculate the score so far for the dealt hand. We'll examine this function later.

Holding and Discarding Cards

Next, you will need a function that is called when the user presses the Hold button below a card:

```
//Hold or discard a card
function Hold(num) {
    if (!dealt) return;
    if (!held[num]) {
        held[num]=true;
        document.images[5+num].src="hold2.gif";
    }
    else {
        held[num]=false;
        document.images[5+num].src="hold.gif";
    }
}
```

This function accepts a parameter indicating the card to hold. The if statement returns from the function if the cards have not yet been dealt. The rest of the function toggles the held flag for the card and displays either a highlighted or plain version of the Hold button to tell the user the card's status.

Drawing New Cards

Next is the Draw function, which is called when the Draw button is clicked. It draws more cards from the deck to replace the cards that the user wants to discard (those that aren't set to Hold). The following JavaScript code defines the Draw function:

```
//Draw new cards
function Draw() {
   var curcard = 6;
   for (i=1; i<6; i++) {
      if (!held[i]) {
      hand[i] = deck[curcard++];
      document.images[i].src = hand[i].fname();
      }
   }
   dealt = false;
   document.images[11].src="deal.gif";
   score += Addscore();
   document.form1.total.value = score;
}
```

Here's how the Draw function works:

- A local variable called curcard is used to indicate the next card to be drawn from the deck. Because five cards have already been drawn, it starts at card number 6.

- The for loop checks each card's status in the held array. If the card is not held, it is replaced with the next card from the deck and the image on the page is updated.

- Because this hand is finished, the dealt variable is set back to false, and the Deal button replaces the Draw button.

- Finally, the Addscore function is called to calculate the score. Unlike the Deal function, this time the score is added to the total score and redisplayed.

Calculating the Score

Last but not least, the Addscore function calculates the score for the current poker hand. The score is one of the following values, loosely based on the odds of different hands:

- One pair (Jacks or better): 1 point
- Two pair: 2 points
- Three of a kind: 3 points
- Straight: 4 points
- Flush: 5 points
- Full house: 10 points

- Four of a kind: 25 points
- Straight flush: 50 points
- Royal flush: 100 points

The following is the complete Addscore function:

```
// Calculate Score
function Addscore() {
   var straight = false;
   var flush = false;
   var pairs = 0;
   var three = false;
   var tally = new Array(14);
// sorted array for convenience
   var nums = new Array(5);
   for (i=0; i<5; i++) {
      nums[i] = hand[i+1].num;
   }
   nums.sort(Numsort);
// flush
   if (hand[1].suit == hand[2].suit &&
       hand[2].suit == hand[3].suit &&
       hand[3].suit == hand[4].suit &&
       hand[4].suit == hand[5].suit) flush = true;
// straight (Ace low)
   if (nums[0] == nums[1] - 1 &&
       nums[1] == nums[2] - 1 &&
       nums[2] == nums[3] - 1 &&
       nums[3] == nums[4] - 1) straight = true;
// straight (Ace high)
   if (nums[0] == 1 && nums[1] == 10 && nums[2] == 11
       && nums[3] == 12 && nums[4] == 13)
       straight = true;
// royal flush, straight flush, straight, flush
   if (straight && flush && nums[4] == 13 && nums[0] == 1) {
      document.form1.message.value="Royal Flush";
      return 100;
   }
   if (straight && flush) {
     document.form1.message.value="Straight Flush";
     return 50;
   }
   if (straight) {
     document.form1.message.value="Straight";
     return 4;
   }
   if (flush) {
     document.form1.message.value="Flush";
     return 5;
   }
```

```
// tally array is a count for each card value
   for (i=1; i<14; i++) {
      tally[i] = 0;
   }
   for (i=0; i<5; i++) {
      tally[nums[i]] += 1;
   }
   for (i=1; i<14; i++) {
      if (tally[i] == 4) {
         document.form1.message.value = "Four of a Kind";
         return 25;
      }
      if (tally[i] == 3) three = true;
      if (tally[i] == 2) pairs += 1;
   }
   if (three && pairs == 1) {
      document.form1.message.value="Full House";
      return 10;
   }
   if (pairs == 2) {
      document.form1.message.value="Two Pair";
      return 2;
   }
   if (three) {
      document.form1.message.value="Three of a Kind";
      return 3;
   }
   if (pairs == 1) {
      if (tally[1] == 2 || tally[11]==2
      || tally[12] == 2 || tally[13]==2) {
         document.form1.message.value="Jacks or Better";
         return 1;
      }
   }
   document.form1.message.value="No Score";
   return 0;
}
```

This function includes some complex calculations, but it isn't too difficult to understand. Here's a breakdown of how it works:

- The var keywords initialize variables, including flags for the various types of poker hands.
- The first for loop creates the nums array, which stores a sorted version of the list of card values in the hand. This makes it easier to detect some hands (such as straights).
- The next if detects a flush (all cards have the same suit).

- Two `if` statements are used to detect a straight (all cards in a sequence). Because Aces can represent either 1 or 13, straights ending in Ace are checked separately.

- An `if` statement detects a royal flush (10, J, Q, K, A) and returns the score.

- Several more `if` statements return the scores for straight flush, straight, and flush hands.

- A `for` loop creates an array called `tally`. This is used to count the number of cards of each value in the hand.

- Several `if` statements use the `tally` array to detect four of a kind, full house, two pair, three of a kind, and pair hands.

- If the previous code detected a pair of cards, a further `if` statement checks whether it's a pair of Jacks or better and return the appropriate score.

- If no scoring hand was detected, the final lines return from the `Addscore` function with no score.

Workshop: Putting It All Together

Listing 22.2 shows the complete draw poker game. In case you don't want to type all this yourself, you can download the complete script from this book's Web site at `http://www.jsworkshop.com/`.

LISTING 22.2   The Complete Draw Poker Game

```html
<html>
<head>
<title>Draw Poker</title>
<script LANGUAGE="JavaScript1.1" type="text/javascript1.1">
var score = 100;
var dealt = false;
var hand = new Array(6);
var held = new Array(6);
var deck = new Array(53);
function DealDraw() {
   if (dealt == true) Draw();
   else Deal();
}
function Deal() {
// fill the deck (in order, for now)
   for (i=1; i<14; i++) {
     deck[i] = new Card(i,"c");
     deck[i+13] = new Card(i,"h");
     deck[i+26] = new Card(i,"s");
     deck[i+39] = new Card(i,"d");
   }
```

LISTING 22.2 Continued

```
// shuffle the deck
   var n = Math.floor(400 * Math.random() + 500);
   for (i=1; i<n; i++) {
       card1 = Math.floor(52*Math.random() + 1);
       card2 = Math.floor(52*Math.random() + 1);
       temp = deck[card2];
       deck[card2] = deck[card1];
       deck[card1] = temp;
   }
// Deal and Display cards
   for (i=1; i<6; i++) {
       hand[i] = deck[i];
       document.images[i].src = hand[i].fname();
       document.images[i+5].src = "hold.gif";
       held[i] = false;
     }
   dealt = true;
   score = score - 1; //deduct one for bet amount
   document.form1.total.value = score;
   document.images[11].src="draw.gif";
   Addscore();
}
//Hold or discard a card
function Hold(num) {
   if (!dealt) return;
   if (!held[num]) {
       held[num]=true;
       document.images[5+num].src="hold2.gif";
   }
   else {
       held[num]=false;
       document.images[5+num].src="hold.gif";
   }
}
//Draw new cards
function Draw() {
   var curcard = 6;
   for (i=1; i<6; i++) {
       if (!held[i]) {
       hand[i] = deck[curcard++];
       document.images[i].src = hand[i].fname();
       }
   }
   dealt = false;
   document.images[11].src="deal.gif";
   score += Addscore();
```

LISTING 22.2 Continued

```
      document.form1.total.value = score;
}
// Make a filename for an image, given Card object
function fname() {
    return this.num + this.suit + ".gif";
}
// Constructor for Card objects
function Card(num,suit) {
   this.num = num;
   this.suit = suit;
   this.fname = fname;
}
// Numeric sort function
function Numsort(a,b) { return a - b; }
// Calculate Score
function Addscore() {
   var straight = false;
   var flush = false;
   var pairs = 0;
   var three = false;
   var tally = new Array(14);
// sorted array for convenience
   var nums = new Array(5);
   for (i=0; i<5; i++) {
      nums[i] = hand[i+1].num;
   }
   nums.sort(Numsort);
// flush
   if (hand[1].suit == hand[2].suit &&
       hand[2].suit == hand[3].suit &&
       hand[3].suit == hand[4].suit &&
       hand[4].suit == hand[5].suit) flush = true;
// straight (Ace low)
   if (nums[0] == nums[1] - 1 &&
       nums[1] == nums[2] - 1 &&
       nums[2] == nums[3] - 1 &&
       nums[3] == nums[4] - 1) straight = true;
// straight (Ace high)
   if (nums[0] == 1 && nums[1] == 10 && nums[2] == 11
       && nums[3] == 12 && nums[4] == 13)
       straight = true;
// royal flush, straight flush, straight, flush
   if (straight && flush && nums[4] == 13 && nums[0] == 1) {
      document.form1.message.value="Royal Flush";
      return 100;
   }
```

22

LISTING 22.2   Continued

```
      if (straight && flush) {
        document.form1.message.value="Straight Flush";
        return 50;
      }
      if (straight) {
        document.form1.message.value="Straight";
        return 4;
      }
      if (flush) {
        document.form1.message.value="Flush";
        return 5;
      }
// tally array is a count for each card value
      for (i=1; i<14; i++) {
        tally[i] = 0;
      }
      for (i=0; i<5; i++) {
        tally[nums[i]] += 1;
      }
      for (i=1; i<14; i++) {
        if (tally[i] == 4) {
          document.form1.message.value = "Four of a Kind";
          return 25;
        }
        if (tally[i] == 3) three = true;
        if (tally[i] == 2) pairs += 1;
      }
      if (three && pairs == 1) {
        document.form1.message.value="Full House";
        return 10;
      }
      if (pairs == 2) {
        document.form1.message.value="Two Pair";
        return 2;
      }
      if (three) {
        document.form1.message.value="Three of a Kind";
        return 3;
      }
      if (pairs == 1) {
        if (tally[1] == 2 || tally[11]==2
        || tally[12] == 2 || tally[13]==2) {
          document.form1.message.value="Jacks or Better";
          return 1;
        }
      }
      document.form1.message.value="No Score";
```

LISTING 22.2   Continued

```
    return 0;
}
</script>
</head>
<body>
<img src="title.gif" width=381 height=81>
<hr>
<form NAME="form1">
<table>
<tr>
  <td> <img border=0 src="blank.gif" height=136 width=106>
  <td> <img border=0 src="blank.gif" height=136 width=106>
  <td> <img border=0 src="blank.gif" height=136 width=106>
  <td> <img border=0 src="blank.gif" height=136 width=106>
  <td> <img border=0 src="blank.gif" height=136 width=106>
  <td> </td>
</tr>
<tr>
  <td> <a href="#" onClick="Hold(1);">
      <img border=0 src="hold.gif" height=50 width=106></a>
  <td> <a href="#" onClick="Hold(2);">
      <img border=0 src="hold.gif" height=50 width=106></a>
  <td> <a href="#" onClick="Hold(3);">
      <img border=0 src="hold.gif" height=50 width=106></a>
  <td> <a href="#" onClick="Hold(4);">
      <img border=0 src="hold.gif" height=50 width=106></a>
  <td> <a href="#" onClick="Hold(5);">
      <img border=0 src="hold.gif" height=50 width=106></a>
</tr>
<tr>
  <td> <B>Total<BR>Score:</B>
      <input TYPE="TEXT" SIZE=6 NAME="total" VALUE="100"></td>
  <td colspan=2> <B>Current <BR>Hand:</B>
      <input TYPE="TEXT" SIZE=20 NAME="message"
      VALUE="Press DEAL to begin.">
  <td>
  <td> <a href="#" onClick="DealDraw();">
      <img border=0 src="deal.gif" height=50 width=106></a>
</tr>
</table>
</form>
</body>
</html>
```

Figure 22.2 shows Internet Explorer's display of the script after a game has been in progress for a while. (You'll notice that I'm losing.)

FIGURE 22.2

The complete game in action.

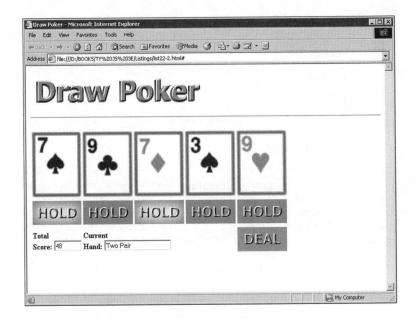

Summary

In this hour, you've created a complete—and hopefully fun—JavaScript application. You've seen how graphics, HTML, and JavaScript can be fitted together to create a complete application.

In the next hour, you'll take another look at Dynamic HTML (DHTML) and create several practical examples using DHTML and JavaScript.

Q&A

Q Is this about as complex as a JavaScript program can get?

A Not by any means. You can write much more complicated scripts that can encompass several different HTML files.

Q I thought the images in the `images` array were indexed starting with 0, but the game uses the indexes 1–5 to display the cards. How does this work?

A The game includes a title graphic at the top, which uses the `images[0]` space. If you add or remove graphics from the top of the page, be sure to change the indexes accordingly.

22

Q **Why use an object to store cards when the filename (such as `10h.gif`) already stores a card's information?**

A Just for convenience. By using an object, you can individually access the card's value and its suit, which are heavily used by the scoring routine.

Quiz

Test your knowledge of the JavaScript techniques you used in this hour by answering the following questions.

Questions

1. Which array can you use to change images in a Web page?

    a. `this`

    b. `document.src`

    c. `document.images`

2. Which of the following is the correct expression for a random integer between 1 and 52?

    a. `Math.random(52)`

    b. `Math.floor(52*Math.random() + 1)`

    c. `Math.floor(52*Math.random())`

3. What are the odds of being dealt a royal flush while playing this game?

    a. 1 in 5,000

    b. 1 in 50,000

    c. 1 in 500,000

Answers

1. c. The `document.images` array can be used to change images on a page.

2. b. Because the `Math.random` method returns a number between 0 and 1, the correct expression is `Math.floor(52*Math.random() + 1)`.

3. c. The odds are about one in half a million, but I didn't really expect you to know that offhand.

Exercises

If you want to gain more experience with the techniques you learned in this hour, try these exercises:

- Modify the draw poker game to allow the player to bet a variable amount instead of one point for each turn, and then adjust the scoring accordingly.

- Add text fields to the draw poker display to keep track of the number of wins (hands that returned a score) and losses (hands with no score) and modify the script to update these fields.

- Using DHTML, modify the game to use regular text instead of form fields to display the score and the status of the current hand. See Part V, "Working with Dynamic HTML," for details.

HOUR 23

Creating DHTML Applications

In Part V, you learned how to use Dynamic HTML (DHTML) to manipulate objects within a Web page. In this hour, you'll further explore DHTML with three practical examples that you can use within Web pages.

Hour 23 covers the following topics:

- Creating a Dynamic Site Map
- Creating DHTML Drop-Down Menus
- Creating a Scrolling Text Box

Creating a Dynamic Site Map

One of the most popular uses for DHTML is to create dynamic, tree-like navigation
maps for sites, with items that can be expanded and collapsed. You can create a dynamic
site map easily using <div> tags to define layers and a simple script.

Defining the Layers

Each category in the site map will be defined with a link to the Toggle function, which
you'll define later. The linked text is a symbol, [+] to indicate that the item can be
expanded or [-] to indicate that it can be collapsed.

```
<b><a ID="xsupport" href="javascript:Toggle('support');">[+]</a>
   Support</b><br>
   <div ID="support" style="display:none; margin-left:2em;">
   <a href="sforum.html">Support Forum</a><br>
   <a href="sforum.html">Contact Support</a><br>
</div>
```

Creating the Script

Each collapsible section of the site map will be defined using a <div> tag. The Toggle
function uses the style.display property to expand or collapse a specified item:

```
<script language="javascript" type="text/javascript">
function Toggle(item) {
   obj=document.getElementById(item);
   visible=(obj.style.display!="none")
   key=document.getElementById("x" + item);
   if (visible) {
     obj.style.display="none";
     key.innerHTML="[+]";
   } else {
      obj.style.display="block";
      key.innerHTML="[-]";
   }
}
</script>
```

This function first uses the visible variable to indicate whether the item is currently visible. If the object is visible, its display property is set to none to collapse it, and the
object's indicator is changed to a [+] symbol. If the object is currently hidden, it is displayed and the indicator is changed to [-].

Creating the HTML Document

To use this function to create the dynamic site map, you can include the script in an
HTML document and use <div> tags to define the map sections. Listing 23.1 shows the
complete HTML document.

LISTING 23.1   Creating a DHTML Site Map

```html
<html>
<head><title>Creating a Navigation Tree</title>
<style>
   A {text-decoration: none;}
</style>
<script language="javascript" type="text/javascript">
function Toggle(item) {
   obj=document.getElementById(item);
   visible=(obj.style.display!="none")
   key=document.getElementById("x" + item);
   if (visible) {
     obj.style.display="none";
     key.innerHTML="[+]";
   } else {
      obj.style.display="block";
      key.innerHTML="[-]";
   }
}
</script>
</head>
<body>
<h1>Navigation Tree Example</h1>
<p>The navigation tree below allows you to expand and
collapse items. You could use this in a frame to provide a
sophisticated navigation system for a site.</p>
<hr>
<b><a ID="xproducts" href="javascript:Toggle('products');">[+]</a>
   Products</b><br>
   <div ID="products" style="display:none; margin-left:2em;">
   <a href="prodlist.html">Product List</a><br>
   <a href="order.html">Order Form</a><br>
   <a href="pricelist.html">Price List</a><br>
   </div>
<b><a ID="xsupport" href="javascript:Toggle('support');">[+]</a>
   Support</b><br>
   <div ID="support" style="display:none; margin-left:2em;">
   <a href="sforum.html">Support Forum</a><br>
   <a href="sforum.html">Contact Support</a><br>
</div>
<b><a ID="xcontact" href="javascript:Toggle('contact');">[+]</a>
   Contact Us</b>
<div ID="contact" style="display:none; margin-left:2em;">
   <a href="contact1.html">Service Department</a><br>
   <a href="contact2.html">Sales Department</a><br>
</div>
</body>
</html>
```

23

This document incorporates the `Toggle` function and a complete set of links and `<div>` sections to define the expandable menu. Figure 23.1 shows the site map in action.

FIGURE 23.1

The dynamic site map in action.

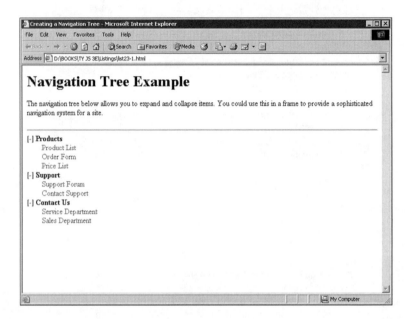

Creating Drop-Down Menus

Another common use for DHTML is to create drop-down menus. Similar to the previous example, this can be accomplished using layers, defined with `<div>` tags, and manipulating their visibility. This time you'll use the `visibility` property to hide or show the layers.

Creating the HTML Document

The HTML document for the drop-down menu example is shown in Listing 23.2. This document uses a `<table>` section to define the menu terms, and `<div>` tags to define the menus that will appear when you move over each menu term.

LISTING 23.2   The HTML Document for the Drop-Down Menu Example

```
<html>
<head>
<title>Drop-Down Menu Example</title>
<script language="JavaScript" type="text/javascript" src="menu.js">
</script>
</head>
```

LISTING 23.2   Continued

```
<body  style="margin-left:0; margin-top:0;">
<table border="0" cellpadding="4">
<tr>
    <td ID="menu-products" width="100" bgcolor="Silver"
      onMouseOver="Menu('products');" onMouseOut="Timeout('products');">
     <a href="products.html"><b>Products</b></a>
    </td>
    <td ID="menu-sales" width="100" bgcolor="Silver"
      onMouseOver="Menu('sales');" onMouseOut="Timeout('sales');">
      <a href="sales.html"><b>Sales</b></a>
    </td>
    <td ID="menu-service" width="100" bgcolor="Silver"
      onMouseOver="Menu('service');" onMouseOut="Timeout('service');">
      <a href="service.html"><b>Service</b></a>
    </td>
</tr>
</table>
<div ID="products" STYLE="position:absolute; visibility: hidden">
  <table width="100%" border="0" cellpadding="4" cellspacing="0">
  <tr> <td width="100%" ID="p1"
    onMouseOver="Highlight('products','p1');"
    onMouseOut="UnHighlight('products','p1');">
  <a href="equip.html">Equipment</a></td></tr>
  <tr> <td width="100%" ID="p2"
    onMouseOver="Highlight('products','p2');"
    onMouseOut="UnHighlight('products','p2');">
  <a href="supplies.html">Supplies</a></td></tr>
  </table>
</div>
<div ID="sales" STYLE="position:absolute; visibility: hidden">
  <table width="100%" border="0" cellpadding="4" cellspacing="0">
  <tr> <td width="100%" ID="s1"
    onMouseOver="Highlight('sales','s1');"
    onMouseOut="UnHighlight('sales','s1');">
  <a href="prices.html">Price List</a></td></tr>
  <tr> <td width="100%" ID="s2"
    onMouseOver="Highlight('sales','s2');"
    onMouseOut="UnHighlight('sales','s2');">
  <a href="order.html">Order Form</a></td></tr>
  <tr> <td width="100%" ID="s3"
    onMouseOver="Highlight('sales','s3');"
    onMouseOut="UnHighlight('sales','s3');">
  <a href="specials.html">Specials</a></td></tr>
  </table>
</div>
<div ID="service" STYLE="position:absolute; visibility: hidden">
  <table width="100%" border="0" cellpadding="4" cellspacing="0">
  <tr> <td width="100%" ID="r1"
```

23

LISTING 23.2   Continued

```
        onMouseOver="Highlight('service','r1');"
        onMouseOut="UnHighlight('service','r1');">
  <a href="support.html">Support</a></td></tr>
  <tr> <td width="100%" ID="r2"
        onMouseOver="Highlight('service','r2');"
        onMouseOut="UnHighlight('service','r2');">
  <a href="cservice.html">Contact Us</a></td></tr>
  </table>
</div>
<h1 align="center">Drop-Down DHTML Menus</h1>
<p>This is a basic test of drop-down DHTML menus. To
test the menus, move the mouse over the menu items above.
</p>
</body>
</html>
```

The menu terms use the onMouseOver event handler to call the Menu function, which will show a menu, and the onMouseOut event handler to call the Timeout function, which will erase the menu after a timeout.

Since this is a complex example, the JavaScript functions will be included in a separate file. Notice that the <script> tag in the header has a src attribute that refers to the file menu.js. For now, save the HTML document.

> As usual, you can download the HTML and JavaScript files for this example from this book's Web site: http://www.jsworkshop.com/.

Creating the JavaScript Functions

The JavaScript functions for this example are stored in the separate menu.js file. Listing 23.3 shows the complete listing for the JavaScript file.

LISTING 23.3   The JavaScript Functions for the Drop-Down Menus

```
var inmenu=false;
var lastmenu=0;
function Menu(current) {
   if (!document.getElementById) return;
   inmenu=true;
   oldmenu=lastmenu;
   lastmenu=current;
```

LISTING 23.3   Continued

```
      if (oldmenu) Erase(oldmenu);
      m=document.getElementById("menu-" + current);
      box=document.getElementById(current);
      box.style.left= m.offsetLeft;
      box.style.top= m.offsetTop + m.offsetHeight;
      box.style.visibility="visible";
      m.style.backgroundColor="Aqua";
      box.style.backgroundColor="Aqua";
      box.style.width="108px";
   }
function Erase(current) {
      if (!document.getElementById) return;
      if (inmenu && lastmenu==current) {
        return;
      }
      m=document.getElementById("menu-" + current);
      box=document.getElementById(current);
      box.style.visibility="hidden";
      m.style.backgroundColor="Silver";
   }
function Timeout(current) {
      inmenu=false;
      window.setTimeout("Erase('" + current + "');",500) ;
   }
function Highlight(menu,item) {
      if (!document.getElementById) return;
      inmenu=true;
      lastmenu=menu;
      obj=document.getElementById(item);
      obj.style.backgroundColor="Silver";
   }
function UnHighlight(menu,item) {
      if (!document.getElementById) return;
      Timeout(menu);
      obj=document.getElementById(item);
      obj.style.backgroundColor="Aqua";
   }
```

This document defines the Menu and Timeout functions called by the event handlers, the Erase function to erase a menu, and the Highlight and UnHighlight functions to highlight the items in each menu as you move over them.

Figure 23.2 shows the menu in action. In the figure, the Products menu is currently displayed.

FIGURE **23.2**

*The Drop-Down menu
example in action.*

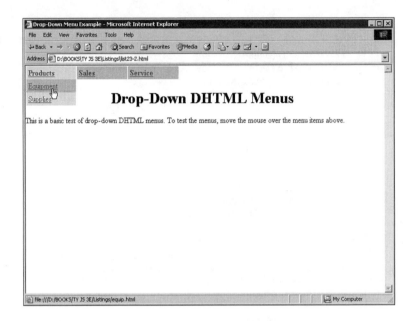

Workshop: Creating a Scrolling Text Box

In Hour 5, "Using Strings and Arrays," you created a simple scrolling message. In Hour 20, "Using Advanced DOM Features," you created a scrolling message using DHTML.

In this section, you'll create a different kind of scrolling message. This one scrolls a large block of text vertically within a window, similar to the credits at the end of a movie. This type of scrolling message is easier to read, and can include links or other HTML features.

Creating the JavaScript Function

This example uses a simple JavaScript function. The following JavaScript code defines the Scroll function:

```
var pos=100;
function Scroll() {
  if (!document.getElementById) return;
  obj=document.getElementById("thetext");
  pos -=1;
  if (pos < 0-obj.offsetHeight+130) return;
  obj.style.top=pos;
  window.setTimeout("Scroll();",30);
}
```

The first line defines a variable, pos, to store the current scroll position. Next, this function subtracts 1 from pos and checks its value. If the scrolling has reached the end, the function exits; otherwise, it sets the object position and calls the Scroll function again using a timeout.

> Notice the if statement at the beginning of the function. This is a simple example of feature sensing, described in Hour 20—if the browser doesn't support the getElementById method, the function exits rather than causing errors.

Creating the HTML Document

To complete the scrolling message, you can create an HTML document that defines the appropriate layers and includes the Scroll function. Listing 23.4 shows the complete HTML document.

LISTING 23.4   The HTML Document for the Scrolling Text Box

```
<html>
<head>
<title>A DHTML Scrolling Window</title>
<script language="JavaScript" type="text/javascript">
var pos=100;
function Scroll() {
  if (!document.getElementById) return;
  obj=document.getElementById("thetext");
  pos -=1;
  if (pos < 0-obj.offsetHeight+130) return;
  obj.style.top=pos;
  window.setTimeout("Scroll();",30);
}
</script>
</head>
<body onLoad="Scroll();">
<h1>Scrolling Window Example</h1>
<p>This example shows a scrolling window created in DHTML. The window
is actually a layer that shows a portion of a larger layer.</p>
<div id="thewindow" style="position:relative;width:180;height:150;
  overflow:hidden; border-width:2px; border-style:solid; border-color:red">
```

LISTING 23.4 Continued

```
<div id="thetext" style="position:absolute;width:170;left:5;top:100">
<p>This is the first paragraph of the scrolling message. The message
is created with ordinary HTML.</p>
<p>Entries within the scrolling area can use any HTML tags. They can
contain <a href="http://www.jsworkshop.com/">Links</a>.</p>
<p>There's no limit on the number of paragraphs that you can include
here. They don't even need to be formatted as paragraphs.</p>
<ul><li>For example, you could format items using a bulleted list.</li></ul>
<p>The scrolling ends when the last part of the scrolling text
is on the screen. You've reached the end.</p>
<p><b>[<a href="javascript:pos=100;Scroll();">Start Over</a>]</b></p>
</div>
</div>
</body>
</html>
```

The <div> tags in this document create two nested layers: One, thewindow, will form the small window for text to display in. The other, thetext, contains the text to scroll.

Since the text doesn't all fit in the small window, you'll only see part of it at a time. The overflow property on the window layer prevents the rest of the content from showing. Your script will manipulate the text window's style.top property to move it relative to the window, creating a scrolling effect.

 The text layer is actually 10 pixels narrower than the window layer. This, along with the left property, creates a small margin of white space on either side of the window, preventing any of the text from being obstructed.

The actual text to scroll is placed within the inner <div> element. You can use any HTML here, although it should be able to wrap to the small window.

Figure 23.3 shows this example in action, after the scrolling text has reached the end.

FIGURE 23.3

The scrolling text box in action.

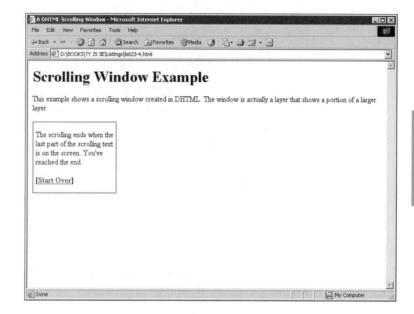

Summary

In this hour, you've explored DHTML further with three practical examples, creating useful navigation features and a more friendly scrolling message.

> You've only scratched the surface of what DHTML can do. To learn more, you may want to consult a DHTML book—one good candidate is *Sams Teach Yourself DHTML in 24 Hours* by Michael Moncur, also published by Sams.

In the next hour, you'll complete your 24-hour tour of JavaScript by looking at the future of JavaScript and learning some useful scripting tips.

Q&A

Q If I use the expandable site map on a page, won't the page's other content move up and down as the items are expanded or collapsed?

A Yes, if the menu and page are in a single window. You can avoid this by placing the menu in a frame or layer, or in a table column.

Q   **In Netscape 6, when I click on an item within the expandable site map or drop-down menu, nothing happens. What's wrong?**

A   You are most likely testing the document in a local file rather than on a Web server. When you click on a link to a file that doesn't exist, some versions of Netscape display an error message and others do nothing. In a real site, since the links would point to actual documents, this wouldn't be a problem.

Q   **When the scrolling text box is viewed in Netscape, why does a scroll bar appear on the right side of the page during the scrolling?**

A   This happens when the hidden text layer is longer than the current browser window would hold—even though the bottom part of it is invisible. This problem doesn't occur in Internet Explorer.

Quiz

Test your knowledge of the JavaScript techniques you used in this hour by answering the following questions.

Questions

1. Which of these properties can you use to show or hide an element of a document and have the remainder of the document expand or collapse to fill the space?

    a. `style.visibility`

    b. `style.display`

    c. `style.collapse`

2. Which HTML tags are typically used to define layers?

    a. `<div> or <body>`

    b. `<span> or <script>`

    c. `<div> or <span>`

3. Which of the following properties prevents the scrolling window text from showing below the window?

    a. `overflow: hidden`

    b. `border-style: solid`

    c. `position: relative`

Answers

1. b. The `style.display` property can hide or show an object and the rest of the document is reformatted accordingly.

2. c. The `<div>` or `<span>` tags are typically used to define layers.

3. a. The `overflow: hidden` property prevents the text from showing below the window.

23

Exercises

If you want to gain more experience with the techniques you learned in this hour, try these exercises:

- Modify the site map example in Listing 23.1 so that all the items are expanded by default.

- Add another menu term and a corresponding menu layer to the drop-down menu in Listing 23.2.

HOUR **24**

JavaScript Tips and Tricks

By now, you should be reasonably confident with JavaScript programming, and you probably have some ideas for improving your pages with this technology. As you reach the end of your 24-hour JavaScript course, it's time to look to the future of JavaScript and the Web, and decide how to further your education.

In Hour 24, you will examine what lies ahead for JavaScript and the Web, and what future technologies may impact your scripting. This hour covers the following topics:

- Where to go to learn more about JavaScript
- How future versions of JavaScript may affect your scripts
- An introduction to XML (Extensible Markup Language)
- How to be sure you're ready for future Web technologies
- A few final JavaScript tips

Learning Advanced JavaScript Techniques

Although you've now learned all of the essentials of the JavaScript language, there is still much to learn. JavaScript can be used to script environments other than the Web, and features such as signed scripts can allow you to create more powerful JavaScript applications.

Here are some ways you can further your JavaScript education:

- See Appendix A, "Other JavaScript Resources," for a list of JavaScript books and Web pages with further information.
- While the core JavaScript language is in place, be sure to follow the latest developments. The Web sites in Appendix A and this book's site (www.jsworkshop.com) will let you know when changes are on the way.
- Be sure to spend some time practicing the JavaScript techniques you've learned throughout this book. You can use them to create much more complex applications than those you've worked with so far.

Future Web Technologies

The Web has practically appeared out of nowhere over the course of a few years, and is continually changing. In the following sections, you will explore some of the upcoming—and already developed—technologies that will affect your pages and scripts.

Future versions of JavaScript

Since this is a book about JavaScript 1.5, you should be well aware that JavaScript has gone through several versions to reach its current status. Fortunately, the core language hasn't changed much through these version changes, and nearly all scripts written for older versions will work on the latest version.

The next version of JavaScript is likely to be version 2.0. While no date has been announced for its release, Netscape's development team and the ECMA agency are working on its specification. Version 2.0's main change will be the addition of true object-oriented features, such as classes and inheritance.

As with previous versions, version 2.0 should be backward compatible with older versions. To be sure your scripts will work under version 2.0, follow the standard language features and do not rely on any undocumented or browser-specific features.

Future DOM Versions

Currently, the W3C DOM level 1 is an official specification, while level 2 is only a recommendation. Level 2 adds features such as event handling and better style sheet support, and is already partially supported by Netscape 6.0, and Internet Explorer 5.0 and later.

In the future, expect better browser support for the DOM, and less compatibility issues between browsers. Future DOM versions will undoubtedly add more features, but no documentation yet exists for these versions.

XML (Extensible Markup Language)

HTML wasoriginally created as a language for the Web, and was based on an older standard for documentation called SGML (Standard Generalized Markup Language). HTML is a much-simplified version of SGML, specifically designed for Web documents.

A relatively new language on the scene is XML (Extensible Markup Language). While XML is also a simplified version of SGML, it isn't nearly as simple as HTML. While HTML has a specific purpose, XML can be used for virtually any purpose.

24

The W3C (World-wide Web Consortium) developed XML, and has published a specification to standardize the language.

Strictly speaking, XML isn't a language in itself—there is no concise list of XML tags because XML has no set list of tags. Instead, XML allows you to create your own languages for whatever purpose you choose.

So what use is a language without any specific commands? Well, XML allows you to define languages for any purpose you choose. If you were storing recipes, for example, you could create tags for ingredients, ingredient quantities, and instructions.

XML uses a DTD (Document Type Definition) to define the tags used in a particular document. The DTD can be in a separate file or built into the document, and specifies which tags are allowed, their attributes, and what they can contain.

XML is already in use today. Although it isn't directly supported by Web browsers, you can use a program on the server to parse XML documents into HTML documents before sending them to the browser.

To return to the recipe example, an XML processor could convert each recipe into HTML. The reason for doing this is simple: By changing the rules in the parser, you could change the entire format of all of the recipes—a difficult task to perform manually if you had thousands of recipes.

XSL (Extensible Stylesheet Language)

XML documents focus strictly on the meaning of the tags—content—and ignore presentation. The presentation of XML can be determined by creating an XSL (Extensible Stylesheet Language) style sheet.

XSL is based on XML, but specifies presentation—parameters such as font size, margins, and table formatting—for an XML document. When you use an XML processing program to create HTML output, it uses an XSL stylesheet to determine the HTML formatting of the output.

> XSL documents are actually XML documents, using their own DTD that specifies stylesheet tags. XSL is a newer W3C specification.

Planning for the Future

In the history of JavaScript, there has never been such a major change to the language that a great number of scripts written using the older version have stopped working. Nevertheless, many scripts have been crippled by new releases—chiefly those that used browser-specific features.

The following sections offer some guidelines you can follow in writing scripts to ensure that the impact of future JavaScript versions and browser releases will be minimal.

Keeping Scripts Compatible

Right now, dynamic HTML (DHTML) is in use on many Web pages. The new W3C DOM standardizes the objects used for dynamic HTML, but it was not available when the vast majority of these pages were created. Thus, they use a number of techniques to offer the latest dynamic features:

- Browser detection is used to separately support Netscape and Internet Explorer, or in some cases a specific browser is required.
- Scripts are written to work around bugs in browsers, or sometimes even take advantage of them.
- The process of writing scripts often involves trial and error rather than consulting official documentation.

While the W3C DOM will solve these issues when it is widely supported, there will always be brand new features that are not part of the official DOM specification and will be subject to change.

There's nothing wrong with using these features—but if you do, you should be aware that you're going to need to test the scripts on several different browsers. Additionally, if you've used non-standard features, you will eventually have to rewrite the scripts to use newer, standard features.

Staying HTML Compliant

One trend as browsers advance is that newer browsers tend to do a better job of following the W3C standard for HTML—and often, relying on it. This means that while a page that uses completely standard HTML will likely work in future browsers, one that uses browser-specific features or workarounds is bound to have problems eventually.

24

In particular, the first release of Netscape 6.0 received many complaints about "breaking" previously working pages. In most cases, the page used bad HTML, and previous browsers happened to handle the error gracefully.

To avoid these problems, try to use completely valid HTML whenever possible. This means not only using standard tags and attributes, but following certain formatting rules: For example, always using both opening and closing <p> tags, and enclosing numbers for table widths and other parameters in quotation marks.

To be sure your documents follow the HTML standard, see Appendix B, "Tools for JavaScript Developers," for suggested HTML validation programs and services. These will examine your document and point out any areas that do not comply with the HTML standard.

Document Everything

Last but not least, be sure you understand everything your scripts are doing. Document your scripts using comments, and particularly document any statements that may look cryptic or were particularly hard to get working properly.

If your scripts are properly documented, it will be a much easier process if you have to modify them to be compatible with a future browser, JavaScript, or DOM version.

A few JavaScript Tips

You've nearly reached the end of your 24-hour JavaScript education. Before you start madly scripting on your latest project, here are a few final tips to keep in mind:

1. First, avoid gratuitous use of JavaScript or its features. While you may get a kick out of watching your page's title wiggle back and forth as your script manipulates it using the DOM, does such a feature really add value to your page?

2. Next, be careful that your scripting doesn't take away normal browser conveniences. As an example, while you can display friendly descriptions on the status line when the user hovers over your links, doing this on links to external sites eliminates the browser's display of the URL, which is a useful feature.

3. Another common example is pages that create their own JavaScript window of a set size. While this is sophisticated, it takes away the normal functionality of the Back and Forward buttons, and often the Status line. Worse, these pages often look quite small and silly when I see them taking up a tiny portion of my large monitor.

4. Be sure you really need it before using a brand-new JavaScript feature. While it may be flashy or even add value to your page, be aware that the latest features will be enjoyed by only those users who are using brand-new browsers, and new features often have unexpected bugs. If you do use new features, be sure to use browser checking to include them only when the latest browsers are in use.

5. Finally, make sure your page scales down gracefully. Test it with older browsers, and with non-JavaScript browsers. While users with these browsers may not be able to see your newest cosmetic improvements, make sure they can at least navigate your page and read its text.

One very scaled-down browser is Lynx, a text-based browser. To find out more about it and try it on your pages, see the Lynx Links site at http://www.trill-home.com/lynx.html.

Workshop: Using Cookies

You've learned quite a bit in your 24-hour exploration of JavaScript. Just to prove that there's more to learn if you choose, here's a final lesson on a useful JavaScript feature for advanced scripts.

Cookies allow you to store one or more variables on the user's computer. This allows your Web pages to remember key information—for example, a username or the current score in an online game.

> Cookies are one of the most controversial—and confusing—Web features. Despite security and privacy fears, this is a feature that is quite useful and quite safe if used properly.

Unlike regular JavaScript variables, cookies are persistent—once you've set one, it will be available to your script each time the same user views your page until the cookie reaches the expiration date you've set. They're a great way to recognize previous visitors or to let the user avoid typing the same information over and over.

Setting a Cookie

Cookies are specific to a single Web page. You can set one or more cookies using the `document.cookie` property. To set a cookie, you just need to specify a name for the cookie, a value, and an expiration date:

```
name=window.prompt("Please enter your name","");
d = new Date();
d.setFullYear(d.getFullYear() + 1);
expires="expires=" + d.toGMTString();
document.cookie="Username=" + name + "; " + expires;
```

This example prompts for a name and sets a cookie called `Username` to store the name. The d variable is used to store the expiration date, which is set one year in the future. If the user name is `Fred`, the cookie value will look something like this:

`Username=Fred; expires= Fri, 25 Apr 2004 08:14:05 UTC`

To delete a cookie, you simply re-set it using an expiration date in the past. You can also set an existing cookie to a new value.

> There is a limit of 20 cookies per domain (including all sites on the domain), so make sure you use as few cookies as possible. You can combine multiple values into a single cookie to avoid this limitation.

Reading a Cookie

As you might have guessed, reading a cookie is as simple as reading the `document.cookie` property. However, this property includes all the cookies for the current page—since there might be more than one, you need to use some string functions to extract the cookie you want. The following example finds the `Username` cookie's value:

24

```
cookies=document.cookie;
startpos=cookies.indexOf("Username") + 9;
endpos=cookies.indexOf(";",startpos);
if (endpos==-1) endpos=cookies.length;
name=cookies.substring(startpos,endpos);
```

This code uses the `indexOf` method to find the position of the `Username=` string that begins the cookie. It adds nine characters to skip over `Username=`, and this is the start position of the value.

The end position is calculated by looking for a semicolon after the start position. Some browsers don't include the semicolon when there's only one cookie, so it sets the end position to the end of the `document.cookie` value if there isn't a semicolon.

Having calculated the start and end positions for the value, the final line of this example uses the `substring` method to read the value for the `Username` cookie.

Putting It All Together

Now that you've learned how to set a cookie and how to read the value of a cookie, you can put them together to make a simple example. This example displays a personalized welcome message when it loads. The first time you load it, it prompts for a name and stores the name in a cookie.

The second time you load this example, it uses the name stored in the cookie and doesn't need to prompt for a name. Listing 24.1 shows the complete example.

LISTING 24.1   Complete Cookie Personalized Welcome Message

```
<html>
<head><title>Cookie Example</title>
</head>
<body>
<h1> Cookie Example</h1>
<script language="javascript1.1" type="text/javascript1.1">
cookies=document.cookie;
startpos=cookies.indexOf("Username") + 9;
    if (startpos<9) {
       // No cookie set
       name=window.prompt("Please enter your name","");
       d = new Date();
       d.setFullYear(d.getFullYear() + 1);
       expires="expires=" + d.toGMTString();
       document.cookie="Username=" + name + "; " + expires;
       document.write("<h2>Welcome, " + name + "!</h2>");
    } else {
       // Cookie was found
```

LISTING 24.1   Continued

```
        endpos=cookies.indexOf(";",startpos);
        if (endpos==-1) endpos=cookies.length;
        name=cookies.substring(startpos,endpos);
    document.write("<h2>Welcome Back, " + name + "!</h2>");
    }
</script>
<p>This example's script uses a cookie to save
the user name. If no cookie is set, it prompts for
a name.</p>
</body>
</html>
```

To test this example, load it into a browser—it should work with Netscape 4 or later or Internet Explorer 4 or later. You'll be prompted for a name, and the next time you load the page it will welcome you back using the name stored in the document's cookie. Figure 24.1 shows the example in action.

24

FIGURE 24.1

The cookie example in action.

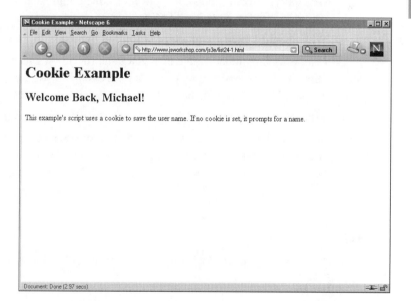

 Some browsers won't store cookies unless the document is on a Web server. If you don't have a server handy, try the online version of this example at this book's Web site: `http://www.jsworkshop.com/`.

Summary

In this hour, you've learned how the future of JavaScript and the Web may affect your Web pages and scripts, and learned some of the upcoming technologies that may change the way you work with the Web. Finally, you learned how to use cookies to store user-specific information.

Time's up—you've reached the end of this book. I hope you've enjoyed spending 24 hours learning JavaScript, and that you'll continue to learn more about it on your own. See Appendix A for starting points to further your knowledge.

Q&A

Q Besides parsing documents into HTML, what other practical uses are there for XML?

A XML is a great way to store any type of marked-up text in a standardized way. Developers of many software applications, including popular word processors, are considering using XML-based files.

Q Why should I care about users of limited browsers, such as Lynx?

A Lynx is used by more people than you think (try it—it's incredibly fast). More importantly, more and more people are accessing the Web with devices such as palmtop PCs and cell phones, which make Lynx look sophisticated by comparison.

Q What if I have a JavaScript question that isn't answered in this book?

A Start with the resources in Appendix A. You should also stop by this book's Web site (`www.jsworkshop.com`) for a list of updates to the book, frequently-asked questions, and a forum where you can discuss JavaScript with the author and other users.

Quiz

Test your knowledge of the topics covered in this Hour by answering the following questions:

Questions

1. Which of the following is the latest DOM recommendation from the W3C?

    a. DOM 1.5

    b. DOM level 1

    c. DOM level 2

2. When should you use a new JavaScript feature?

    a. Immediately

    b. As soon as it's supported by browsers

    c. As soon as it's part of a standard, and browsers that support it are widely available

3. Which of the following is an important way of making sure your scripts will work with future browsers?

    a. Follow HTML, JavaScript, and DOM standards.

    b. Spend an hour a day downloading the newest browsers and testing your scripts.

    c. Wait until the very last browsers are released before writing any scripts.

Answers

1. c. DOM level 2 is the latest W3C recommendation.

2. c. Wait until JavaScript features are standardized and widely available before implementing them.

3. a. Following HTML, JavaScript, and DOM standards is an important way of making sure your scripts will work with future browsers.

Exercises

To further your knowledge of JavaScript and the latest Web technologies, perform the following exercise:

- Examine the list of Web sites in Appendix A, and browse them to learn about JavaScript and the Web's future.

24

Part VII
Appendices

Appendix

Appendix **A**

Other JavaScript Resources

While you've learned a lot about JavaScript in 24 hours, there's still a lot to know. If you'd like to move on to advanced features of JavaScript or learn more, the resources listed in this appendix will be helpful.

Other Books

The following books, also from Sams.net, discuss JavaScript and DHTML in more detail:

- *Sams Teach Yourself JavaScript in a Week*, by Arman Danesh. ISBN 1-57521-195-5.

- *JavaScript Unleashed*, by Richard Wagner, et al. ISBN 1-57521-306-0.

- *JavaScript Developer's Dictionary*, by Alexander J. Vincent and John Krutsch. ISBN 0-672-32201-3.

- *Sams Teach Yourself DHTML in 24 Hours*, by Michael Moncur. ISBN 0-672-323-2-8.

JavaScript Web Sites

The following Web sites will help you learn more about JavaScript:

- JavaScript Developer Central, part of Netscape's DevEdge site, includes links to a wide variety of JavaScript resources.

  `http://developer.netscape.com/tech/javascript/index.html`

- Netscape's JavaScript Reference is the definitive JavaScript reference.

  `http://developer.netscape.com/docs/manuals/js/client/jsref/index.htm`

- Website Abstraction has a number of sample scripts and JavaScript tutorials, including information about the new W3C DOM.

  `http://wsabstract.com/`

Web Site Development

The following sites have news and information about Web technologies, including JavaScript, XML, and DHTML, as well as basic HTML:

- WebReference.com has information and articles about Web technologies ranging from Java to plug-ins.

  `http://www.webreference.com/`

- HTMLcenter has reviews, news, and tutorials about HTML, JavaScript, and other Web technologies.

  `http://www.htmlcenter.com/`

- BrowserWatch has the latest news about new browsers and plug-ins.

  `http://browserwatch.internet.com/`

- The W3C (World Wide Web Consortium) is the definitive source for information about the HTML and CSS standards.

  `http://www.w3.org/`

Dynamic HTML Web Sites

You'll find the following resources useful for learning more about DHTML and CSS:

- The Web Design Group has several useful references about HTML and CSS.

  `http://www.htmlhelp.com/`

- WebReference.com's DHTML Lab has many DHTML tutorials and examples, both for the new DOM and for 4.0 browsers.

  `http://www.webreference.com/dhtml/`

CGI Resources

Sometimes JavaScript and DHTML can't do everything you need. The following Web sites have information about CGI and server-side programming languages:

- The CGI Resource Index has links to thousands of CGI scripts. You can copy some of these to your own server, while others are remotely hosted services.

  http://cgi.resourceindex.com/

- Perl is the original language for CGI programming, and still among the most popular. Find out more about this language at Perl.com.

  http://www.perl.com/

- PHP is a newer open-source language that works on Web servers, and its simplicity makes it a perfect choice for those experienced with JavaScript. Full documentation is available at the official PHP site.

  http://www.php.net/

- The PHP Resource Index has links to many freely available PHP programs.

  http://php.resourceindex.com/

In addition, you might find the following books useful:

- *Sams Teach Yourself CGI in 24 Hours*, by Rafe Colburn, ISBN 0-672-31880-6.
- *Sams Teach Yourself PHP4 in 24 Hours*, by Matt Zandstra, ISBN 0-672-31804-0.
- *Sams Teach Yourself Perl in 24 Hours*, by Clinton Pierce, ISBN 0-672-31773-7.

A

This Book's Web Site

As with everything else on the Internet, JavaScript is constantly changing, and it's sometimes hard for a printed book to keep up. For this reason, I've created a Web site to accompany this book:

http://www.jsworkshop.com/

At this site you'll find the following:

- The latest news about JavaScript and the Web in general
- Updated links to other JavaScript pages and resources
- Corrections and clarifications for this book
- Answers to this book's Exercises sections
- Tips and tricks for new JavaScript techniques

- Online versions of the examples in this book, which you can copy and use yourself, as well as graphics and other files required for the examples
- Updated examples showing JavaScript's capabilities
- A chance to communicate with the author and other JavaScript users in the JavaScript Forum

APPENDIX B

Tools for JavaScript Developers

One of the best things about JavaScript is that it requires no specialized tools—all you need to start scripting is a Web browser and a simple text editor. Nonetheless, tools are available that will make scripting easier. Some of these are described in this appendix.

HTML and Text Editors

While they aren't specifically intended for scripting, a wide variety of HTML editors are available. These allow you to easily create Web documents, either by automating the process of entering tags, or by presenting you with an environment for directly creating styled text.

HomeSite

HomeSite, from Macromedia, is a full-featured HTML editor. It is similar to a text editor, but includes features to automatically add HTML tags, and to easily create complicated HTML elements such as tables.

HomeSite also includes a number of JavaScript features, such as creating tags automatically and coloring script commands to make them easy to follow.

A demo version of HomeSite is available for download from Macromedia's site:

`http://www.macromedia.com/software/homesite/`

HomeSite also includes a basic version of TopStyle from Bradsoft, an editor for Cascading Style Sheets. You can find out more about TopStyle at their Web site:

`http://www.bradsoft.com/topstyle/`

FrontPage

Microsoft FrontPage is a popular WYSIWYG (What You See Is What You Get) HTML editor that allows you to easily create HTML documents. The latest version, FrontPage 2000, includes a component to create simple scripts automatically.

You can download FrontPage from Microsoft's site:

`http://www.microsoft.com/frontpage/`

NetObjects ScriptBuilder

NetObjects ScriptBuilder is a development environment for JavaScript that provides a sophisticated editor, and tools to create simple scripts automatically. You can learn more about it from the NetObjects Web site:

`http://www.netobjects.com/`

BBEdit

For Macintosh users, BBEdit is a great HTML editor that also includes JavaScript features. You can download it from Bare Bones Software's Web site:

`http://www.bbedit.com/`

Text Editors

Often, a simple text editor is all you need to work on an HTML document or script. Here are some editors that are available for download:

- TextPad, from Helios Software Solutions, is a Windows text editor intended as a replacement for the basic Notepad accessory. It's a fast, useful editor, and also includes a number of features for working with HTML. TextPad is shareware, and a fully-working version can be downloaded from its official site:

  `http://www.textpad.com/`

- UltraEdit-32, from IDM Computer Solutions, is another good Windows text editor, with support for hexadecimal editing for binary files as well as simple text editing. The shareware version is available for download here:

  `http://www.ultraedit.com/`

- SlickEdit, from MicroEdge, is a sophisticated programmer's editor for Windows and UNIX platforms:

  `http://www.slickedit.com/`

HTML Validators

Writing Web pages that comply with the HTML specifications is one way to avoid JavaScript errors, as well as to ensure that your pages will work with future browser versions. Here are some automated ways of checking the HTML compliance of your pages:

- CSE HTML Validator, from AI Internet Solutions, is an excellent stand-alone utility for Windows that checks HTML documents against your choice of HTML versions. It can also be integrated with HomeSite, TextPad, and several other HTML and text editors. While the Pro version of this product is commercial, a Lite version is available for free download. Visit their Web site:

  `http://www.htmlvalidator.com/`

- The W3C's HTML Validation Service is a Web-based HTML validator. Just enter your URL, and it will be immediately checked for HTML compliance. Access this service at this URL:

  `http://validator.w3.org/`

- The WDG HTML Validator offers a different perspective, and is also an easy-to-use Web-based service. Access it at this URL:

  `http://www.htmlhelp.com/tools/validator/`

B

Debugging Tools

You might find the following tools useful in debugging your JavaScript applications:

- Netscape's JavaScript debugger allows you to set breakpoints, display variable values, and perform other debugging tasks. It works with Netscape 4.x.

  `http://developer.netscape.com/software/jsdebug.html`

- Netscape's Mozilla team is working on a debugger for Netscape 5 and 6. Find out more here:

  `http://www.mozilla.org/projects/venkman/`

- Microsoft Script Debugger works with JavaScript and VBScript in Internet Explorer.

  `http://msdn.microsoft.com/library/en-us/sdbug/Html/sdbug_1.asp`

- WebReview.com has an excellent tutorial that covers the basics of JavaScript debugging.

  `http://www.webreview.com/2000/10_06/webauthors/10_06_00_1.shtml`

APPENDIX C

Glossary

ActiveX A technology developed by Microsoft to allow components to be created, primarily for Windows computers. ActiveX components, or controls, can be embedded in Web pages.

anchor In HTML, a named location within a document, specified using the <a> tag. Anchors can also act as links.

applet A Java program that is designed to be embedded in a Web page.

argument A parameter that is passed to a function when it is called. Arguments are specified within parentheses in the function call.

array A set of variables that can be referred to with the same name and a number, called an index.

attribute A property value that can be defined within an HTML tag. Attributes specify style, alignment, and other aspects of the element defined by the tag.

Boolean A type of variable that can store only two values: true and false.

browser sensing   A scripting technique that detects the specific browser in use by clients to provide compatibility for multiple browsers.

Cascading Style Sheets (CSS)   The W3C's standard for applying styles to HTML documents. CSS can control fonts, colors, margins, borders, and positioning.

concatenate   The act of combining two strings into a single, longer string.

conditional   A JavaScript statement that performs an action if a particular condition is true, usually using the `if` statement.

decrement   To decrease the value of a variable by one. In JavaScript, this can be done with the decrement operator, `--`.

debug   The act of finding errors, or bugs, in a program or script.

deprecated   A term the W3C applies to HTML tags or other items that are no longer recommended for use, and may not be supported in the future. For example, the `<font>` tag is deprecated in HTML 4.0, since style sheets can provide the same capability.

Document Object Model (DOM)   The set of objects that JavaScript can use to refer to the browser window and portions of the HTML document. The W3C (World Wide Web Consortium) DOM is a standardized version supported by the latest browsers, and allows access to every object within a Web page.

Dynamic HTML (DHTML)   The combination of HTML, JavaScript, CSS, and the DOM, which allows dynamic Web pages to be created. DHTML is not a W3C standard or a version of HTML.

element   A single member of an array, referred to with an index. In the DOM, an element is a single node defined by an HTML tag.

event   A condition, often the result of a user's action, that can be detected by a script.

event handler   A JavaScript statement or function that will be executed when an event occurs.

expression   A combination of variables, constants, and operators that can be evaluated to a single value.

feature sensing   A scripting technique that detects whether a feature, such as a DOM method, is supported before using it to avoid browser incompatibilities.

function   A group of JavaScript statements that can be referred to using a function name and arguments.

global variable A variable that is available to all JavaScript code in a Web page. It is declared (first used) outside any function.

Hypertext Markup Language (HTML) The language used in Web documents. JavaScript statements are not HTML, but can be included within an HTML document.

increment To increase the value of a variable by one. In JavaScript, this is done with the increment operator, ++.

interpreter The browser component that interprets JavaScript statements and acts on them.

Java An object-oriented language developed by Sun Microsystems. Java applets can be embedded within a Web page. JavaScript has similar syntax, but is not the same as Java.

JavaScript A scripting language for Web documents, loosely based on Java's syntax, developed by Netscape. JavaScript is now supported by the most popular browsers.

layer An area of a Web page that can be positioned and can overlap other sections in defined ways. Layers are also known as positionable elements.

local variable A variable that is available to only one function. It is declared (first used) within the function.

loop A set of JavaScript statements that are executed a number of times, or until a certain condition is met.

method A specialized type of function that can be stored in an object, and acts on the object's properties.

Navigator A browser developed by Netscape, and the first to support JavaScript.

node In the DOM, an individual container or element within a Web document. Each HTML tag defines a node.

object A type of variable that can store multiple values, called properties, and functions, called methods.

operator A character used to divide variables or constants used in an expression.

parameter A variable sent to a function when it is called, also known as an argument.

property A variable that is stored as part of an object. Each object can have any number of properties.

rule In CSS, an individual element of a style block that specifies the style for an HTML tag, class, or identifier.

C

scope   The part of a JavaScript program that a variable was declared in and is available to.

selector   In a CSS rule, the first portion of the rule that specifies the HTML tag, class, or identifier that the rule will affect.

statement   A single line of a script or program.

string   A group of text characters that can be stored in a variable.

tag   In HTML, an individual element within a Web document. HTML tags are contained within angle brackets, as in <body> and <p>.

text node   In the DOM, a node that stores a text value rather than an HTML element. Nodes that contain text, such as paragraphs, have a text node as a child node.

variable   A container, referred to with a name, that can store a number, a string, or an object.

VBScript   A scripting language developed by Microsoft, with syntax based on Visual Basic. VBScript is supported only by Microsoft Internet Explorer.

World Wide Web Consortium (W3C)   An international organization that develops and maintains the standards for HTML, CSS, and other key Web technologies.

XHTML (Extensible Hypertext Markup Language)   A new version of HTML developed by the W3C. XHTML is similar to HTML, but conforms to the XML specification.

XML (Extensible Markup Language)   A generic language developed by the W3C (World Wide Web Consortium) that allows the creation of standardized HTML-like languages, using a DTD (Document Type Definition) to specify tags and attributes.

APPENDIX D

JavaScript Quick Reference

This appendix is a quick reference for the JavaScript language. It includes the built-in objects and the objects in the basic object hierarchy, JavaScript statements, and built-in functions.

Built-in Objects

The following objects are built in to JavaScript. Some can be used to create objects of your own; others can only be used as they are. Each is detailed below.

Array

You can create a new array object to define an array—a numbered list of variables. (Unlike other variables, arrays must be declared.) Use the new keyword to define an array, as in this example:

```
students = new Array(30)
```

Items in the array are indexed beginning with 0. Refer to items in the array with brackets:

```
fifth = students[4];
```

Arrays have a single property, length, which gives the current number of elements in the array. They have the following methods:

- join quickly joins all of the array's elements together, resulting in a string. The elements are separated by commas, or by the separator you specify.
- reverse returns a reversed version of the array.
- sort returns a sorted version of the array. Normally this is an alphabetical sort; however, you can use a custom sort method by specifying a comparison routine.

String

Any string of characters in JavaScript is a string object. The following statement assigns a variable to a string value:

```
text = "This is a test."
```

Since strings are objects, you can also create a new string with the new keyword:

```
text = new String("This is a test.");
```

String objects have a single property, length, which reflects the current length of the string. There are a variety of methods available to work with strings:

- substring returns a portion of the string.
- toUpperCase converts all characters in the string to uppercase.
- toLowerCase converts all characters in the string to lowercase.
- indexOf finds an occurrence of a string within the string.
- lastIndexOf finds an occurrence of a string within the string, starting at the end of the string.
- link creates an HTML link using the string's text.
- anchor creates an HTML anchor within the current page.

There are also a few methods that allow you to change a string's appearance when it appears in an HTML document:

- string.big displays big text, using the <big> tag in HTML 3.0.
- string.blink displays blinking text, using the <blink> tag in Netscape.
- string.bold displays bold text, using the <b> tag.

- `string.fixed` displays fixed-font text, using the `<tt>` tag.
- `string.fontcolor` displays the string in a colored font, equivalent to the `<font-color>` tag in Netscape.
- `string.fontsize` changes the font size, using the `<fontsize>` tag in Netscape.
- `string.italics` displays the string in italics, using the `<i>` tag.
- `string.small` displays the string in small letters using the `<small>` tag in HTML 3.0.
- `string.strike` displays the string in a strike-through font, using the `<strike>` tag.
- `string.sub` displays subscript text, equivalent to the `<sub>` tag in HTML 3.0.
- `string.sup` displays superscript text, equivalent to the `<sup>` tag in HTML 3.0.

Math

The Math object is not a "real" object, since you can't create your own objects. A variety of mathematical constants are also available as properties of the Math object:

- `Math.E` is the base of natural logarithms (approximately 2.718).
- `Math.LN2` is the natural logarithm of two (approximately 0.693).
- `Math.LN10` is the natural logarithm of 10 (approximately 2.302).
- `Math.LOG2E` is the base 2 logarithm of e (approximately 1.442).
- `Math.LOG10E` is the base 10 logarithm of e (approximately 0.434).
- `Math.PI` is the ratio of a circle's circumference to its diameter (approximately 3.14159).
- `Math.SQRT1_2` is the square root of one half (approximately 0.707).
- `Math.SQRT2` is the square root of two (approximately 2.7178).

The methods of the Math object allow you to perform mathematical functions. The methods are listed below in categories.

Algebraic Functions

- `Math.acos` calculates the arc cosine of a number, in radians.
- `Math.asin` calculates the arc sine of a number.
- `Math.atan` calculates the arc tangent of a number.
- `Math.cos` calculates the cosine of a number.
- `Math.sin` returns the sine of a number.
- `Math.tan` calculates the tangent of a number.

D

Statistical and Logarithmic Functions

- `Math.exp` returns *e* (the base of natural logarithms) raised to a power.
- `Math.log` returns the natural logarithm of a number.
- `Math.max` accepts two numbers, and returns whichever is greater.
- `Math.min` accepts two numbers, and returns the smaller of the two.

Basic Math and Rounding

- `Math.abs` calculates the absolute value of a number.
- `Math.ceil` rounds a number up to the nearest integer.
- `Math.floor` rounds a number down to the nearest integer.
- `Math.pow` calculates one number to the power of another.
- `Math.round` rounds a number to the nearest integer.
- `Math.sqrt` calculates the square root of a number.

Random Numbers

- `Math.random` returns a random number between 0 and 1.

Date

The Date object is a built-in JavaScript object that allows you to conveniently work with dates and times. You can create a date object any time you need to store a date, and use the date object's methods to work with the date:

- `setDate` sets the day of the month.
- `setMonth` sets the month. JavaScript numbers the months from 0 to 11, starting with January (0).
- `setYear` sets the year. `SetFullYear` is a four-digit, Y2K-compliant version.
- `setTime` sets the time (and the date) by specifying the number of milliseconds since January 1, 1970.
- `setHours`, `setMinutes`, and `setSeconds` set the time.
- `getDate` gets the day of the month.
- `getMonth` gets the month.
- `getYear` gets the year.
- `getTime` gets the time (and the date) as the number of milliseconds since January 1, 1970.
- `getHours`, `getMinutes`, and `getSeconds` get the time.

- `getTimeZoneOffset` gives you the local time zone's offset from GMT.
- `toGMTString` converts the date object's time value to text, using GMT (Greenwich Mean Time, also known as UTC).
- `toLocalString` converts the date object's time value to text, using local time.
- `Date.parse` converts a date string, such as "June 20, 2003" to a date object (number of milliseconds since 1/1/1970).
- `Date.UTC` converts a date object value (number of milliseconds) to a UTC (GMT) time.

Creating and Customizing Objects

This is a brief summary of the keywords you can use to create your own objects and customize existing objects. These are documented in detail in Hour 15, "Creating Custom Objects."

Creating Objects

There are three JavaScript keywords used to create and refer to objects:

- `new` is used to create a new object.
- `this` is used to refer to the current object. This can be used in an object's constructor function or in an event handler.
- `with` makes an object the default for a group of statements. Properties without complete object references will refer to this object.

To create a new object, you need an object constructor function. This simply assigns values to the object's properties using `this`:

```
function Name(first,last) {
   this.first = first;
   this.last = last;
}
```

You can then create a new object using `new`:

```
Fred = new Name("Fred","Smith");
```

Customizing Objects

You can add additional properties to an object you have created just by assigning them:

```
Fred.middle = "Clarence";
```

D

Properties you add this way apply only to that instance of the object, not to all objects of the type. A more permanent approach is to use the `prototype` keyword, which adds a property to an object's prototype (definition). This means that any future object of the type will include this property. You can include a default value:

```
Name.prototype.title = "Citizen";
```

You can use this technique to add properties to the definitions of built-in objects as well. For example, this statement adds a property called `num` to all existing and future string objects, with a default value of 10:

```
string.prototype.num = 10;
```

JavaScript Statements

This is an alphabetical listing of the statements available in JavaScript and their syntax.

Comments

Comments are used to include a note within a JavaScript program, and are ignored by the interpreter. There are two different types of comment syntax:

```
//this is a comment
/* this is also a comment */
```

Only the second syntax can be used for multiple-line comments; the first must be repeated on each line.

break

This statement is used to break out of the current `for` or `while` loop. Control resumes after the loop, as if it had finished.

continue

This statement continues a `for` or `while` loop without executing the rest of the loop. Control resumes at the next iteration of the loop.

for

Defines a loop, usually to count from one number to another using an index variable. In this example, the variable i counts from 1 to 9:

```
for (i=1;i<10;i++;) { statements }
```

for ... in

This is a different type of loop, used to iterate through the properties of an object, or the elements of an array. This statement loops through the properties of the Scores object, using the variable x to hold each property in turn:

```
for (x in Scores) { statements }
```

function

Defines a JavaScript function that can be used anywhere within the current document. Functions can optionally return a value with the return statement. This example defines a function to add two numbers and return the result:

```
function add(n1,n2) {
   result = n1 + n2;
   return result;
}
```

if ... else

This is a conditional statement. If the condition is true, the statements after the if statement are executed; otherwise, the statements after the else statement (if present) are executed. This example prints a message stating whether a number is less than or greater than 10:

```
if (a > 10) {
   document.write("Greater than 10");
}
else {
   document.write("10 or less");
}
```

A shorthand method, known as the "hook and colon" conditional, can also be used for these types of statements, where ? indicates the if portion and : indicates the else portion. This statement is equivalent to the example above:

```
document.write((a > 10) ? "Greater than 10" : "10 or less");
```

Conditional statements are explained further in Hour 6, "Testing and Comparing Values."

return

This statement ends a function, and optionally returns a value. The return statement is necessary only if a value is returned.

D

var

This statement is used to declare a variable. If you use it within a function, the variable is guaranteed to be local to that function. If you use it outside the function, the variable is considered global. Here's an example:

```
var students = 30;
```

Since JavaScript is a loosely-typed language, you do not need to specify the type when you declare the variable. A variable is also automatically declared the first time you assign it a value:

```
students = 30;
```

Using var will help avoid conflicts between local and global variables. Note that arrays are not considered ordinary JavaScript variables; they are objects. See Hour 5, "Using Strings and Arrays," for details.

while

The while statement defines a loop that iterates as long as a condition remains true. This example waits until the value of a text field is "go":

```
while (document.form1.text1.value != "go") {statements }
```

JavaScript Built-in Functions

The functions in the following sections are built into JavaScript, rather than being methods of a particular object.

eval

This function evaluates a string as a JavaScript statement or expression, and either executes it or returns the resulting value. In the following example, a function is called using variables as an argument:

```
a = eval("add(x,y);");
```

eval is typically used to evaluate an expression or statement entered by the user.

parseInt

Finds an integer value at the beginning of a string and returns it. If there is no number at the beginning of the string, "NaN" (not a number) is returned.

parseFloat

Finds a floating-point value at the beginning of a string and returns it. If there is no number at the beginning of the string, "NaN" (not a number) is returned.

D

APPENDIX E

DOM Quick Reference

This appendix presents a quick overview of the DOM objects available, including the basic Level 0 DOM and the W3C Level 1 DOM.

DOM Level 0

The Level 0 DOM includes objects that represent the browser window, the current document, and its contents. The following is a basic summary of Level 0 DOM objects.

For detailed information about the properties and methods of each of the objects in the Level 0 DOM, consult Netscape's JavaScript Reference: `http://developer.netscape.com/docs/manuals/js/client/jsref/index.htm`.

Window

The `window` object represents the current browser window. If multiple windows are open or frames are used, there may be more than one window object. These are given aliases to distinguish them:

- `self` represents the current window, as does `window`. This is the window containing the current JavaScript document.
- `top` is the window currently on top (active) on the screen.
- `parent` is the window that contains the current frame.
- The `frames` array contains the window object for each frame in a framed document.

The window object has three child objects:

- `location` stores the location (URL) of the document displayed in the window.
- `document` stores information about the current Web page.
- The `history` object contains a list of sites visited before or after the current site in the window.

Location

The `location` object contains information about the current URL being displayed by the window. It has a set of properties to hold the different components of the URL:

- `location.hash` is the name of an anchor within the document, if specified.
- `location.host` is a combination of the host name and port.
- `location.hostname` specifies the host name.
- `location.href` is the entire URL.
- `location.pathname` is the directory to find the document on the host, and the name of the file.
- `location.port` specifies the communication port.

E

- `location.protocol` is the protocol (or *method*) of the URL.
- `location.query` specifies a query string.
- `location.target` specifies the TARGET attribute of the link that was used to reach the current location.

History

The `history` object holds information about the URLs that have been visited before and after the current one in the window, and includes methods to go to previous or next locations:

- `history.back` goes back to the previous location.
- `history.forward` goes forward to the next location.
- `history.go` goes to a specified offset in the history list.

Document

The `document` object represents the current document in the window. It includes the following child objects:

- `document.forms` is a collection with an element for each form in the document.
- `document.links` is a collection containing elements for each of the links in the document.
- `document.anchors` is a collection with elements for each of the anchors in the document.
- `document.images` contains an element for each of the images in the current document.
- `document.applets` is a collection with references to each embedded Java applet in the document.

Navigator

The `navigator` object includes information about the current browser version:

- `appCodeName` is the browser's code name, usually "Mozilla."
- `appName` is the browser's full name.
- `appVersion` is the version number of the browser. (Example: "4.0(Win95;I)".)

- `userAgent` is the user-agent header, which is sent to the host when requesting a web page. It includes the entire version information, such as "Mozilla/4.5(Win95;I)."
- `plugIns` is a collection, which contains information about each currently-available plug-in (Netscape only).
- `mimeTypes` is a collection containing an element for each of the available MIME types (Netscape only).

DOM Level 1

The Level 1 DOM is the first cross-browser DOM standardized by the W3C. Its objects are stored under the `document` object of the Level 0 DOM.

Basic Node Properties

Each object has certain common properties:

- `nodeName` is the name of the node (not the ID). The name is the tag name for HTML tag nodes, `#document` for the document node, and `#text` for text nodes.
- `nodeType` is a number describing the node's type: 1 for HTML tags, 3 for text nodes, and 9 for the document.
- `nodeValue` is the text contained within a text node.
- `innerHTML` is the HTML contents of a container node.
- `id` is the value of the `ID` attribute for the node.
- `classname` is the value of the `class` attribute for the node.

Relationship Properties

The following properties describe an object's relationship with others in the hierarchy:

- `firstChild` is the first child node for the current node.
- `lastChild` is the last child object for the current node.
- `childNodes` is an array of all of the child nodes under a node.
- `previousSibling` is the sibling before the current node.
- `nextSibling` is the sibling after the current node.
- `parentNode` is the object that contains the current node.

Offset Properties

While not part of the W3C DOM, both Netscape and Internet Explorer support the following properties that provide information about a node's position:

- offsetLeft is the distance from the left-hand side of the browser window or containing object to the left edge of the node object.
- offsetTop is the distance from the top of the browser window or containing object to the top of the node object.
- offsetHeight is the height of the node object.
- offsetWidth is the width of the node object.

Style Properties

The style child object under each DOM object includes its style sheet properties. These are based on attributes of a style attribute, <style> tag, or external style sheet. See Hour 18, "Working with Style Sheets," for details on these properties.

Node Methods

The following methods are available for all DOM nodes:

- appendChild(node) adds a new child node to the node after all of its existing children.
- insertBefore(node,oldnode) inserts a new node before the specified existing child node.
- replaceChild(node,oldnode) replaces the specified old child node with a new node.
- removeChild(node) removes an existing child node.
- hasChildNodes() returns a Boolean value of true if the node has one or more children, or false if it has none.
- cloneNode() returns a copy of the current node.
- getAttribute(*attribute_name*) gets the value of the attribute you specify and stores it in a variable.
- setAttribute(*attribute_name*, *value*) sets the value of an attribute.
- removeAttribute(*attribute_name*) removes the attribute you specify.
- hasAttributes() simply returns true if the node has attributes, and false if it has none.

Document object methods and properties

The following are methods and properties of the `document` object:

- `document.getElementById(ID)` returns the element with the specified ID attribute.

- `document.getElementsByTagName(tag)` returns an array of the elements with the specified tag name. You can use the asterisk (*) as a wildcard to return an array containing all of the nodes in the document.

- `document.createElement(tag)` creates a new element with the specified tag name.

- `document.createTextNode(text)` creates a new text node containing the specified text.

- `document.documentElement` is an object that represents the document itself, and can be used to find information about the document.

INDEX

A

M

X-Z

SAMS Teach Yourself JavaScript in 24 Hours

What you should already have to get the most out of this book...

- Familiarity with the basic workings of your computer, your operating system, and the Internet
- At least basic skills in creating Web pages with HTML
- The aptitude and the desire to create dynamic content with JavaScript

Some books that may help...

Sams Teach Yourself HTML and XHTML in 24 Hours

This book will get you up and running with HTML in no time.

Sams Teach Yourself the Internet in 24 Hours

A how-to on getting connected and learning how the Internet works.

What this book will help you learn...

- The fundamentals of JavaScript development
- How to write script for both Internet Explorer and Netscape Browsers.
- How to manipulate Cascading Style Sheets (CSS) with JavaScript

Related titles...

Sams Teach Yourself DHTML in 24 Hours

Put DHTML to work for you.

Sams Teach Yourself PHP in 24 Hours

As an alternative, technologies such as PHP provide many of the same capabilities in a consistent, easy-to-use package.

Where you may want to go from here...

- Expand your abilities as a Web developer by gaining a more complete knowledge of JavaScript
- Expand your repertoire by learning other programming languages such as Java

Possible titles to look for...

Pure JavaScript

This book contains insightful programming techniques, complete with well-commented code examples.

Sams Teach Yourself Java 2 in 24 Hours

This book will increase your ability to add interactivity to your Web development.